KT-524-614

Tell Me Lies

Propaganda and Media
Distortion in the Attack on Iraq

Edited by
David Miller

Pluto Press

LONDON • STERLING, VIRGINIA

First published 2004 by
Pluto Press
345 Archway Road, London N6 5AA
and 22883 Quicksilver Drive, Sterling, VA 20166–2012, USA

www.plutobooks.com

British Library Cataloguing in Publication Data
A catalogue record for this book is available from the British Library

ISBN   0 7453 2202 6 hardback
ISBN   0 7453 2201 8 paperback

Library of Congress Cataloging in Publication Data applied for

10   9   8   7   6   5   4   3   2   1

Designed and produced for Pluto Press by
Chase Publishing Services, Fortescue, Sidmouth, EX10 9QG, England
Typeset from disk by Stanford DTP Services, Northampton, England
Printed and bound in the European Union by
MPG Books, Bodmin, Cornwall, England

Contents

Acknowledgements

This has been a book produced at some speed between mid-May and mid-August 2003. It could not have been done without the commitment and help of all the contributors, who have often produced articles under very heavy pressure of other commitments and certainly to tight deadlines. I had anticipated that it might be difficult to fill the book in so short a period, but as it turned out I was deluged with offers and no one refused my requests for chapters. Even more astonishing there were only a couple of unavoidable drop outs. In the end there was too much material, some of which I have had to hack down for reasons of space. My apologies for any offence to authors' sensibilities for this! Pluto also appreciated the need to get the book out fast. My thanks to everyone there for their efforts.

People who have helped in big and small ways in putting this together deserve thanks. Thanks to all the contributors for their chapters and especially to Faisal Bodi, David Cromwell, David Crouch, Tim Gopsill, John Pilger, Andy Rowell, Norman Solomon, John Stauber, Mark Thomas, Granville Williams, for other contributions. Thanks also to Carmel Brown, Cindy Baxter, Susan Casey of MWAW, Louise Christian, James Curran, Jeremy Dear, Lindsey German, Ken Loach, Eveline Lubbers, Robert McChesney, Mike Marqusee, John Meed, Seumas Milne, Andrew Murray, and last but not least, the indefatigable Barry White of the CPBF.

The book could not have been completed without alternative media and the myriad of information made available by activists and switched-on journalists on and off the web. Mainstream media organisations contain many dissidents who often do what they can to counter corporate and government priorities. They all deserve our support as workers and truth tellers. Thanks especially to all those who have leaked memos and other inside information to me and others – always gratefully received. Dissidents are important for what they can do now, but also for their potential future role in the creation of genuinely free and independent media. This is a notion which – post-Seattle and post-Iraq – once more seems just about within the bounds of the thinkable. Thanks are also due to dissidents outside the mainstream, who have become incredibly important resources for intellectual self-defence. To Media Lens, PR Watch, the Institute for Public Accuracy, to all the people who have posted on the Media Watch list, to Fairness and Accuracy in Reporting, to Media Workers Against the War, to Pacifica Radio (and especially its Bay area, California affiliate KPFA) and to Z Net. Special mention should be made of the inspiring work of Glen Rangwala who uncovered the plagiarism in the "dodgy" dossier and has forensically monitored government statements for lies, misinformation and evasions. His website at <http://middleeastreference.org.uk> is an essential resource.

I would like to acknowledge my debt first of all to the anti-war movement which has inspired me and countless others to add our voices to a truly global protest. The radicalising sense, not just of being part of a protest movement, but of being a small part in a *collective* whole can only be bad news for our rulers. I would also like to thank the myriad of activists in the movement with whom I have talked, argued, protested, and the rest. In particular I owe a debt to the members of the Stirling University anti-war group, the Glasgow Branch of the NUJ and especially to Glasgow Southside Against War. I should also mention a personal debt to David Maguire, Patsy King, and to my highly esteemed colleague and friend William Dinan who kept his head when all around him were losing theirs. A huge thank you to Emma Miller for her sustaining commitment, anger and humour in the face of the adversity of the "war on terror" and the relentless advance of corporate power; for her committed research on development and globalisation and for her participation in our hobby of shouting at television news. Lastly, thanks and love to Caitlin and Lewis Miller – especially for their repertoire of anti-war slogans (Who let the bombs drop?...).

Some of the chapters in this book have appeared before in various forms. The original sources are acknowledged below. Chapters 1–4 originally appeared in the *New Statesman* on 3 February 2003, 17 February 2003, 17 March 2003 and 14 April 2003, respectively. Chapter 5 originally appeared in the *Independent on Sunday* on 20 April 2003. Chapter 6 is based on two articles which originally appeared in *PR Watch* in the last quarter of 2002 and the first quarter of 2003. Chapter 11 originally appeared in *British Journalism Review*, June 2003. Chapter 12 is adapted from various pieces which originally appeared in *Free Press*. Chapter 14 originally appeared in the *Independent* on 3 April 2003. Chapter 19 originally appeared in *Z Magazine*, June 2003. Chapter 23 has been adapted from a Media Lens alert on 6 June 2003. Chapter 24 was originally broadcast on Friday 23 May 2003 on Pacifica Radio's *Peace Watch* in the US. Chapter 32 was originally published in the *Guardian* on 4 February 2003. The cartoons on pages 13 and 39 by Steve Bell originally appeared in the *Guardian* on 1 April 2003 and 10 January 2003 respectively. The cartoon by Polyp on page 241 was originally published in *Red Pepper* in June 2003. The photomontage by Steve Caplin on page 127 was commissioned for this volume.

Every effort has been made to trace copyright holders of any third-party material included in this book.

Foreword

When the US and UK troops invaded Iraq I like many became obsessed with trying to find out what was happening to the civilian population, including the conscripted civilians forced to fight. I felt that I had to follow every detail of this one-sided fight and would sit glued to breakfast TV trying to get a handle on what had occurred the previous evening, while my children demanded a return to kids programmes. I received the news of deaths through friendly fire or the latest fake report of a chemical weapon hoard being discovered by the US military through a barrage of under-10 heckling of "Turn it over! This is rubbish! Mum ... Dad's watching the news again!", whilst peanut buttered toast was waved angrily in my direction. In retrospect I should have joined them shouting and waving bits of breakfast at the news. It certainly would be a more appropriate response than actually watching it with some vague hope of ... well ... er ... hearing some actual news.

With barely enough coffee in my system to survive the early morning onslaught of GMTV/BBC presenters I would channel hop. Skipping and flashing through presenters in studio to *in situ* with the embedded journalists. The BBC had coffee tables that transformed into battle maps, to give us that cosy neighbourly analysis while cooing about how careful the bombers were to avoid civilian casualties and giving credence to the most incredible military claims of finds of chemical or biological weapons. Then they would cut to their khaki-clad desert colleagues hanging out with the troops fulfilling what looked like some sort of weird homoerotic/Duke of Edinburgh award/*Apocalypse Now* fantasy. They would tell us that they couldn't tell us where they were but that they were winning and how the lads they were travelling with were all a great bunch. This wasn't so much reporting, more like a sub-Royal Tournament commentary. Then it would be back to GMTV and discussion and interview from a set of presenters I would just about trust to give me correct information on foundation creams for make-overs, but little else.

What was fantastic was to turn off the news. I actually had a greater clarity on the situation when I didn't watch the news. "Ah-ha!" some media hack might say. "That's because the news challenged your preconceptions and without them being challenged you found it easier to cling to your interpretation of events." Not so. Basra and the reporting surrounding the city's capture by UK troops is a good example of what media folk came to call "the fog of war" and what ordinary mortals called distortions or lies. First it was ours, then only a bit of it was ours, then Saddam's men were killing civilians trying to leave, then we had a bit less than first thought, then it turns out the military decided that it wasn't that important a place anyway.

This was not "fog", it was the media reporting exactly what they were told without properly questioning it. This was mainlining uncut propaganda.

The news editors from the UK were completely wedded to the embedded journalist, they thought it would fill the gaps in their 24-hour news scheduling. In a careless moment they might even have thought that embedded reporters would return to the idea of great war journalists travelling with the troops enduring their hardships and then reporting the truth back home. Instead we had an entirely one-sided vision of the war, with a lot of testosterone.

If the broadcast media had any plan to present a view that was anything other than base propaganda then surely they should have had embedded journalists in the Iraqi hospitals. Reporting on the civilian end of the war. Then perhaps viewers might see that the narrow jingoistic view of the invasion was precisely that. The TV might even have started to broadcast the consequences of this conflict.

At the time of writing, the Hutton inquiry had just questioned Dr Kelly's widow. The BBC had tried to portray themselves as avid defenders of the truth standing up to the government and Alistair Campbell's vicious spin machine. However, it is hard to see how the BBC stood up to the government in its broadcasting during the invasion. How did the reporting of the apparent collapse of the anti-war movement challenge the government? How did parroting the US and UK military press releases challenge the government? Even in Dr Kelly's death the media carried on the propaganda war, "Dossier Claims First Victim" was one of the headlines, as if some 20,000 dead Iraqis didn't count, and callously ignoring the dead coalition troops the media had proudly claimed to support.

For many though the propaganda has not worked. In fact it has had the opposite effect. The appetite for alternative news sources is immense, whether it be the Indymedia sites reporting actions and demonstrations that the mainstream media continually ignore, or the amazing work of iraqbodycount.org which collates the maximum and minimum figures of reported Iraqi civilian fatalities. From Chomsky to Pilger to Klein bookshelves are scoured in search of information and ideas on how to challenge the status quo. This invasion has been an incredible political event for thousands of people, where their actions and those of countless others have been marginalised by the mainstream media in favour of the pro-war camp. It is not often that the rift between the world's people and their leaders is so thoroughly exposed. The media might be failing to provide us with the information that we need but in the quest to find it a whole new generation of dissent is being galvanised by it.

Mark Thomas
London, September 2003

Introduction

David Miller

The title of this book recalls Adrian Mitchell's famous poem "Tell Me Lies About Vietnam". Mitchell himself performed the poem at the anti-war rally in Trafalgar Square on 13 October 2001, changing the end of each verse to Iraq, Palestine and Afghanistan respectively. Since 11 September 2001 the propaganda machine in the US (and UK) has been cranked up to levels not seen outside the 1939–45 war. It should be no surprise that the content of the propaganda cranked out quietly to selected journalists or with fanfare in the form of several dossiers or grandstanding appearances before the United Nations, should be riddled with deception. Governments have long believed that – to misquote Wilfred Owen – *dulce et decorum est pro patria decipio*. But it does remain difficult to find a straightforward espousal of this thesis in the mainstream media. Much of the media continue to assume that the statements of government officials and politicians are characterised by what Mark Curtis calls a "basic benevolence".[1] They may lie here or there, or they may act in a foolish or misguided way, but to advance the proposition that they are calculating liars, in full consciousness of the outcomes of their policies is beyond the pale. Thus discussions of propaganda strategy and deliberate deception remain rare.

For the sake of clarity, let us say a few words about lies – to combat the accusation of erecting a mirror image propaganda from the margins. Lies are falsehoods the status of which the liar is aware. Of course it is difficult to prove intention in these matters even in personal relations. In governmental circles it is more difficult as there is always someone else who can take the rap. I didn't know that this information was false. I took it in good faith from Alastair Campbell, MI6, the Office of Special Plans, Italian intelligence, Iraqi defectors (delete according to taste). A further muddying element in official misinformation is that the system of relations between journalists and government in and out of war is based on confidence and trust. Off the record briefing, disguised sources, and the like are a fundamental part of the system and are fully exploited by government in the US and UK. One of the "most insidious" – because least checkable

– ways of exploiting the system is when "propaganda stories are planted on willing journalists, who disguise their origin from their readers".[2] The key to this is that the stories are deniable. That is to say that – since the source will not be identified – government can deny any role in the information. This is a system of institutionalised lying which deliberately seeks to cover its tracks.

A further question is the distinction betweeen big and little lies. Was the justification for war "an honourable deception"[3] as former Cabinet minister Clare Short has said of Tony Blair's state of mind? Or was it, as Paul Wolfowitz of the Pentagon has put it, for reasons of "bureaucracy [that] we settled on the one issue that everyone could agree on"?[4] The size of the lie will depend in part on the status of the liar and in part on the consequences of the lie. But little lies have a way of meshing together. The tangled webs they weave when first they practise to deceive – as the saying has it. Little lies can become webs of deceit especially when they are directed to some overall purpose such as presenting the military and the government in a favourable light and attempting to promote – or at least not undermine – big lies. In the first week of the attack on Iraq there were numerous examples of little lies. The *Daily Mirror* counted 13 separate cases often made up of more than one deception. These included the alleged firing of Scud missiles, the "discovery" of a chemical warfare factory, the "liberation" of Umm Qasr, the "uprising" in Basra and others.[5] Later, British army press officers with the Forward Press Information Centre claimed that as civilians were attempting to leave Basra "the local militia engaged ... the civilians with possibly the inference that they should all get back in, which was exactly the reaction that they got". This claim was picked up on television news that evening as fact: "This is one of the bridges where today civilians scattered as Iraqi fighters opened fire on them" (BBC1, *News at Ten*, 28 March 2003). Later the UK Defence Secretary Geoff Hoon announced the story in the House of Commons as yet another example of "brutal suppression" by the Iraqi regime. Yet – according to the eyewitness reports of BBC journalists filming a documentary titled *Fighting the War* – the Iraqis were in fact engaging the British army:

> It's the British soldiers who are being fired at ... It's not until the bridge is clear of people that [Iraqi] mortar rounds are fired towards it ... In reality it is the British who are controlling movement across the bridge, both in and out of the city.[6]

But these little lies – even cumulatively – pale in comparison with the really big lie, which elements of the US government and MI6 have reportedly been building through "I/Ops" or Information Operations, since at least 1997.[7] This is the notion that Iraq posed a threat to the west by virtue of its programme on weapons of mass destruction and (latterly) by virtue of its links with international terrorism. Both of these justifications were categorically false. The question is only whether those at the top knew that they were false.

One of the key claims – mentioned four separate times in the September 2002 dossier *Iraq's Weapons of Mass Destruction: The Assessment of the British Government* – was that WMD could be "ready within 45 minutes of an order to use them".[8] This was not the only false claim made by the US and UK governments in the attempt to justify war. Glen Rangwala has produced a briefing paper identifying some 36 separate falsehoods.[9] But it illustrates the key point. The dossier claimed that "much information about Iraqi weapons of mass destruction is already in the public domain from UN reports and from Iraqi defectors. This points clearly to Iraq's continuing possession, after 1991, of chemical and biological agents' (p. 5) and Iraq has "continued to produce chemical and biological agents". The problem with these statements is not just that they are false but that they are fundamental misrepresentations of the sources cited by the government, notably UN reports and evidence from the key defector, Hussein Kamel, Saddam Hussein's son in law. Briefly these sources indicate that the Iraqi government had destroyed 90–95 per cent of their chemical and biological agents and that any that remained (with the single exception of mustard gas) was in a form which would have degraded to uselessness within ten years. In the case of the mustard gas, if any actually remained, the quantity was so small that it would only effectively poison an area of some 5.2 square kilometres. The sources also indicate a complete lack of evidence that new production had occurred.[10]

So the notion that there was any significant threat from Iraq from chemical and biological attack was wrong and they knew it was wrong. On the possibility of using the weapons within 45 minutes the dossier noted that Iraq "can deliver chemical and biological agents using an extensive range of artillery shells, free-fall bombs, sprayers and ballistic missiles ... The Iraq military are able to deploy these weapons within 45 minutes of a decision to do so" (p. 17). This neatly conflates the alleged "intelligence" on 45 minutes with long-range ballistic missiles. In fact, Iraq did not have any such missiles and the original intelligence assessment was only, according to John Scarlett of the Joint Intelligence Committee, that "battlefield mortar shells or small calibre weaponry" could be deployed in 45 minutes. Again, both Blair and Campbell were in a position to know this since it was their own intelligence. (Blair, as Prime Minister, sees all intelligence reports.) In other words, the 45 minutes claim involved at least three separate deceptions: on the existence of the agent in weaponised form; on the existence of the delivery mechanism; and on the application of the 45 minutes claim to long-range delivery systems. Weaving these various deceptions into a wholly false picture of a "current" Iraqi threat required deliberate deception, but deception with a purpose; the purpose was to present the deception in such a way as to encourage the media to draw the obvious conclusion. That it did so is more than evident in the headline in the *London Evening Standard* that day, "45 Minutes from Attack" (24 September 2003), or in the *Daily Express* the next day, "Saddam Can Strike in 45 Minutes" (25 September 2003).

An examination of the language used in official pronouncements shows that ministers and officials – in this case Alastair Campbell and Tony Blair – took considerable care not to be caught out. But at the same time they stretch language so that words appear to mean the opposite of their dictionary definitions. This can be seen in their use of off the record and confidential briefings and leaks, but also in the extreme care taken in the use of language in set piece – on the record – encounters.

One thread in the web of deceit, exposed at the Hutton inquiry, illustrates the seeming inability of those in power to do anything but dissemble. Campbell claimed before the Foreign Affairs Committee that the first draft of the September dossier had been seen by him on 9 September and had included the controversial 45 minutes claim. At Hutton, it emerged that he had chaired the meeting on 5 September at which an earlier draft was discussed. Asked to explain, Campbell replied simply that the previous draft was a different document.

> that is not what I define as the WMD dossier ... these were different products that were being prepared in different parts of Government. The one that mattered was the one that John Scarlett was putting together ... I think in my mind, certainly, they were always separate.[11]

This playing with words characterises the whole affair.

Blair too, was very careful in his use of language which exploited the media thirst for dramatic threats. In a key address to the House of Commons Liaison Committee, Blair said: "I think it is important that we do everything we can to try to show people the link between the issue of weapons of mass destruction and these international terrorist groups, mainly linked to al-Qaeda." Seconds later Blair acknowledged that "I know of nothing linking Iraq to the September 11 attack and I know of nothing either that directly links al-Qaeda and Iraq to recent events in the UK."[12]

The final position seemed to be that although there was no connection it was dangerous to leave weapons of mass destruction in the hands of Hussein in case at some future date these ended up with terrorists. The "link" in other words is a hypothetical one. Via the medium of spin this is deliberately translated into a "real" link. As Blair put it in the House of Commons: "*at some point in a future not too distant*, the threat will *turn into reality*. The threat therefore is not imagined. The history of Saddam and weapons of mass destruction is not American or British propaganda. The history and the present threat are real."[13] Note the dishonesty of the language here as Blair appears to say the threat is both "real" and "present" while at the same time a potential threat in the "not too distant" future which will "turn into" reality.

On the strength of this hypothetical future risk up to 40,000 Iraqis were killed. The ability of the US and UK governments to get away with these killings depends in part on their ability to muddy the waters by means of propaganda and deceit. The attack on Iraq shows the integration of propaganda and lying into the core of government strategy. It shows how such a strategy, planned and executed by a relatively small cabal (in Downing St, the White House and Pentagon), in the face of opposition from within their own ranks, to invade and occupy a sovereign country, can be successful. This does seem to me to elevate the Iraqi threat story into the premier league of big lies.

But we also need to explain the seeming inability of a large majority of the political elite to see through the lies. Some of this is easily explained in terms of political calculation and in terms of fear. But, there is a further element in the psychosis of government which is that members of the elite come to believe their own lies and seem unable to break free of the operating assumptions of the system. Even outside the charmed circle of ministerial office, they come to believe that the world seen through the distorting lens of their own self interest is how the world really is. Of course this will change with the relative strength of the forces of opposition. We cannot explain the pathetic evasions and misunderstandings contained in both the Foreign Affairs Committee and the Intelligence and Security Committee reports on Iraq, together with their occasional glimpses of truth, without understanding that perceptions of the world can be markedly distorted by ideology – the moulding of perceptions by interests – and by political circumstance.

Most crucially the Iraq lie shows the immense gulf between the democratic wishes of the population and the priorities of the political elite. The elite can simply ignore the will of the people of the UK and the majority of global opinion. It can control or bypass the institutions of democracy such as Congress or the House of Commons by means both of deception and the long-term sapping of their practical democratic power. It shows that democracy in both the US and UK is institutionally corrupt, and that there is a need for fundamental changes in the system of national and global governance for them to be objectively recognisable as democratic. The most important legacy of the attack on Iraq then, may be to expose to the world the crisis of liberal democracy and this may well prove in the longer term to be the biggest chink in the armour of the American empire and its UK vassal.

ABOUT THIS BOOK

Tell Me Lies is intended to be an antidote to the distraction and disinformation served up by the mainstream media. It is about lies and misinformation and how – all too often – the mainstream media act as ciphers for the powerful. The book had its origins in a meeting convened in the HQ of the National Union of Journalists in central London on 9 April 2003 as the statue of Saddam Hussein being pulled down by the US military outside the journalists' Palestine Hotel was beamed around the world. At that stage – the temporary high point of US and UK propaganda success – at least two things were clear to the meeting. That there was a desperate need to counter the lies and misinformation dominating most of the mainstream media and that the situation in Iraq was already a disaster in human, social, political and military terms.

Towards the end of the meeting – attended by representatives from the NUJ, Media Workers Against the War, Stop the War Coalition,

Campaign for Press and Broadcasting Freedom, Campeace, Greenpeace and a sprinkling of others – someone mooted the idea of a book on the media and misinformation and someone else noted that if a book was to be done it would have to be done "quick". Well, here it is. Not as quick as we at times imagined, but not bad. Our concerns about the plight of the Iraqi people, the voracious appetite for oil and control of the US neo-cons and their comrades in the transnational corporations have been more than borne out. Wild-sounding theories about a second Vietnam whispered in April, now seem only common sense descriptions of the brutality of the US and UK occupation and the strength of Iraqi resistance. But I don't think that anyone foresaw the powerful impact that the anti-war movement would have on the machinery of UK government as it proceeded to show signs of disintegrating during the summer of 2003. The Hutton inquiry has certainly laid bare some elements of the apparatus of lying. But for all the spectacle of previously secret emails and memos and the damage it has evidently done to the government much of the mainstream media have evaluated the hearing in terms of whether it was a good or bad day for the government or the BBC. Much of the debate on the 45 minutes claim seems to have misun-derstood the nature of the claim and the depth of deception involved even in making the claim that they did. Key sections of the mainstream media have pursued a seam of inquiry which claims to be interested in nailing Blair for lying, while neglecting to notice the proverbial elephant of deceit in their living room.

This book is a product of the dishonesty of governments and mis-reporting by the mainstream media. It has not been produced to enrich the authors and – after permissions etc. have been paid – all the royalties will be donated to organisations and initiatives attempting to counter misinformation and misreporting.

PLAN OF THE BOOK

This book is divided into four, not always neat, parts. The first reprints five of John Pilger's dispatches covering the run-up to the 15 February demonstration, the invasion of Iraq and the declaration of "victory". The second part is on propaganda. Here are pieces from the PR Watch team on the "roll out" of the US propaganda campaign beginning in earnest in September 2002 and, by former US propagandist Nancy Snow, on the apparatus of US "public diplomacy" otherwise known as foreign propaganda. Next is an historical account by Des

Freedman, of the relations between the military and the media pointing out that "embedding" of journalists has a past. Mark Curtis follows this up with a strong account of the contempt for democracy and elitist assumptions embodied in UK government propaganda practice. David Miller continues the theme by examining the apparatus of propaganda in the US and UK and how the UK branch has been transformed since 11 September 2001. Phillip Knightley gives his view on the media politics of the attack on Iraq directing our attention in particular to the Pentagon's disdain for independent reporting. Stephen Dorril focuses on the role of the intelligence services in misinformation and advances the argument that the intelligence services themselves – rather than simply government spin – are the originators of much of the misinformation which surfaces in the media. Andy Rowell takes us on to the terrain of the content of propaganda and focuses on the motivation for the conflict. According to the US and UK governments, the attack on Iraq was not about oil. Rowell – an expert on the oil industry – demolishes this claim drawing on evidence from within the industry.

The third part focuses on the role of the media in relation to Iraq and the Middle East more broadly. Mark Steel delivers a broadside against the media for their inability or unwillingness to challenge obvious lies from government. Justin Lewis and Rod Brookes report on their detailed study of British television coverage of the war revealing the pro-war bias of the main television networks. They note that Channel 4 News was consistently more dispassionate, although it too showed a pro-war orientation, and that Sky, ITN and the BBC were more consistently pro-war in their coverage. Douglas Kellner examines the US networks' coverage of the war on terror and the attack on Iraq showing the way in which the "war on terror" swept along a compliant media. Norman Solomon takes up this theme, pointing to research showing how marginal dissent has been in the US media and the personal identification of many mainstream news personnel with government policy in "war".

Julian Petley takes the sanitising of the conflict as his starting point, arguing that the broadcasters' refusal to show images of carnage is not merely a question of "taste and decency", but is profoundly political and anti-humanitarian. Edward Herman dissects the legitimation of US strategy, arguing that the US media function to "normalise" aggression by the world's leading rogue state. Patricia Holland examines the coverage of child victims in the attack on Iraq and other conflicts, arguing for an appreciation of the way in which such images are used to marshal emotional responses, in an ambivalent cavalcade of exploitation. Granville Williams asks us to cast our minds back to the attempted suppression of the Pentagon Papers as he examines how the economic interests of media corporations can interfere with news reporting. Moving on to the attack on Iraq he highlights similar processes in relation to both the US and UK media. Growing up in Iraq, Abdul Hadi Jiad was a childhood fan of the BBC. He went on to work for the BBC World Service and he tells about the problems of covering the Middle East and Iraq properly. He finishes with his sudden sacking by BBC management just before the attack on Iraq. David Edwards and David Cromwell are interested in the way in which the mainstream British media operate, in effect, as propaganda agencies for the powerful. They note in particular the failure of the mainstream media (especially television news and the liberal broadsheets) to expose government deception over weapons of mass destruction before the attack on Iraq.

Robert Fisk has reported on the Middle East for more than 20 years. In this interview with the US independent radio network Pacifica, he discusses some of the problems of reporting the Middle East and reflects on the way the media system demands only certain perspectives on conflict. Focusing on the Israel/Palestine conflict Tim Llewellyn provides a critique from the inside of the BBC's failure to properly cover the Palestinian story. The pro-Israeli bias of the UK and US media is one of the great unmentionables of civilised conversation. The result is – as Greg Philo and Maureen Gilmour show – that there is an astonishing "black hole" in public knowledge about the conflict as well as about other key international events. This lack of knowledge performs a key ideological function for western governments, reinforcing perceptions that western policy, past and present, is merely benign and defensive.

The final part of the book is devoted to alternatives to the mainstream, and the problems which face them. Faisal Bodi of Al Jazeera gives an account of the role of the satellite network in providing alternative coverage of the attack on Iraq. The importance of this is that it fatally undermined US and UK propaganda ploys, which would otherwise have had much longer shelf lives. Tim Gopsill discusses the ability of journalists to cover Iraq independently and the risks faced by those reporters who went "unilateral". The conclusion is that the biggest risk to independent journalism are US forces and their masters in the Pentagon. Yvonne Ridley gives an account of her experience of covering Afghanistan and Iraq. She also discusses her transformation from ordinary journalist to prominent peace campaigner. At some point – for so many people – the gap between lies and reality just becomes too wide to ignore. David Crouch describes the campaigning work of Media Workers Against War, and the involvement of journalists in attempting to counter misinformation and to protest against war. Like Al Jazeera the internet became extremely important in the attack on Iraq. Alistair Alexander discusses the role of the internet in providing first-hand access to wider sources of information and its use in organising the global anti-war movement. Finally, Noam Chomsky discusses the global anti-war movement. In an interview recorded before the attack on Iraq, Chomsky sets out his analysis of the potential strength and power of protest.

This book is intended to be an aid to understanding. But understanding alone is not enough. The ability to fight war depends not just on propaganda and media distortion but on the ability to use these in political and military action. Opposing war also depends not just on words and alternative understandings but on action and protest. If this book enables people to understand propaganda and misreporting and encourages them to seek out alternative information as a kind of intellectual self defence, that is good. But the more important thing is the moment when people decide that opposition also requires action. Action can take many forms, including media activism. But, media activism must also be seen as part of a bigger struggle, which, in the end, involves civil disobedience. It requires millions of us to speak and act "knowing and fearing" as John Pilger puts it, "that we cannot be silenced".

11 September 2003

NOTES

1. Mark Curtis, *Web of Deceit*, London: Vintage, 2003.
2. David Leigh, "Britain's Security Services and Journalists: The Secret Story", *British Journalism Review*, Vol. 11, No. 2, 2000, pp. 21–6.
3. House of Commons Select Committee on Foreign Affairs, Oral Evidence, <http://www.publications.parliament.uk/pa/cm200203/cmselect/cmfaff/uc813-i/uc81302.htm>.
4. United States Department of Defense, "Deputy Secretary Wolfowitz Interview with Sam Tannenhaus, Vanity Fair", News Transcript, Friday 9 May 2003, <http://www.dod.mil/transcripts/2003/tr20030509-depsecdef0223.html>.

5. Justine Smith, "The Fog of War: Conflict's Truth Obscured by Official Lies", *Daily Mirror*, 28 March 2003, pp. 16–17.
6. *Fighting the War*, BBC1, 29 June 2003.
7. Seymour Hersh, "Who Lied to Whom?" *New Yorker*, 31 March 2003.
8. *Iraq's Weapons of Mass Destruction: The Assessment of the British Government*, 24 September 2002, <http://www.number-10.gov.uk/output/Page271.asp>.
9. See <http://middleeastreference.org.uk>.
10. See the forensic deconstruction of these claims on Glen Rangwala's site, <http://www.middleeastreference.org.uk>.
11. Transcript of Alastair Campbell's evidence, 19 August 2003, <http://www.the-hutton-inquiry.org.uk/content/transcripts/hearing-trans12.htm>.
12. Select Committee on Liaison, Minutes of Evidence, 23 January 2003, <http://www.parliament.the-stationery-office.co.uk/pa/cm200203/cmselect/cmliaisn/334-i/3012102.htm>.
13. My emphasis, House of Commons, Tuesday 24 September 2002 <http://www.parliament.the-stationery-office.co.uk/pa/cm200102/cmhansrd/vo020924/debtext/20924–01.htm>.

Part I
The Media War

1
A Great Betrayal

John Pilger

3 February 2003

The Palestinian writer Ghada Karmi has described "a deep and unconscious racism [that] imbues every aspect of western conduct toward Iraq". She wrote:

> I recall that a similar culture prevailed in the UK during the 1956 Suez crisis and the 1967 Arab-Israeli war, when Nasser was the arch-villain and all Arabs were crudely targeted. Today, in Britain, such overt anti-Arabness is unacceptable, so it takes subtler forms. Saddam-bashing, a sport officially sanctioned since 1991, has made him the perfect surrogate for anti-Arab abuse.

Reading this, I turned up the *Observer's* tribute to its great editor, David Astor, who died in 2001. In opposing the British attack on Suez in 1956, Astor, said the paper, "took the government to task for its bullying and in so doing defined the *Observer* as a freethinking paper prepared to swim against the tide". In a famous editorial, Astor had described "an endeavour to re-impose 19th-century imperialism of the crudest kind". He wrote: "Nations are said to have the governments they deserve. Let us show that we deserve better." The present-day *Observer* commented that "the richness of [Astor's] language and relevance of the sentiments resonate today".

The absence of irony in this statement is bleak. Little more than a year later, in its editorial of 19 January 2003, the *Observer* finally buried David Astor and his principled "freethinking" legacy. Pretending to wring its hands, the paper announced it was for attacking Iraq: a position promoted by its news and feature pages for more than a year now, notably in its barren "investigations" seeking to link Iraq with both the anthrax scare and al-Qaeda. The paper that stood proudly against Eden on Suez is but a supplicant to the warmongering Blair, willing to support the very crime the judges at

Nuremberg deemed the most serious of all: an unprovoked attack on a sovereign country offering no threat.

Not a word in the *Observer*'s editorial mentioned the great crime committed by the British and American governments against the ordinary people of Iraq. Withholding more than $5 billion worth of humanitarian supplies approved by the Security Council, Washington, with Blair's backing, maintains a medieval blockade against Iraq. Cancer treatment equipment, water treatment equipment, painkillers, children's vaccines, to name a few of the life-giving essentials that are maliciously withheld, have resulted in the deaths of tens of thousands of vulnerable people, mostly infants under the age of five. Extrapolating from the statistics, the American scholars John Mueller and Karl Mueller conclude that "economic sanctions have probably already taken the lives of more people in Iraq than have been killed by all weapons of mass destruction".

When the *Observer* celebrates the overthrow of Saddam Hussein, with pictures of exhausted Iraqis "thanking" their liberators, will it explain to its readers that as many as a million people, mostly children, could not attend the festivities thanks to the barbaric policies of the British and American governments? No. A contortion of intellect and morality that urges participation in what has been described as "a firestorm of 800 missiles in two days" censors by omission.

We come back to Ghada Karmi's references to the veiled racism that propels every western attack on Arabs, from Churchill's preference in 1921 for "using poison gas on uncivilised tribes" to the use of depleted uranium in the 1991 Gulf slaughter. This racism applies, quintessentially, to her homeland, Palestine. While the Iraq pantomime plays, America's proxy, Israel, has begun the next stage of its historic ethnic cleansing of Palestinians. On 21 January 2003, the town of Nazlat 'Iza in the northern West Bank was invaded by a force of armoured personnel carriers, tanks and 60-ton, American-made Israeli bulldozers. Sixty-three shops were demolished, along with countless homes and olive groves. Little of this was reported outside the Arab world. Some parts of the West Bank have been under curfew for a total of 214 days. Whole villages are under house arrest. People cannot get medical care; ambulances have been prevented from reaching hospitals; women have lost their new-born babies in agony and pools of blood at military checkpoints. Fresh water is permanently scarce, and food; in some areas, more than half the children are seriously undernourished. One image unforgettable to me is the sight of children's kites flying from the windows and yards of their prison-homes.

Then there is the slaughter. During the month of November 2002, more than 50 Palestinian civilians were killed by the Israelis – a record by one calculation. These included a 95-year-old woman, 14 young children and a British UN worker, shot in the back by an Israeli sniper. Human rights groups say the deaths occurred mostly in circumstances in which there was no exchange of gunfire. "The Israelis have killed sixteen Palestinians within 48 hours," said Dr Mustafa Barghouti in Ramallah on 27 January. "That's an average of one Palestinian every three hours. The silence about this is simply unconscionable."

While Blair damns Iraq for the chemical weapons that a swarm of inspectors cannot find, he has quietly approved the sale of chemical weapons to Israel, a terrorist and rogue state by any dictionary meaning of those words. While he accuses Iraq of defying the United Nations, he is silent about the 64 UN resolutions Israel has ignored – a world record.

The Israeli terrorists, who subjugate and brutalise a whole nation, demolishing homes and shops, expelling and killing and "systematically torturing" (Amnesty) day after day, are not mentioned in the *Observer* editorial. No "decisive action" (the *Observer*'s words) is required against the prima facie war criminals Ariel Sharon and General Shaul Mofaz, who, along with their predecessors, have caused a degree of suffering of which Saddam Hussein and al-Qaeda can only dream. There is no suggestion that the British force heading for the Middle East should "intervene" in the "republic of fear" that Israel has created in Palestine in defiance of the world, and "displace" them. There is not a word about the weapons of mass destruction that Sharon repeatedly flaunts ("the Arabs may have the oil, but we have the matches").

To most people in Europe, and across the world, these double standards offend common decency. Overhear people on the bus and in the pub if you need to know why. This decency, combined with a critical public intelligence, is not understood by the suburban propagandists, whose fondness for and imagined closeness to power mark their servility to it. The same power and its court were defined succinctly by that distinguished scholar of international politics, the late Professor Hedley Bull. "Particular states or groups of states", he wrote, "that set themselves up as the authoritative judges of the world common good, in disregard of the view of others, are in fact a menace."

2
The Lies of Old

John Pilger

17 February 2003

In "Dulce et decorum est", his classic poem from the First World War, Wilfred Owen described young soldiers, doomed to die, "like old beggars under sacks", and a man's "hanging face, like a devil's sick of sin".

> If you could hear, at every jolt, the blood
> Come gargling from the froth-corrupted lungs,
> Obscene as cancer, bitter as the cud
> Of vile, incurable sores on innocent tongues,–
> My friend, you would not tell with such high zest
> To children ardent for some desperate glory,
> The old Lie: Dulce et decorum est
> Pro patria mori.

What has changed since Owen wrote those words, not long before his own death in the trenches? In the Gulf War in 1991, the slaughter of Iraqi conscripts was conducted in a similar industrial way. Three brigades of the United States 1st Mechanized Infantry Division used snow ploughs mounted on tanks and combat earth movers, mostly at night, to bury terrified Iraqi teenagers, many of them still alive, including the wounded, in more than 70 miles of trenches. A brigade commander, Colonel Anthony Moreno, said: "For all I know, we could have killed thousands."

The policy of General Norman Schwarzkopf, the American field commander, was that the Iraqi dead were not to be counted. "This is the first war in modern times", said one of his aides, "where every screwdriver, every nail, is accounted for." As for human beings, "I don't think anybody is going to come up with an accurate count for Iraqi dead."

In fact, Schwarzkopf did provide figures to Congress, indicating that at least 100,000 Iraqi soldiers had been killed. He offered no estimate of civilian deaths. Almost a year later, the Medical Education

Trust in London published a comprehensive study of casualties. Up to a quarter of a million men, women and children were killed or died in the aftermath of the American-led attack.

As in 1914–18, the war was a bloodfest, with one difference. Almost all the casualties were on one side, and as many as half of them were civilians. A quarter of the 148 American soldiers who died were killed by other Americans. Most of the British who died were also killed by Americans, including nine blown to bits by an American tank. Little of this was reported at the time. The massacre of conscripts and the wounded was revealed six months later by one tenacious reporter, Knut Royce, in New York's *Newsday*. Although journalists sent to report the Gulf War enjoyed extraordinary communications, their editors allowed them to be corralled in a censorial "pool" system.

Little had changed since 1914–18 when *The Times* correspondent Sir Philip Gibbs (compliant media stars were knighted then; nowadays it's more likely to be an OBE and wealth) wrote: "We were our own censors ... some of us wrote the truth ... apart from the naked realism of horrors and losses, and criticism of the facts which did not come within the liberty of our pen." When the Gulf War was over, the BBC's foreign editor, John Simpson, reported from Baghdad: "As for the human casualties, tens of thousands of them, or the brutal effect the war had on millions of others ... we didn't see much of that." If the Gulf War was the most "covered" war in history, it was also the most covered-up. With honourable exceptions, the massacre of so many human beings was not considered news.

Every effort is now being made to repeat this travesty, this "old lie". In his interview on 6 February with the Prime Minister, the BBC's Jeremy Paxman's only reference to the human cost of the Bush/Blair adventure was to repeat a question from a woman in his audience. "She asked you", said Paxman to Tony Blair, "about the deaths of innocent people. I mean, as a Christian, how do you feel about innocent people dying?" He then allowed Blair to get away with a self-serving answer that included the lie that, prior to NATO's attack on Yugoslavia, he "let the peace negotiations go on for several more weeks in order to try and get them sorted".

Paxman made no mention of a United Nations estimate, based on World Health Organisation figures, that "as many as 500,000 people could require treatment as a result of direct and indirect injuries" and that an attack was "likely to cause an outbreak of diseases in epidemic if not pandemic proportions". Neither did he ask Blair how he could justify attacking a nation where almost half the population were children, and a large proportion of them were stricken from the consequences of an American- and British-driven blockade. If the American and British governments had no quarrel with the Iraqi people and wished to liberate them, Paxman might have asked, quoting Blair himself, why was the United States currently blocking more than $5 billion worth of humanitarian supplies approved by the Security Council?

No, the BBC's inquisitor was more concerned with the complexities of a second UN resolution, a fig leaf, an amoral contrivance. The clear implication was that as long as the killing of large numbers of innocent human beings was backed by a second resolution, "the problem" was solved. That the Security Council's principal members were themselves the sources of numerous human rights crimes was not deemed relevant.

Suppressing the human cost of war is the "old lie" in Wilfred Owen's wonderful poem. Yet in 2003, a privileged establishment journalist paid large amounts of public money ensured that the Prime Minister did not have to justify the old lie, just as he ensured that Blair did not have to explain the hypocrisy and double standards of Britain's long and cynical role in Iraq. He even allowed Blair contemptuously to dismiss "the oil thing" as a "conspiracy theory". With the lives of thousands in the balance, he asked Blair if he prayed with George W. Bush.

The opposition of the great majority of the British people, and of people all over the world, to an unprovoked attack on another country has illuminated the indecency of those who claim to speak for and share the public's essentially liberal values. From behind a humanitarian mask, they promote killing. To this "liberal" lobby, it is wrong to kill innocent people if you are Saddam Hussein (evil) and right to kill them if you are Tony Blair (good). The actual deaths and the crime of killing are irrelevant; the attitude of their killers is what matters.

On 3 February, I pointed out that the *Observer*, in its editorial of 19 January, had finally buried the principled "freethinking" legacy of its great editor, David Astor. The paper that had stood against British imperialism's attack on Egypt in 1956 announced it was for attacking Iraq. Coming to the defence of the *Observer*'s betrayal of its history and readers was the Guardian group's latest right-wing provocateur, David Aaronovitch, who exemplifies the mask-wearers. Promoting himself as a "liberal", Aaronovitch is a former apparatchik of the Communist Party that supported the crushing of the Hungarian uprising in 1956. The transition from Party hack to pro-Bush warmonger is a smooth road trodden by many. The obscenity of those like Aaronovitch is crystallised in three words in his *Observer* column of 2 February. The attack on Iraq, he wrote, will be "the easy bit".

"The easy bit" will be an onslaught of hundreds of missiles on a defenceless population, resulting in countless, and uncounted, civilian casualties. Defending the right of rapacious power to do what it likes when it likes, from Hungary to Iraq, Aaronovitch's "easy bit" is the callous dismissal of the lives of innocent people who will be cut to pieces by cluster bombs, dropped by American and British pilots from a safe height. "Shooting fish in a barrel", the American aircraft carrier pilots called it in 1991.

Unlike the witness-nothing windbags, who appear almost to yearn for war, I have seen the victims of cluster bombs. From many snapshots, here is one. Two children writhe on a dirt floor, their bodies displaying hundreds of small open wounds. They have been showered with tiny plastic objects from an American "pellet bomb", the prototype of the cluster bomb. As the darts move through their vital organs, they die a terrible death, the equivalent of swallowing acid.

"For many of us [supporting an attack on Iraq]," wrote Aaronovitch, "this has become the most difficult and painful judgement to make." Painful? What pain will he feel? Pain is what the children on the dirt floor felt. Pain is what dying Iraqi infants, who are denied painkillers by the Anglo-American blockade, feel. Ask Denis Halliday, the former UN assistant secretary general and UN humanitarian co-ordinator for Iraq, who watched them die and demanded that the embargo's enforcers, such as Blair, join him and hear the children's screams.

Who among the "liberals" who say their motive for backing Bush and Blair is to "liberate" the Iraqi people has spoken out against this medieval siege that has "liberated" hundreds of thousands of Iraqis from life? Their specious compassion is like that of the man who stands besides a torturer, reassuring the victim that his ordeal will end if he accepts the torturer's terms. "Nothing about Iraq is hard for Pilger," wrote Aaronovitch. "He was opposed to the containment of Saddam through the enforcement of the no-fly zones, dismissive of the threats to the Kurdish people of the north." Once again, the unworthy victims are airbrushed. The fishermen, farmers, shepherds and their families and sheep, slaughtered by marauding "coalition" aircraft, are simply omitted. Their deaths are documented in a United Nations security section report and verified by the UN humanitarian co-ordinator for Iraq.

As for "the threats to the Kurdish people of the north", year after year, Kurdish villages in northern Iraq have been viciously attacked by the Turkish military, guardians of NATO. They carry out their atrocities under cover of the illegal "no-fly zones" and with the complicity of the US and Britain, which routinely ground their own planes so that their Turkish allies can get on with killing the Kurds. This is rarely reported. In his seminal essay "The Banality of Evil", Edward S. Herman described the important state function of certain journalists and commentators as "normalising the unthinkable for the general public". What it is wonderful to see these days is that they have failed. There has never been a time of such overwhelming popular opposition to a war before it began. What Aaronovitch calls "the left" are people of decency and common sense from right across the political spectrum.

I read a letter recently by a former conservative Australian politician, writing on behalf of other Australian Tories. Its deeply offended and angry tone is representative of the feelings of millions. It says:

> Wilful mixing of the "war against terrorism" with alleged threat from Iraq is an insult to our intelligence, and if there's one thing I like less than mindless war, it's being treated like an idiot by people not bright enough to know we know or too full of their own importance to care. George Bush Junior is the worst leader of a major democracy I have observed for more than 50 years.

Today, all over the world, the common decency of the majority of humanity is ranged against Bush and Blair and their suburban propagandists, who can either listen and draw back and save countless lives – or they can do as Bertolt Brecht suggested in "The Solution":

> The Secretary of the Writers' Union
> Had leaflets distributed in the Stalinallee
> Stating that the people
> Had forfeited the confidence of the government
> And could win it back only
> By redoubled efforts. Would it not be easier
> In that case for the government
> To dissolve the people
> And elect another?

3
The Case for
Civil Disobedience

John Pilger

17 March 2003

How have we got to this point, where two western governments take us into an illegal and immoral war against a stricken nation with whom we have no quarrel and who offers us no threat: an act of aggression opposed by almost everybody and whose charade is transparent?

How can they attack, in our name, a country already crushed by more than twelve years of an embargo aimed mostly at the civilian population, of whom 42 per cent are children – a medieval siege that has taken the lives of at least half a million children and is described as genocidal by the former United Nations humanitarian co-ordinator for Iraq?

How can those claiming to be "liberals" disguise their embarrassment, and shame, while justifying their support for George Bush's proposed launch of 800 missiles in two days as a "liberation"? How can they ignore two United Nations studies which reveal that some 500,000 people will be at risk? Do they not hear their own echo in the words of the American general who said famously of a Vietnamese town he had just levelled: "We had to destroy it in order to save it"?

"Few of us", Arthur Miller once wrote, "can easily surrender our belief that society must somehow make sense. The thought that the State has lost its mind and is punishing so many innocent people is intolerable. And so the evidence has to be internally denied."

These days, Miller's astuteness applies to a minority of warmongers and apologists. Since 11 September 2001, the consciousness of the majority has soared. The word "imperialism" has been rescued from agitprop and returned to common usage. America's and Britain's planned theft of the Iraqi oilfields, following historical precedent, is well understood. The false choices of the Cold War are redundant, and people are once again stirring in their millions. More and more of them now glimpse American power, as Mark Twain wrote, "with its banner of the Prince of Peace in one hand and its loot-basket and its butcher-knife in the other".

What is heartening is the apparent demise of "anti-Americanism" as a respectable means of stifling recognition and analysis of American Imperialism. Intellectual loyalty oaths, similar to those rife during the Third Reich, when the abusive "anti-German" was enough to silence dissent, no longer work. In America itself, there are too many anti-Americans filling the streets now: those whom Martha Gellhorn called "that life-saving minority who judge their government in moral terms, who are the people with a wakeful conscience and can be counted upon".

Perhaps for the first time since the late 1940s, Americanism as an ideology is being identified in the same terms as any rapacious power structure; and we can thank Bush and Dick Cheney and Donald Rumsfeld and Condoleezza Rice for that, even though their acts of international violence have yet to exceed those of the "liberal" Bill Clinton.

"My guess", wrote Norman Mailer recently,

> is that, like it or not, or want it or not, we are going to go to war because that is the only solution Bush and his people can see. The dire prospect that opens, therefore, is that America is going to become a mega-banana republic where the army will have more and more importance in our lives. And, before it is all over, democracy, noble and delicate as it is, may give way ... Indeed, democracy is the special condition that we will be called upon to defend in the coming years. That will be enormously difficult because the combination of the corporation, the military and the complete investiture of the flag with mass spectator sports has set up a pre-fascist atmosphere in America already.

In the military plutocracy that is the American state, with its unelected president, venal Supreme Court, silent Congress, gutted Bill of Rights and compliant media, Mailer's "pre-fascist atmosphere" makes common sense. The dissident American writer William Rivers Pitt pursues this further. "Critics of the Bush administration", he wrote,

> like to bandy about the word "fascist" when speaking of George. The image that word conjures is of Nazi storm troopers marching

in unison towards Hitler's Final Solution. This does not at all fit. It is better, in this matter, to view the Bush administration through the eyes of Benito Mussolini. Dubbed "the father of fascism", Mussolini defined the word in a far more pertinent fashion. "Fascism," he said, "should more properly be called corporatism, since it is the merger of state and corporate power."

Bush himself offered an understanding of this on 26 February 2003 when he addressed the annual dinner of the American Enterprise Institute. He paid tribute to "some of the finest minds of our nation [who] are at work on some of the greatest challenges to our nation. You do such good work that my administration has borrowed twenty such minds. I want to thank them for their service."

The "twenty such minds" are crypto-fascists who fit the definition of William Rivers Pitt. The Institute is America's biggest, most important and wealthiest "think-tank". A typical member is John Bolton, under-secretary for arms control, the Bush official most responsible for dismantling the 1972 Anti-Ballistic Missile Treaty, arguably the most important arms control agreement of the late twentieth century. The Institute's strongest ties are with extreme Zionism and the regime of Ariel Sharon. Last month, Bolton was in Tel Aviv to hear Sharon's view on which country in the region should be next after Iraq. For the expansionists running Israel, the prize is not so much the conquest of Iraq but Iran. A significant proportion of the Israeli air force is already based in Turkey with Iran in its sights, waiting for an American attack.

Richard Perle is the Institute's star. Perle is chairman of the powerful Defense Policy Board at the Pentagon, the author of the insane policies of "total war" and "creative destruction". The latter is designed to subjugate finally the Middle East, beginning with the $90 billion invasion of Iraq.

Perle helped to set up another crypto-fascist group, the Project for the New American Century. Other founders include Vice President Cheney, Defense Secretary Rumsfeld and Deputy Defense Secretary Paul Wolfowitz. The Institute's "mission report", "Rebuilding America's Defences: strategy, forces and resources for a new century", is an unabashed blueprint for world conquest. Before Bush came to power, it recommended an increase in arms spending by $48 billion so that America "can fight and win multiple, simultaneous major theater wars". This has come true. It said that nuclear war-fighting should be given the priority it deserved. This has come true. It said that Iraq should be a primary target. And so it is. And it dismissed the issue of Saddam Hussein's "weapons of mass destruction" as a convenient excuse, which it is.

Written by Wolfowitz, this guide to world domination puts the onus on the Pentagon to establish a "new order" in the Middle East under unchallenged US authority. A "liberated" Iraq, the centrepiece of the new order, will be divided and ruled, probably by three American generals; and after a horrific onslaught, known as Shock and Awe.

Vladimir Slipchenko, one of the world's leading military analysts, says the testing of new weapons is a "main purpose" of the attack on Iraq. "Nobody is saying anything about it," he said last month.

In May 2001, in his first presidential address, Bush spoke about the need for preparation for future wars. He emphasised that the armed forces needed to be completely high-tech, capable of conducting hostilities by the no-contact method. After a series of live experiments – in Iraq in 1991, Yugoslavia, Afghanistan – many corporations achieved huge profits. Now the bottom line is $50–60bn a year.

He says that, apart from new types of cluster bombs and cruise missiles, the Americans will use their untested pulse bomb, known also as a microwave bomb. Each discharges two megawatts of radiation which instantly puts out of action all communications, computers, radios, even hearing aids and heart pacemakers. "Imagine, your heart explodes!" he said.

In the future, this Pax Americana will be policed with nuclear, biological and chemical weapons used "pre-emptively", even in conflicts that do not directly engage US interests. In August, the Bush administration will convene a secret meeting in Omaha, Nebraska, to discuss the construction of a new generation of nuclear weapons, including "mini nukes", "bunker busters" and neutron bombs. Generals, government officials and nuclear scientists will also discuss the appropriate propaganda to convince the American public that the new weapons are necessary.

Such is Mailer's pre-fascist state. If appeasement has any meaning today, it has little to do with a regional dictator and everything to do with the demonstrably dangerous men in Washington. It is vitally important that we understand their goals and the degree of their ruthlessness. One example: General Pervez Musharraf, the Pakistani dictator, was last year deliberately allowed by Washington to come within an ace of starting a nuclear war with India – and to continue supplying North Korea with nuclear technology – because he agreed to hand over al-Qaeda operatives. The other day, John Howard, the Australian prime minister and Washington mouthpiece, praised Musharraf, the man who almost blew up west Asia, for his "personal courage and outstanding leadership".

In 1946, Justice Robert Jackson, chief prosecutor at the Nuremberg trials, said: "The very essence of the Nuremberg charter is that individuals have international duties which transcend national obligations of obedience imposed by the state." With an attack on Iraq almost a certainty, the millions who filled London and other capitals on the weekend of 15–16 February 2003, and the millions who cheered them on, now have these transcendent duties. The Bush gang, and Tony Blair, cannot be allowed to hold the rest of us captive to their obsessions and war plans. Speculation on Blair's political future is trivia; he and the robotic Jack Straw and Geoff Hoon must be stopped now, for the reasons long argued in these pages and on hundreds of platforms. And, incidentally, no one should be distracted by the latest opportunistic antics of Clare Short, whose routine hints of "rebellion", followed by her predictable inaction, have helped to give Blair the time he wants to subvert the UN.

There is only one form of opposition now: it is civil disobedience leading to what the police call civil unrest. The latter is feared by undemocratic governments of all stripes.

The revolt has already begun. In January 2003, Scottish train drivers refused to move munitions. In Italy, people have been blocking dozens of trains carrying American weapons and personnel, and dockers have refused to load arms shipments. US military bases have been blockaded in Germany, and thousands have demonstrated at Shannon airport which, despite Ireland's neutrality, is being used by the US military to refuel its planes en route to Iraq.

"We have become a threat, but can we deliver?" asked Jessica Azulay and Brian Dominick of the American resistance movement. "Policy-makers are debating right now whether or not they have to heed our dissent. Now we must make it clear to them that there will be political and economic consequences if they decide to ignore us."

My own view is that if the protest movement sees itself as a world power, as an expression of true internationalism, then success need not be a dream. That depends on how far people are prepared to go. The young female employee of the Gloucestershire-based top-secret

Government Communications Headquarters (GCHQ), who was charged in March 2003 with leaking information about America's dirty tricks operation on members of the Security Council, shows us the courage required.

In the meantime, the new Mussolinis are on their balconies, with their virtuoso rants and impassioned insincerity. Reduced to wagging their fingers in a futile attempt to silence us, they see millions of us for the first time, knowing and fearing that we cannot be silenced.

4

Crime Against Humanity

John Pilger

14 April 2003

Did I read the following words in *Catch-22*? Surely, they were meant to be ferociously ironic? Alas, I doubt that whoever designed the *Observer's* page three last Sunday had Joseph Heller in mind when he wrote the weasel headline: "The moment young Omar discovered the price of war". These cowardly words accompanied a photograph of an American marine reaching out to comfort 15-year-old Omar, having just participated in the mass murder of his father, mother, two sisters and brother during the unprovoked invasion of their homeland, in breach of the most basic law of civilised peoples.

No true epitaph for them in Britain's famous liberal newspaper; no honest headline, such as: "This American marine murdered this boy's family". No photograph of Omar's father, mother, sisters and brother dismembered and blood-soaked by automatic fire. Versions of the *Observer's* propaganda picture have been appearing in the Anglo-American press since the invasion began: tender cameos of American troops reaching out, kneeling, ministering to their "liberated" victims.

And where were the pictures from the village of Furat, where 80 men, women and children were reportedly rocketed to death? Apart from the *Daily Mirror*, where were the pictures, and footage, of small children holding up their hands in terror while Bush's thugs forced their families to kneel in the street? Imagine that in a British high street.

"To initiate a war of aggression", said the judges in the Nuremberg trial of the Nazi leadership, "is not only an international crime; it is the supreme international crime differing only from other war crimes in that it contains within itself the accumulated evil of the whole." In stating this guiding principle of international law, the judges specifically rejected German arguments of the "necessity" for pre-emptive attacks against other countries.

Nothing Bush and Blair, their cluster-bombing boys and their media court do now will change the truth of their great crime in Iraq. It is a matter of record, understood by the majority of humanity, if not by those who claim to speak for "us". As Denis Halliday said of the Anglo-American embargo against Iraq, it will "slaughter them in the history books". It was Halliday who, as then assistant secretary general of the United Nations, set up the "oil for food" programme in Iraq in 1996 and quickly realised that the UN had become an instrument of "a genocidal attack on a whole society". He resigned in protest, as did his successor, Hans von Sponeck, who described "the wanton and shaming punishment of a nation".

I have mentioned these two men often in the past, partly because their names and their witness have been airbrushed from most of the media. I well remember Jeremy Paxman bellowing at Halliday on *Newsnight* shortly after his resignation: "So are you an apologist for Saddam Hussein?" That helped set the tone for the travesty of journalism that now daily, almost gleefully, treats criminal war as sport. In a leaked email, a BBC executive described the BBC's war coverage as "extraordinary – it almost feels like World Cup football when you go from Umm Qasr to another theatre of war somewhere else and you're switching between battles".

He is talking about murder. That is what the Americans do, and no one will say so, even when they are murdering journalists. They bring to this one-sided attack on a weak and mostly defenceless people the same racist, homicidal intent I witnessed in Vietnam, where they had a whole programme of murder called Operation Phoenix. This runs through all their foreign wars, as it does through their own divided society. Take your pick of the current onslaught. Last weekend, a column of their tanks swept heroically into Baghdad and out again. They murdered people along the way. They blew off the limbs of women and the scalps of children. Hear their voices on the unedited and unbroadcast videotape: "We shot the shit out of it." Their victims overwhelm the morgues and hospitals – hospitals already denuded of drugs and painkillers by America's deliberate withholding of $5.4 billion in humanitarian goods, approved by the Security Council and paid for by Iraq.

Heller would appreciate the sideshows. Take the British helicopter pilot who came to blows with an American who had almost shot him down. "Don't you know the Iraqis don't have a fucking air force?" he shouted. Did this pilot reflect on the truth he had uttered, on the whole craven enterprise against a stricken Third World country and his own part in this crime? I doubt it. The British have been the most skilled at delusion and lying. By any standard, the Iraqi resistance to the high-tech Anglo-American machine was heroic. With ancient tanks and mortars, small arms and desperate ambushes, they panicked the Americans and reduced the British military class to one of its specialities – mendacious condescension.

The Iraqis who fight are "terrorists", "hoodlums", "pockets of Ba'ath Party loyalists", "kamikaze" and "feds" (fedayeen). They are not real people: cultured and cultivated people. They are Arabs. This vocabulary of dishonour has been faithfully parroted by those enjoying it all from the broadcasting box. "What do you make of Basra?" asked *The Today Programme*'s presenter of a former general embedded in the studio. "It's hugely encouraging, isn't it?" he replied. Their mutual excitement, like their plummy voices, are their bond.

On the same day, in a *Guardian* letter, Tim Llewellyn, a former BBC Middle East correspondent, pointed us to evidence of this "hugely encouraging" truth – fleeting pictures on Sky News of British soldiers smashing their way into a family home in Basra, pointing their guns at a woman and manhandling, hooding and manacling young men, one of whom was shown quivering with terror.

Is Britain "liberating" Basra by taking political prisoners and, if so, based on what sort of intelligence, given Britain's long unfamiliarity with this territory and its inhabitants. The least this ugly display will do is remind Arabs and Muslims everywhere of our Anglo-Saxon double standards – we can show your prisoners in ... degrading positions, but don't you dare show ours.

The BBC executive says the suffering of Umm Qasr is "like World Cup football". There are 40,000 people in Umm Qasr; desperate refugees are streaming in and the hospitals are overflowing. All this misery is due entirely to the "coalition" invasion and the British siege, which forced the United Nations to withdraw its humanitarian aid staff. CAFOD, the Catholic relief agency, which has sent a team to Umm Qasr, says the standard humanitarian quota for water in emergency situations is 20 litres per person per day. CAFOD reports hospitals entirely without water and people drinking from contaminated wells. According to the World Health Organisation, 1.5 million people across southern Iraq are without water, and epidemics are inevitable. And what are "our boys" doing to alleviate this, apart from staging childish, theatrical occupations of presidential palaces, having fired shoulder-held missiles into a civilian city and dropped cluster bombs?

A British colonel laments to his "embedded" flock that "it is difficult to deliver aid in an area that is still an active battle zone". The logic of his own words mocks him. If Iraq was not a battle zone, if the British and the Americans were not defying international law, there would be no difficulty in delivering aid.

There is something especially disgusting about the lurid propaganda coming from these PR-trained British officers, who have not a clue about Iraq and its people. They describe the liberation they are bringing from "the world's worst tyranny", as if anything, including death by cluster bomb or dysentery, is better than "life under Saddam". The inconvenient truth is that, according to UNICEF, the Ba'athists built the most modern health service in the Middle East. No one disputes the grim, totalitarian nature of the regime; but Saddam Hussein was careful to use the oil wealth to create a modern secular society and a large and prosperous middle class. Iraq was the only Arab country with a 90 per cent clean water supply and with free education. All this was smashed by the Anglo-American embargo. When the embargo was imposed in 1990, the Iraqi civil service organised a food distribution system that the UN's Food and Agriculture Organisation described as "a model of efficiency ... undoubtedly saving Iraq from famine". That, too, was smashed when the invasion was launched.

Why are the British yet to explain why their troops have to put on protective suits to recover dead and wounded in vehicles hit by American "friendly fire"? The reason is that the Americans are using solid uranium coated on missiles and tank shells. When I was in southern Iraq, doctors estimated a sevenfold increase in cancers in areas where depleted uranium was used by the Americans and British in the 1991 war. Under the subsequent embargo, Iraq, unlike Kuwait, has been denied equipment with which to clean up its contaminated battlefields. The hospitals in Basra have wards overflowing with children with cancers of a variety not seen before 1991. They have no painkillers; they are fortunate if they have aspirin.

With honourable exceptions (Robert Fisk; Al Jazeera), little of this has been reported. Instead, the media have performed their pre-ordained role as imperial America's "soft power": rarely identifying "our" crime, or misrepresenting it as a struggle between good intentions and evil incarnate. This abject professional and moral failure now beckons the unseen dangers of such an epic, false victory, inviting its repetition in Iran, Korea, Syria, Cuba, China.

George Bush has said: "It will be no defence to say: 'I was just following orders.'" He is correct. The Nuremberg judges left in no doubt the right of ordinary soldiers to follow their conscience in an illegal war of aggression. Three British soldiers have had the courage to seek status as conscientious objectors. They face court martial and imprisonment; yet virtually no questions have been asked about them in the media. George Galloway has been pilloried for asking the same question as Bush, and he and Tam Dalyell, Father of the House of Commons, are being threatened with withdrawal of the Labour whip.

Dalyell, 41 years a member of the Commons, has said the Prime Minister is a war criminal who should be sent to The Hague. This is not gratuitous; on the prima facie evidence, Blair is a war criminal, and all those who have been, in one form or another, accessories should be reported to the International Criminal Court. Not only did they promote a charade of pretexts few now take seriously, they brought terrorism and death to Iraq. A growing body of legal opinion around the world agrees that the new court has a duty, as Eric Herring of Bristol University wrote, to investigate "not only the regime, but also the UN bombing and sanctions which violated the human rights of Iraqis on a vast scale". Add the present piratical war, whose spectre is the uniting of Arab nationalism with militant Islam. The whirlwind reaped by Blair and Bush is just beginning. Such is the magnitude of their crime.

5
The Unthinkable is Becoming Normal

John Pilger

20 April 2003

Last Sunday, seated in the audience at the Bafta television awards ceremony, I was struck by the silence. Here were many of the most influential members of the liberal elite, the writers, producers, dramatists, journalists and managers of our main source of information, television; and not one broke the silence. It was as though we were disconnected from the world outside: a world of rampant, rapacious power and great crimes committed in our name by our government and its foreign master. Iraq is the "test case", says the Bush regime, which every day sails closer to Mussolini's definition of fascism: the merger of a militarist state with corporate power. Iraq is a test case for western liberals, too. As the suffering mounts in that stricken country, with Red Cross doctors describing "incredible" levels of civilian casualties, the choice of the next conquest, Syria or Iran, is "debated" on the BBC, as if it were a World Cup venue.

The unthinkable is being normalised. The American essayist Edward Herman wrote:

> There is usually a division of labor in doing and rationalizing the unthinkable, with the direct brutalizing and killing done by one set of individuals ... others working on improving technology (a better crematory gas, a longer burning and more adhesive napalm, bomb fragments that penetrate flesh in hard-to-trace patterns). It is the function of the experts, and the mainstream media, to normalize the unthinkable for the general public.

Herman wrote that following the 1991 Gulf War, whose nocturnal images of American bulldozers burying thousands of teenage Iraqi conscripts, many of them alive and trying to surrender, were never shown. Thus, the slaughter was normalised. A study released just before Christmas 1991 by the Medical Educational Trust revealed that more than 200,000 Iraqi men, women and children were killed or died as a direct result of the American-led attack. This was barely reported, and the homicidal nature of the "war" never entered public consciousness in this country, let alone America.

The Pentagon's deliberate destruction of Iraq's civilian infrastructure, such as power sources and water and sewage plants, together with the imposition of an embargo as barbaric as a medieval siege, produced a degree of suffering never fully comprehended in the west. Documented evidence was available, volumes of it; by the late 1990s, more than 6,000 infants were dying every month, and the two senior United Nations officials responsible for humanitarian relief in Iraq, Denis Halliday and Hans von Sponeck, resigned, protesting the embargo's hidden agenda. Halliday called it "genocide".

As of last July, 2002, the United States, backed by the Blair government, was wilfully blocking humanitarian supplies worth $5.4 billion, everything from vaccines and plasma bags to simple painkillers, all of which Iraq had paid for and the Security Council had approved.

Last month's attack by the two greatest military powers on a demoralised, sick and largely defenceless population was the logical extension of this barbarism. This is now called a "victory", and the flags are coming out. Last week, the submarine HMS *Turbulent* returned to Plymouth, flying the Jolly Roger, the pirates' emblem. How appropriate. This nuclear-powered machine fired some 30 American Tomahawk cruise missiles at Iraq. Each missile cost £700,000: a total of £21 million. That alone would provide desperate Basra with food, water and medicines.

Imagine: what did Commander Andrew McKendrick's 30 missiles hit? How many people did they kill or maim in a population nearly half of which are children? Maybe, Commander, you targeted a palace with gold taps in the bathroom, or a "command and control facility", as the Americans and Geoffrey Hoon like to lie. Or perhaps each of your missiles had a sensory device that could distinguish George Bush's "evil-doers" from toddlers. What is certain is that your targets did not include the Ministry of Oil.

When the invasion began, the British public was called upon to "support" troops sent illegally and undemocratically to kill people with whom we had no quarrel. "The ultimate test of our professionalism" is how Commander McKendrick describes an unprovoked attack on a nation with no submarines, no navy and no air force, and now with no clean water and no electricity and, in many hospitals, no anaesthetic with which to amputate small limbs shredded by shrapnel. I have seen elsewhere how this is done, with a gag in the patient's mouth.

One child, Ali Ismaeel Abbas, the boy who lost his parents and his arms in a missile attack, has been flown to a modern hospital in Kuwait. Publicity has saved him. Tony Blair says he will "do everything he can" to help him. This must be the ultimate insult to the memory of all the children of Iraq who have died violently in Blair's war, and as a result of the embargo that Blair enthusiastically endorsed. The saving of Ali substitutes a media spectacle of charity for our right to knowledge of the extent of the crime committed against the young in our name. Let us now see the pictures of the "truckload of dozens of dismembered women and children" that the Red Cross doctors saw.

As Ali was flown to Kuwait, the Americans were preventing Save the Children from sending a plane with medical supplies into northern Iraq, where 40,000 are desperate. According to the UN, half the population of Iraq has only enough food to last a few weeks. The head of the World Food Programme says that 40 million people around the world are now seriously at risk because of the distraction of the humanitarian disaster in Iraq.

And this is "liberation"? No, it is bloody conquest, witnessed by America's mass theft of Iraq's resources and natural wealth. Ask the crowds in the streets, for whom the fear and hatred of Saddam Hussein have been transferred, virtually overnight, to Bush and Blair and perhaps to "us".

Such is the magnitude of Blair's folly and crime that the contrivance of his vindication is urgent. As if speaking for the vindicators, Andrew Marr, the BBC's political editor, reported: "[Blair] said they would be able to take Baghdad without a bloodbath, and that in the end the Iraqis would be celebrating. And on both of those points he has been proved conclusively right."

What constitutes a bloodbath to the BBC's man in Downing Street? Did the murder of the 3,000 people in New York's Twin Towers qualify? If his answer is yes, then the thousands killed in Iraq during the past month is a bloodbath. One report says that more than 3,000 Iraqis were killed within 24 hours or less. Or are the vindicators saying that the lives of one set of human beings have less value than those recognisable to us? Devaluation of human life has always been essential to the pursuit of imperial power, from the Congo to Vietnam, from Chechnya to Iraq.

If, as Milan Kundera wrote, "the struggle of people against power is the struggle of memory against forgetting", then we must not forget. We must not forget Blair's lies about weapons of mass destruction which, as Hans Blix now says, were based on "fabricated evidence". We must not forget his callous attempts to deny that an American missile killed 62 people in a Baghdad market. And we must not forget the reason for the bloodbath. Last September, in announcing its National Security Strategy, Bush served notice that America intended to dominate the world by force. Iraq was indeed the "test case". The rest was a charade.

We must not forget that a British defence secretary has announced, for the first time, that his government is prepared to launch an attack with nuclear weapons. He echoes Bush, of course. An ascendant mafia now rules the United States, and the Prime Minister is in thrall to it. Together, they empty noble words – liberation, freedom and democracy – of their true meaning. The unspoken truth is that behind the bloody conquest of Iraq is the conquest of us all: of our minds, our humanity and our self-respect at the very least. If we say and do nothing, victory over us is assured.

Part 2
Propaganda Wars

6
War Is Sell

Laura Miller, John Stauber
and Sheldon Rampton

"From a marketing point of view, you don't introduce new products in August," White House Chief of Staff Andrew H. Card Jr told the *New York Times* in September 2002. Card was explaining what the *Times* characterised as a "meticulously planned strategy to persuade the public, the Congress, and the allies of the need to confront the threat from Saddam Hussein".

Officially, President George W. Bush is claiming that he sees war as an option of last resort, and many members of the American public seem to have taken him at his word. In reality, say journalists and others who have closely observed the key players in decision-making positions at the White House, they have already decided on war.

In November, key Pentagon adviser Richard Perle stunned British members of parliament when he told them that even a "clean bill of health" from UN chief weapons inspector Hans Blix would not stop a US attack on Iraq. "Evidence from one witness on Saddam Hussein's weapons programme will be enough to trigger a fresh military onslaught," reported the *Mirror* of London, paraphrasing Perle's comments at an all-party meeting on global security.

"America is duping the world into believing it supports these inspections," said Peter Kilfoyle, a member of the British Labour Party and a former British defence minister. "President Bush intends to go to war even if inspectors find nothing. This makes a mockery of the whole process and exposes America's real determination to bomb Iraq."

Even the US Central Intelligence Agency, hardly a pacifist organisation, has come under pressure from White House and Pentagon hawks unhappy with the CIA's reluctance to offer intelligence assessments that would justify an invasion. "The Pentagon is bringing relentless pressure to bear on the agency to produce intelligence reports more supportive of war with Iraq," reported Robert Dreyfuss in the *American Prospect* in December. "Morale inside the US national-security apparatus is said to be low, with career staffers feeling intimidated and pressured to justify the push for war." Much of the pro-war information cited by the White House comes from the Iraqi National Congress (INC), a front group established in the early 1990s by the Rendon Group. "Most Iraq hands with long experience in dealing with that country's tumultuous politics consider the INC's intelligence-gathering abilities to be nearly nil," Dreyfuss stated.

The Pentagon's critics are appalled that intelligence provided by the INC might shape US decisions about going to war against Baghdad. At the CIA and at the State Department, Ahmed Chalabi, the INC's leader, is viewed as the ineffectual head of a self-inflated and corrupt organization skilled at lobbying and public relations, but not much else.

RENDON TO THE RESCUE

"I am not a National Security strategist or a military tactician," says John W. Rendon Jr, whose DC-based PR firm was recently hired by the Pentagon to win over the hearts and minds of Arabs and Muslims worldwide. "I am a politician," Rendon said in a 1998 speech to the National Security Conference (NSC), "and a person who uses communication to meet public policy or corporate policy objectives. In fact, I am an information warrior, and a perception manager. This is probably best described in the words of Hunter S. Thompson, when he wrote 'When things turn weird, the weird turn pro.'"

The Rendon Group's contract with the Pentagon was awarded on a no-bid basis, reflecting the government's determination to hire a firm already versed in running overseas propaganda operations. Rendon specialises in "assisting corporations, organizations, and governments achieve their policy objectives". Past clients include the CIA, USAID, the government of Kuwait, Monsanto Chemical Company, and the official trade agencies of countries including Bulgaria, Russia and Uzbekistan. "Through its network of international offices and strategic alliances," the Rendon Group website boasts, "the company has provided communications services to clients in more than 78 countries, and maintains contact with government officials, decision-makers, and news media around the globe."

The Pentagon stipulates that the Rendon Group will receive $400,000 for four months of work. Details are confidential, but according to the *San Jose Mercury News*, Rendon will be monitoring international news media, conducting focus groups, creating a website about the US campaign against terrorism, and recommending "ways the US military can counter disinformation and improve its own public communications".

RENDON AND DESERT STORM

In dollar terms, Rendon's Pentagon contract resembles the $100,000 monthly retainer that it received in the early 1990s from the Kuwaiti government as part of a multi-million-dollar PR campaign denouncing Iraq's 1990 invasion and mobilising public support for Operation Desert Storm.

The Rendon Group's website states that during the Gulf War, it "established a full-scale communications operation for the Government of Kuwait, including the establishment of a production studio in London producing programming material for the exiled Kuwaiti Television". Rendon also provided media support for exiled government leaders and helped Kuwaiti officials after the war by "providing press and site advance to incoming congressional delegations and other visiting US government officials". Several of Rendon's non-governmental clients also have headquarters in Kuwait: Kuwait Petroleum Corporation, Kuwait University, American Housing Consortium, American Business Council of Kuwait, and KPMG/Peat Marwick.

The Rendon Group's work in Kuwait continued after the war itself had ended. "If any of you either participated in the liberation of Kuwait City ... or if you watched it on television, you would have seen hundreds of Kuwaitis waving small American flags," John Rendon said in his speech to the NSC. "Did you ever stop to wonder how the people of Kuwait City, after being held hostage for seven long and painful months, were able to get hand-held American flags? And for that matter, the flags of other coalition countries? Well, you now know the answer. That was one of my jobs."

Rendon was also a major player in the CIA's effort to encourage the overthrow of Saddam Hussein. In May 1991, then-President George Bush Sr signed a presidential finding directing the CIA to create the conditions for Hussein's removal. The hope was that members of the Iraqi military would turn on Hussein and stage a military coup. The CIA did not have the mechanisms in place to make that happen, so they hired the Rendon Group to run a covert anti-Saddam propaganda campaign. Rendon's post-war work involved producing videos and radio skits ridiculing Saddam Hussein, a travelling photo exhibit of Iraqi atrocities, and radio scripts calling on Iraqi army officers to defect.

A February 1998 report by Peter Jennings cited records obtained by ABC News which showed that the Rendon Group spent more than $23 million in the first year of its contract with the CIA. It worked closely with the Iraqi National Congress, an opposition coalition of 19 Iraqi and Kurdish organisations whose main tasks were to "gather information, distribute propaganda and recruit dissidents". According to ABC, Rendon came up with the name for the Iraqi National Congress and channelled $12 million of covert CIA funding to it between 1992 and 1996.

ClandestineRadio.com, a website which monitors underground and anti-government radio stations in countries throughout the world, credits the Rendon Group with "designing and supervising" the Iraqi Broadcasting Corporation (IBC) and Radio Hurriah, which began broadcasting Iraqi opposition propaganda in January 1992 from a US government transmitter in Kuwait. According to a September 1996 article in *Time* magazine, six CIA case officers supervised the IBC's eleven hours of daily programming and Iraqi National Congress activities in the Iraqi Kurdistan city of Arbil. These activities came to an abrupt end on 31 August 1996, when the Iraqi army invaded Arbil and executed all but twelve out of 100 IBC staff workers along with about 100 members of the Iraqi National Congress.

FOCUS, PEOPLE, FOCUS

The techniques being used to sell a war in Iraq are familiar PR strategies. The message is developed to resonate with the targeted audiences through the use of focus groups and other types of market research and media monitoring. The delivery of the message is tightly controlled. Relevant information flows to the media and the public through a limited number of well-trained messengers, including seemingly independent third parties.

A seamless blend of private and public money and organisations are executing their war campaign in the face of a sinking US economy and increasing public opposition to attacking Iraq. But with a Republican-controlled Congress and a largely pliant corporate media, there is little to challenge the White House agenda. Its diplomatic and political manoeuvres have been tightly choreographed in concert with a handful of right-wing think-tanks, the newly concocted Committee for the Liberation of Iraq, and well-connected PR and lobby firms that now dominate media coverage of US foreign policy in the Middle East.

According to the *New York Times*, intensive planning for the "Iraq rollout" began in July 2002. Bush advisers checked the Congressional calendar for the best time to launch a "full-scale lobbying campaign". The effort started the day after Labor Day as Congress reconvened and Congressional leaders received invitations to the White House and the Pentagon for Iraq briefings with Vice President Dick Cheney, Secretary of Defense Donald Rumsfeld and CIA director George Tenet. White House communications aides scouted locations for the President's 11 September address, which served as a prelude to his militaristic speech to the United Nations Security Council.

The *Washington Post* reported in July that the White House had created an Office of Global Communications (OGC) to "coordinate the administration's foreign policy message and supervise America's image abroad". In September, *The Times* of London reported that the OGC would spend $200 million for a "PR blitz against Saddam Hussein" aimed "at American and foreign audiences, particularly in Arab nations sceptical of US policy in the region". The campaign would use "advertising techniques to persuade crucial target groups that the Iraqi leader must be ousted".

The Bush administration has not hesitated to use outright disinformation to bolster the case for war. In December, CBS *60 Minutes* interviewed a former CIA agent who investigated and debunked the oft-mentioned report that 11 September airplane hijacker Mohammed Atta met with an Iraqi intelligence official in Prague several months before the deadly attacks on 11 September. "Despite a lack of evidence that the meeting took place," the CBS report noted, "the item was cited by administration officials as high as Vice President Dick Cheney and ended up being reported so widely that two-thirds of Americans polled by the Council on Foreign Relations believe Iraq was behind the terrorist attacks of 9/11".

THE BATTLE OF THE BAND

"We're getting the band together," said White House Communications director Dan Bartlett in September. The "band", explained *Newsweek*'s Martha Brant, refers to "the people who brought you the war in Afghanistan – or at least the accompanying public-relations campaign. Now they're back for a reunion tour on Iraq".

A group of young White House up-and-comers, the "band" was meeting daily on a morning conference call to plan media strategy with the aim of controlling "the message within the administration so no one – not even Vice President Dick Cheney – freelances on Iraq", Brant wrote. Its main players are Bartlett, Office of Global Communications director Tucker Eskew, and James Wilkinson, former Deputy Communications director who has now been reassigned to serve as spokesperson to General Tommy Franks at US Central Command in Qatar. Other frequent participants in the planning sessions have included top Pentagon spokesperson Victoria Clarke, Cheney adviser Mary Matalin, and Secretary of State Colin Powell's mouthpiece, Richard Boucher.

Meanwhile, the State Department is providing media training to Iraqi dissidents to "help make the Bush administration's argument for the removal of Saddam Hussein", reported *PR Week* on 2 September. Muhammed Eshaiker, who serves on the board of the Iraqi Forum for Democracy, was one of the State Department trainees. "Iraqis in exile were not really taking advantage of the media opportunities," he said during an interview on National Public Radio. "We probably stumble and wait and say, well, I mean what's the use – everybody knows [Hussein's] a criminal, so what's the use if we just add another story or another crime? But everything counts! If we keep hammering on the same nail, the nail is going to find its way through."

US Secretary of Defense Donald H. Rumsfeld has used an informal "strategic communications" group of Beltway lobbyists, PR people and Republican insiders to hone the Pentagon's message. Pentagon public affairs head Victoria Clarke, who used to run Hill & Knowlton's DC office, is reported to have assembled the Rumsfeld group. Participants "intermittently offer messaging advice to the Pentagon", reported *PR Week* on 26 August. One of the Rumsfeld group's projects is linking the anti-terrorism cause with efforts to convince the public "of the need to engage 'rogue states' – including Iraq – that are likely to harbor terrorists".

According to military analyst William Arkin, Rumsfeld's group is doing more than merely spinning rationales for attacking Iraq. Writing for the 24 November *Los Angeles Times*, Arkin called Rumsfeld's communication strategy "a policy shift that reaches across all the armed services", as "Rumsfeld and his senior aides are revising missions and creating new agencies to make 'information warfare' a central element of any US war".

"Information warfare" blurs the line between distributing factual information and psychological warfare. During the current build-up against Iraq, for example, the Bush administration's statements have been calculated to create confusion about whether an actual US invasion is imminent. Such confusion can be a useful weapon against an enemy, forcing Saddam Hussein to divide his efforts between diplomatic initiatives and military preparations. The confusion is so complete, however, that even the American people have little idea what their leaders are actually planning.

THE COMMITTEE FOR THE INVASION OF IRAQ

The anti-Hussein public relations work is also being done by a number of front groups and pundits with close ties to the Pentagon and White House. These private-sector war boosters are making the rounds of TV news programmes and newspaper editorial pages. What won't be apparent to the average US media consumer are the many tangled connections that exist between them.

The newly formed Committee for the Liberation of Iraq (CLI) sits at the centre of the PR campaign, which is co-ordinated closely with other groups that are actively promoting an attack on Iraq, including the Washington Institute for Near East Policy, Middle East Forum, Project for a New American Century, the American Enterprise Institute, Hudson Institute, Hoover Institute, and the clients of media relations firm Benador Associates. CLI sends its message to American citizens through meetings with newspaper editorial boards and journalists, framing the debate and providing background materials written by a close-knit web of supporters. CLI also works closely with Condoleezza Rice and other administration officials to sponsor foreign policy briefings and dinners. "It is also encouraging its members to hold lectures around the US, creating opportunities to penetrate local media markets," reported *PR Week* on 25 November. "Members have already been interviewed on MSNBC and Fox News Channel, and articles have appeared in the *Washington Post* and the *New York Times*."

The CLI's mission statement says the group "was formed to promote regional peace, political freedom and international security by replacing the Saddam Hussein regime with a democratic government that respects the rights of the Iraqi people and ceases to threaten the community of nations". CLI representatives have made it clear that they plan to focus the debate on regime change, regardless of what weapons inspectors find or don't find inside Iraq. Although CLI uses humanitarian buzzwords on its website and strives for a bipartisan look, its leadership and affiliations are decidedly right-wing, militaristic and very much in step with the Bush administration. CLI president Randy Scheunemann is a well-connected Republican military and foreign policy adviser who has worked as National Security Advisor for Senators Trent Lott and Bob Dole. He also owns Orion Strategies, a small government-relations PR firm.

CLI is ostensibly "an independent entity", although it is expected to "work closely with the administration", the *Washington Post*'s Peter Slevin reported on 4 November.

> At a time when polls suggest declining enthusiasm for a US-led military assault on Hussein, top officials will be urging opinion makers to focus on Hussein's actions in response to the United Nations resolution on weapons inspections – and on his past and present failings. They aim to regain momentum and prepare the political ground for his forcible ouster, if necessary.

According to former Secretary of State George Schultz, who chairs CLI's advisory board, the Committee "gets a lot of impetus from the White House", essentially serving as a public outlet for some of the Bush administration's more hawkish thinking.

CLI also has a number of direct connections with the American Enterprise Institute (AEI) and other conservative think-tanks that focus on the Middle East. According to reporter Jim Lobe,

> the CLI appears to be a spin-off of the Project for a New American Century (PNAC), a front group consisting mainly of neo-conservative Jews and heavy-hitters from the Christian Right, whose public recommendations on fighting the "war against terrorism" and US backing for Israel in the conflict in the occupied territories have anticipated to a remarkable degree the administration's own policy course.

PNAC was founded by William Kristol and Robert Kagan, both of whom sit on PNAC's board of directors. Kristol edits the conservative *Weekly Standard* and is also a CLI advisory board member. Kagan was George Shultz's speechwriter during his tenure as President Reagan's Secretary of State. CLI is chaired by another PNAC director – Bruce P. Jackson, a former vice president at Lockheed Martin who also served as an aide to former Secretaries of Defense Frank Carlucci and Dick Cheney.

Other CLI advisory board members include:

- former House Speaker Newt Gingrich
- former Senator Bob Kerrey
- Teamster President James Hoffa Jr
- retired Generals Barry McCaffrey, Wayne Downing and Buster Glosson
- Jeane Kirkpatrick, a White House and Pentagon adviser under former Presidents Reagan and Bush who is currently an AEI senior fellow
- Danielle Pletka, AEI vice president for Foreign and Defense Policy
- former CIA director James Woolsey
- top Pentagon adviser and AEI fellow Richard Perle, who helped sell the 1991 war in the Persian Gulf as co-chair of the Committee for Peace and Security in the Gulf (CPSG). According to journalist Jim Lobe, CPSG "worked closely with both the Bush Sr. administration in mobilizing support of the war, particularly in Congress, and with a second group financed by the Kuwaiti monarchy called Citizens for a Free Kuwait. CPSG also received a sizable grant from the Wisconsin-based Lynde & Harry Bradley Foundation, a major funder of both PNAC and AEI."
- former New York Democratic Representative Stephen Solarz, who was Perle's former co-chair at CPSG.

TRUST US, WE'RE EXPERTS

A number of Iraq hawks, including Perle and Woolsey, are clients of Eleana Benador, whose PR firm, Benador Associates, doubles as an "international speakers bureau". Other Benador clients, many of whom have a prior history of advancing aggressive military policies and promoting dirty wars, include:

- conservative *Washington Post* columnist Charles Krauthammer, who criticised the *New York Times* in August for reporting that prominent Republicans were dissenting from Bush's Iraq war plans
- dissident Iraqi nuclear scientist Dr Khidir Hamza

- Alexander Haig, former US Secretary of State under Ronald Reagan
- Michael Ledeen, another AEI fellow and a prominent figure in the Reagan administration's Iran/Contra scandal who helped broker the covert arms deal between the US and Iran.

In a 14 October article for WorkingForChange.com, Bill Berkowitz reported that Benador's "high-powered media relations" company gets her clients "maximum exposure on cable's talking-head television programs and [places] their op-ed pieces in a number of the nation's major newspapers". Benador and her clients have assumed a prominent role in shaping the public debate over US Middle East policy.

Benador Associates lists 34 speakers on its website, at least nine of whom are connected with the American Enterprise Institute, the Washington Institute and the Middle East Forum. "Although these three privately-funded organizations promote views from only one end of the political spectrum," notes British journalist Brian Whitaker, "the amount of exposure that they get with their books, articles and TV appearances is extraordinary." The Washington Institute publishes books, places newspaper articles, holds luncheons and seminars, and testifies before Congress. Whitaker calls it "the most influential of the Middle East think tanks". Its board of advisers include Alexander Haig, along with CLI advisory board members Richard Perle, George Shultz and Jeane Kirkpatrick. The Washington Institute "takes credit for placing up to 90 articles written by its members – mainly 'op-ed' pieces – in newspapers during the last year", Whitaker writes. "Fourteen of those appeared in the *Los Angeles Times*, nine in *New Republic*, eight in the *Wall Street Journal*, eight in the *Jerusalem Post*, seven in the *National Review Online*, six in the *Daily Telegraph*, six in the *Washington Post*, four in the *New York Times* and four in the *Baltimore Sun*."

The Middle East Forum (MEF) is headed by Daniel Pipes, a frequent guest on TV public affairs shows. It publishes *Middle East Quarterly* and *Middle East Intelligence Bulletin*, an email newsletter sent free to journalists, academics and other interested groups. MEF also sponsors Campus Watch, a project that "monitors and critiques Middle East studies in North America, with an aim to improving them". What this means in practice is that Campus Watch attacks university professors and departments that are perceived as harbouring pro-Arab sympathies, "working for the mullahs" or encouraging "militant

Islam". Its website provides a form to report on "Middle East-related scholarship, lectures, classes, demonstrations, and other activities relevant to Middle East studies" and lists academics that "Campus Watch has identified as apologists for Palestinian and Islamist violence". Like Benador, MEF provides its own "list of experts ... to guide television and radio bookers" and to speak in other venues. Three of MEF's experts, in fact, are also listed on Benador's list: Khalid Durán, director of the Council on Middle Eastern Affairs; Michael Rubin, an AEI visiting fellow and Pentagon adviser, and Meyrav Wurmser, director of the Center for Middle East Policy at the conservative Hudson Institute and the former executive director of the Middle East Media Research Institute. MEF's list of experts also includes two staff members from the Washington Institute as well as PNAC/CLI's William Kristol.

7
Brainscrubbing: The Failures of US Public Diplomacy After 9/11

Nancy Snow

No one f——— knows what they're f——— doing at [the State Department's Bureau of] Public Diplomacy[1]

There's another reason why the subway stop for the US State Department is called Foggy Bottom. Originally a reference to the boggy atmosphere of this particular section of Washington DC where diplomats earned hardship pay in the pre-air-conditioned dog days, Foggy Bottom has become an apt metaphor for an administration in search of clarity on public diplomacy after 9/11. While the war in Iraq continued to rage on 1 April 2003, Secretary of State Colin Powell was being asked to explain public diplomacy efforts in the Arab world. It was over 18 months since 11 September 2001 and just one month after Under-Secretary of State for Public Diplomacy Charlotte Beers had resigned her office.

Question: Do you think the United States has done enough in terms of public diplomacy in the Arab world? Are you disappointed with these efforts? I know administration officials are going on television over there, but what more can be done? And are you disappointed?

Secretary Powell: We're doing as much as we can. We're always looking for new ways of carrying our message to the Arab world. We do spend a great deal of time on Arab television and we are looking for every channel that we can use. We are sending a lot of material out to our embassies and our embassies are in touch with the governments and with the publics of the countries in which those embassies are located. I also hope that as the operation progresses and as we are able to break the back of Iraqi resistance, which we most certainly will be doing in the days ahead, and people are no longer intimidated, people are no longer terrified by the Fedayeen or by the intelligence and security apparatus that, for the most part, has these people trapped in their towns and villages, we are confident that when the people are free to speak and understand that the United States and its coalition partners have come in peace to provide them with a better life, images will flow from that that I think will make the case that the United States and its coalition partners came for a specific purpose, a number of specific purposes: one, to get rid of the weapons of mass destruction and break this nexus between rogue states' weapons of mass destruction and terrorism, and now that that regime did not comply with its international obligations, remove it and put in place a representative government that will provide a better life for the Iraqi people; get rid of the torture chambers; get rid of a regime that would cut the tongues out of people who would resist it. This kind of barbaric behaviour has no place in the world, and I think that message will eventually come through.

Richard Holbrooke, the former Clinton-appointed US Ambassador to the United Nations, lamented to the US press just one month after al-Qaeda terrorists toppled New York City's World Trade Center towers that the US effort to persuade the world has been "a disaster" and a "confused mess". Among the problems, Holbrooke said, were

the failure to open a sustained public discussion with key Muslim intellectuals over how the Koran has been twisted by extremists into an endorsement of murder, the failure to publicise the fact that hundreds of those killed in the World Trade Center were Muslims [and] the failure to find credible, Arabic-speaking Muslims to speak the truth about [Osama] bin Laden.

As Holbrooke mused shortly after 9/11: "How can a man in a cave out-communicate the world's leading communications society?" As you'll read at the end of this chapter, he still is.

Part of the challenge for the US government to explain itself to the world is definitional. Public diplomacy efforts are not monolithic and as a result, the right hand of government (one agency) may not know what the left hand (another agency) is doing to reach out to an overseas target. The State Department has its USIA-inspired traditional public diplomacy efforts (international exchanges like the Fulbright Program, Office of International Visitors, Speakers Program) while the Pentagon has its black propaganda here-today, gone-tomorrow Office of Strategic Influence (OSI). Not to be outdone, the White House initiated its own Office of Global Communications in early 2003 as an outgrowth of the post-9/11 Coalition Information Centers (CIC) in London and Islamabad.

Propaganda, a term that the United States government for the most part eschews, is defined by NATO as "any information, ideas, or special appeals disseminated to influence the opinion, emotions, attitudes or behaviour of any specified group in order to benefit the sponsor, either directly or indirectly". Interestingly, the rest of the world embraces the concept of propaganda as not only what the United States is quite gifted in generally – benefiting the sponsor – but also what the US government utilises on a regular basis as part of its salesmanship on American foreign policy efforts. Another lesser-known military term for influence is psychological operations (psyops) that NATO defines as "planned psychological activities in peace and war directed at enemy, friendly and neutral audiences in order to influence attitudes and behaviour affecting the achievement of political and military objectives". Examples of psyops include the US military aircraft Commando Solo dropping leaflets over Iraq and Afghanistan and the Middle East Radio Project that includes Radio Sawa ("together") to the Middle East and Radio Farda targeting Iran.

By far, the most widely used generic and friendly term for what it is that the US government does to officially influence and persuade international audiences is public diplomacy. Public diplomacy is formally defined by the US State Department, America's foreign policy and diplomacy arm, as "the cultural, educational and informational programs, citizen exchanges or broadcasts used to promote the national interest of the United States through understanding, informing and influencing foreign audiences". The US Advisory Commission on Public Diplomacy, a State Department adjunct of federally appointed commissioners, defines public diplomacy as a general ideal: "The open exchange of ideas and information is an inherent characteristic of open societies. Its global mission is central to foreign policy. And it remains indispensable to national interests, ideals and leadership roles in the world." More practically applied, public diplomacy efforts are tapped when the US message and mission is under attack. In May 2002, I asked Norman Pattiz, chair of the Middle East Committee on the Broadcasting Board of Governors that oversees US broadcasting efforts, why the US had a need for Radio Sawa and Radio Farda.[2] He succinctly replied: "To combat hate media", which I took to mean any media that was decidedly anti-US or anti-Israel in tone or content. Pattiz and I do battle over the term propaganda. He told the *Los Angeles Times* in April 2003 that what he's doing is not propaganda but telling the truth. "Our mission is a journalistic mission. We don't do propaganda and we don't do psychological operations."[3] Well maybe he doesn't do those things, but the US government does and the world knows it. According to the BBG website, Radio Farda, which means "Radio Tomorrow" in Persian,

> is a joint effort of two BBG entities: Radio Free Europe/Radio Liberty (RFE/RL) and Voice of America (VOA). Operated from Washington, D.C. and Prague, Czech Republic, Radio Farda produces fresh news and information at least twice an hour, with longer news programming in the morning and the evening. Radio Farda also broadcasts a combination of popular Persian and Western music. The station operates 24 hours a day on medium wave (AM 1593 and AM 1539), digital audio satellite, and on the internet as well as 21 hours a day on shortwave. Radio Farda complements the VOA's Persian-language radio and television broadcasts into Iran.

The English language version of Radio Farda included a headline report on 15 June 2003, "Bush Sees Yearning for Freedom in Iran Protests." In his clearest comment so far in support of the demonstrations that have broken out on campuses and streets around Iran, US President George Bush said on Sunday in Kennebunkport, Maine, "This is the beginning of people expressing themselves toward a free Iran, which I think is positive," Homayoun Majd reported from Washington. Naturally, the Iranian government took notice of this little trial balloon US-backing of regime change, given the recent goings on in the region and denounced the US President's meddling in internal affairs.[4] Radio Sawa, the brainchild of Pattiz, was piloted in March 2002 and is now fully operational. Pattiz loves to brag about the growing audience numbers from Sawa, which parrot those of a commercial radio station. Some of those higher audience numbers may have to do with the fact that Radio Sawa is, like Farda, a non-commercial 24/7 Arabic-language service aimed at listeners under 30, who, if given the choice, probably prefer a network without commercials and that features American and international pop tunes with only intermittent news inserts on the quarter hour. Pattiz has stated repeatedly that Sawa is no magic bullet but rather just a government-operated station that utilises the same marketing principles of his own Westwood One commercial stations.

Kenneth Tomlinson, former chairman of the Broadcasting Board of Governors believes that Al Jazeera, the so-called CNN of the Middle East and another hate media operation to Pattiz and others, must not go unanswered in the Middle East. Tomlinson spearheaded a US-funded "Arabic language venture", consisting of $500 million for non-military international broadcasts and an initial start-up funding of $30 million for a Middle East TV Network (METN), Radio Sawa, Radio Free Iraq, "the most important public-diplomacy initiative of our time". All of these efforts have been met with mixed reaction from their target Middle Eastern audience. Some listeners say that while they do listen to US broadcasts, this does not translate into support for US policies.

The success of Pattiz's and Tomlinson's lobbying efforts in Washington DC show how just one or two people with enough political power can push their pet projects through Congress. Many of the resources that had once been given to public diplomacy – to explaining the US and US values to the world – were eliminated after the Cold War and the Middle East region in particular vis-à-vis American broadcasting was barely a whisper. Radio Sawa was a direct challenge to the VOA's Arab-language service, which for years had garnered a listening audience of barely 1 to 2 per cent of Arabs and virtually no one under the age of 30, some 60 per cent of the population in the region. Radio Sawa represents a controversial break with traditional US international broadcasting efforts that favoured news and government-slanted editorials. In 2002, VOA's shortwave Arabic services were gutted and their in-depth news, analysis and government-information programming eliminated in favour of Radio Sawa's dumbed-down headline-news format. Radio Sawa's advocates say the new system reaches far more people and attracts more listener loyalty than the old Voice. In Norman Pattiz's view, the US must come in through the back door using pop influence rather than the front door using overt propaganda. But Newton Minow, former Federal Communications Commission chairman, calls all these efforts

> late and, in my view, too timid. They are tactical, not strategic. They are smart, not visionary. The cost of putting Radio Free Afghanistan on the air and underwriting its annual budget, for example, is less than even one Comanche helicopter. We have

many hundreds of helicopters, which we need to destroy tyranny, but they are insufficient to secure freedom. In an asymmetric war, we must also fight on the idea front.

Minow recommends spending 1 per cent of the US defence budget, about $3.3 billion, on international communication efforts, or six times the present rate.

Public diplomacy spending in the post-Cold War decade leading up to 11 September 2001 was abysmal. As the US Advisory Commission and Council on Foreign Relations figures have pointed out, the US spends about $1 billion on public diplomacy, or just about 4 per cent of the US government's international affairs budget compared to $25 billion on traditional diplomacy efforts (negotiations, international meetings, embassy outreach). More than $30 billion is spent on intelligence and counter-intelligence like the CIA and National Security Agency, both of which have little if any public oversight. During my employment at the US Information Agency from 1992 to 1994, the bottom was beginning to fall out from public diplomacy funding. From 1993 to 2001, funding for educational and cultural exchange programmes declined by one-third and from 1995 to 2001 the number of international exchange participants fell from 45,000 to less than 30,000. As these numbers declined, so did the potential pool of citizen diplomats who could continue their lobbying efforts on behalf of US efforts in public diplomacy. In summer 2002, the Council on Foreign Relations' Independent Task Force on Public Diplomacy noted that "the U.S. government spends only $5 million annually on foreign public opinion polling. This amount does not cover the research costs of an average U.S. Senate campaign and it is a tiny fraction of the $6 billion spent by the U.S. private sector to gauge overseas opinion."[5]

On 21 January 2003, after suffering too many political and propaganda defeats around the world, Bush issued Executive Order 13283 establishing a White House Office of Global Communications (OGC).[6] The OGC, according to the executive order, advises national leadership on

the most effective means for the United States government to ensure consistency in messages that will promote the interests of the United States abroad, prevent misunderstanding, build support for and among coalition partners of the United States and inform international audiences.

Strategy, Bush said in the executive order, is paramount:

> The office shall co-ordinate the formulation among appropriate
> agencies of messages that reflect the strategic communications
> framework and priorities of the United States, and shall facilitate
> the development of a strategy among the appropriate agencies to
> effectively communicate such messages.

The office, Bush stipulated, "shall co-ordinate closely and regularly"
with the presidential national-security adviser. The most prominent
publication of the OGC was its pre-bombing, pre-ultimatum,
Apparatus of Lies: Saddam's Disinformation and Propaganda 1990–2003,
which, along with Colin Powell's show-and-tell at the United Nations
in February 2003, were designed to be the one-two punch of the
administration's justification for taking out Saddam Hussein's regime.

Charlotte Beers' tenure at the US State Department (October
2001–March 2003) will be remembered as doing more to raise the
profile of US public diplomacy than any predecessor. With a name
like Beers who formerly sold Uncle Ben's Rice and was tasked to sell
Uncle Sam, how could the global media resist? To her credit, Beers
did inherit a broken public-diplomacy apparatus and never could
mesh her soft-power State Department efforts with the Bush administration's military speak. Beers came in to a Department that
inherited a very watered-down version of the US Information Agency
in 1999. By the time Beers was nominated in March 2001 and
months before 11 September, US-run cultural and educational
facilities around the world, called America Houses, as well as valuable
English-language libraries, had been shut down after the Cold War
and never revitalised. Government scholarships for foreign students
to study in the United States, including the flagship Fulbright
Program, fell from their Reagan-era peak of 20,000 a year (when I
went to Germany on a Fulbright scholarship) to mere thousands.
Under Beers, the State Department wasted $15 million on a "Shared
Values" campaign designed to broadcast slick advertisements of
happy Muslim-Americans over TV networks of Islamic countries
around the world. The campaign flopped after receiving bad reviews
in the few countries in which the ads were aired and after client states
such as Egypt refused to allow the State Department to purchase air
time on their state-run networks. The plug was pulled in February
2003 shortly before Beers departed for stated health reasons.

As a "graduate" of the Clinton era in public diplomacy, I know that US public diplomacy efforts were either taken for granted or put on the back burner after the Cold War. The sentiment inside Washington was that America had ideologically triumphed over communism and that America's story was "selling itself" through American media, film, television, and 24-hour commercial news networks like CNN. The Clinton administration emphasised American commercial and corporate ties to public diplomacy through NAFTA and Fast Track trade legislation, while the diplomatic explaining of interests, values and positions withered on the vine. Even since 9/11, when public diplomacy was vaulted into the public consciousness, US diplomats have struggled to get the American message across at their respective embassies. In September 2002, a US ambassador to a West European country told *Insight* magazine that he was unable to explain President Bush's policy toward Iraq because the State Department had not provided the proper policy guidance and talking points. Some diplomats didn't even have the most basic tools. In a cost-saving measure, the Clinton administration had shut down US consulates in cities all over the world. In Zurich, Switzerland's financial capital, journalists for the country's leading newspapers told *Insight* that they could not sit down with any US government representatives to answer questions about Iraq because the consulate remained closed.

"Meanwhile, American marketing talent continues to successfully sell Madonna's music, Pepsi Cola and Coca-Cola, Michael Jordan's shoes and McDonald's hamburgers around the world," notes Minow, now Annenberg Professor of Communications, Law and Policy at Northwestern University. "Our film, television and computer-software industries dominate their markets world-wide. Yet, the United States government has tried to get its message of freedom and democracy out to the 1 billion Muslims in the world and can't seem to do it."

Why can't it do it?

The ultimate reason for the failure of US public diplomacy efforts since 9/11 is the American disconnect, which operates at two levels. During the Cold War, Kennedy and Khrushchev initiated a hotline between the two superpowers. Now the US might want to reissue a hotline to the entire world because its phone lines of communication have been cut. The first disconnection is that between American Power, which is economic and military in orientation and self-interested in purpose, and American Values, which are both inwardly and outwardly espoused and universally embraced.

US public diplomacy efforts generally favour "glittering generalities" like nebulous American values of freedom and democracy that are rarely defined. American Power is rarely acknowledged by the US government through its public diplomacy efforts to the outside world. The world sees how such power is used, while the US government doesn't acknowledge or explain its reasons for maintaining American Power. Charlotte Beers referred to this disconnect as the proverbial elephant in the living room. American Power, since the Cold War, has only been used to preserve the status quo in the Middle East and Arab audiences see how it has kept in place US-friendly Arab autocrats. *New York Times* writer Thomas Friedman notes that after the Cold War ended and America supported, and celebrated, the flowering of democracy from Eastern Europe to Latin America, the Arab world was excluded. The reason for this is because those of us working in Washington in the early 1990s were so relieved to have "defeated" the Red Menace that we focused our conversion efforts on the new ex-communists instead of the protracted Arab/Israeli or Middle Eastern conflicts, which we left to the war hawks to handle.

The second disconnect is between global media coverage versus American media, particularly during the war in Iraq. The European press in particular viewed the war through a prism that highlighted the human costs, difficulties and risks, whereas American press coverage favoured more how "our" side was doing and the wow factor associated with the state-of-the-art technology of media embeds. The US media covered some of the anti-war protests in the US, but generally in the context of the overhead helicopter shot of people taking to the streets. There was almost no dissenting voice on the American broadcast airwaves once the war had started, although anti-war author Howard Zinn, author of *A People's History of the United States*, did make a cameo the first day of bombing on the American public broadcasting programme, *The News Hour with Jim Lehrer*. This disconnect between how the American press portrays global consciousness on issues versus a global media that tends to react to American Power projection in the world presents a unique challenge to the Washington propagandists whose military and economic superpower message continues to dominate public policy and public dialogue and, most notably, American press coverage.

Kathleen Cahill wrote in the *Washington Post* two months after the war in Iraq ended, that the American reputation on the global street has gone from bad to worse. The most recent Pew Global Attitudes Project poll, which surveyed 16,000 people in 20 countries between 28 May and 15 June 2003, reported that the news is "They don't like us. Worse, they don't trust us."[7] Osama bin Laden, missing in action for well over a year, showed that his poll numbers "to do the right thing in world affairs" remained high among many Arabs and Muslims (71 per cent of Palestinians agreed, while 58 per cent polled yes in Indonesia; in Jordan, 55 per cent; in Morocco, 49 per cent; in Pakistan, 45 per cent). Such suspicious minds toward the US in general and the vaulting of stateless violent ideologues like bin Laden negatively impact the ongoing US-led global war on terrorism and related homeland security initiatives. Truth is, until and unless the United States is attacked again at home, many Americans are likely to remain indifferent to the rise in anti-Americanism. We have made our bed and its name is security over credibility. There was one positive outcome, which may serve as a hook for future US public diplomacy efforts, which by design can only improve. Cahill notes that,

> In the silver lining department, there was this: Large majorities in most Muslim countries surveyed said that Western-style democracy could work well in their countries. In Kuwait, 83 percent of those polled agreed; in Nigeria, 75 percent; in Lebanon, 71 percent; in Jordan, 69 percent; in Morocco, 64 percent; in Pakistan, 57 percent; in the Palestinian areas, 54 percent; and in Turkey, generally viewed as the strongest Muslim democracy, 50 percent agreed.

Emphasis here is Western, not American. There's the rub. The most recent waxing nostalgic over the lost gains in US public diplomacy comes from the conservative Heritage Foundation in Washington DC, whose April 2003 report, "How to Reinvigorate U.S. Public Diplomacy", underscores the urgency of PD failures in an age of the internet, Al Jazeera and instantaneous global communication:

> In the information age, it is remarkable that the United States government has been hesitant to embrace and effectively implement mass communication to support America's defense and foreign policy goals. In recent times, only the Reagan Administration consistently factored communication strategies

into meeting its domestic and international political challenges. Now, when Washington wants public diplomacy to come to the rescue, it seems to expect public diplomacy to deliver goodwill instantly among foreign publics without first establishing the necessary foundation of mutual trust and understanding. Instead, reflex should become habit. Public diplomacy is effective only when it builds on long-term relationships that identify common interests between people and capitalise on them. It must be strategic, consistent, and flexible in its use of channels and, above all, must encourage two-way communication.[8]

Without US willingness to listen and learn, even when the news has gone from bad to worse, it won't be possible to build those long-term relationships.

NOTES

1. J. Michael Wallter, *Insight on the News*, 14 April 2003. When asked by *Insight* about the State Department's public-diplomacy efforts, a senior National Security Council official burst into this exasperated stream of profanities.
2. See the Broadcasting Board of Governors' home page at <http://www.ibb.gov/>.
3. Josh Getlin, "US Nightly News Shows to Make Their Iraqi Television Debut; Some fear the White House-backed program espousing a free press will create a backlash", *Los Angeles Times*, 15 April 2003.
4. See "Iran Faults U.S. for 5 Days of Protests; Demonstrations Lauded By Bush as 'Positive'" by Karl Vick, *Washington Post*, 16 June 2003; and "Iran: Ripe for Revolution?", *Christian Science Monitor* editorial, 16 June 2003.
5. Council on Foreign Relations, *Public Diplomacy: A Strategy for Reform*, July 2002.
6. Read about the White House Office of Global Communications at <http://www.whitehouse.gov/ogc/index.html>.
7. Kathleen Cahill, "They Don't Like Us. Worse, They Don't Trust Us", *Washington Post*, 15 June 2003.
8. Stephen Johnson and Helle Dale, "How to Reinvigorate US Public Diplomacy", Heritage Foundation, Washington DC, 23 April 2003.

8
Misreporting War Has a Long History

Des Freedman

The use by the British and US governments of lies, distortion and misrepresentation to justify their war on Iraq was largely echoed and amplified by the media of those countries. Despite a clear anti-war majority in Britain and a significant anti-war minority in the US, most media outlets supported the war and failed systematically to challenge the arguments for an invasion or to expose the brutality and consequences of the war. It was a shocking but not an unprecedented situation that both institutions, despite many tensions and arguments, have traditionally shared the same assumptions and objectives in the pursuit of military victory.

It is often argued (mostly by journalists) that governments and reporters have fundamentally conflicting interests, particularly in times of war. While the former is concerned to close off access to information, the latter is dedicated to uncovering and disseminating information. The first part of this scenario is hardly controversial – few governments would deny that controlling information flows during wartime is a legitimate task. Suppressing information that might aid the enemy, producing propaganda to win consent and maintain support for war, and imposing guidelines on how the media are allowed to cover war are, by now, long-established (and problematic) features of military conflict. More contentious is the second assertion: that journalists are impartial and independent monitors of military conduct. This assumes that correspondents are able and willing to shrug off both ideological and organisational restrictions to keep a watchful eye on the activities of military combatants and to challenge the arguments of those in control.

The man credited with founding the tradition of the independent war reporter certainly did confront the general running of British operations in the Crimea in the 1850s. William Howard Russell covered the war for *The Times* (the first civilian to do so as all previous "reporting" had been provided by soldiers themselves) and condemned the atrocious military leadership and the appalling conditions of the troops. His reports were widely publicised and led to the resignation of the general and the collapse of the government. Russell, however, did not challenge the underlying reasons for the war, simply the way in which it was carried out. "The one thing he never doubted or criticised", argues Phillip Knightley in his history of war correspondents, "was the institution of war itself."[1] This is a theme we see again and again.

In order to deal with people like Russell and to cope with the growing demands of newspapers, Britain developed a system of media controls. During the First World War, censorship operated through the Press Bureau, set up to provide information favourable to the war effort and to suppress any information that was not. Correspondents and photographers were kept away from the front and threatened with being shot if they got too close. This infuriated newspaper editors and inspired the first "unilaterals", those correspondents who dared to ignore the military and investigate on their own. One such reporter, Philip Gibbs of the *Daily Chronicle*, wrote later about how these reporters "were arrested, put into prison, caught again in forbidden places, re-arrested and expelled from France".[2] Gibbs himself had previously covered the war in the Balkans, mostly playing billiards in the Hotel Bulgarie in Sofia,[3] much as later correspondents would cover US wars in Iraq and Kuwait from the comfort of luxury hotels in Qatar and Saudi Arabia.

The government quickly realised that such harrassment was counter-productive. One newspaper argued that press censorship was undermining enthusiasm for the war and that more coverage would increase recruitment to the army.[4] In May 1915, a few correspondents were finally allowed to report from the front, not as "unilaterals" but as fully accredited army staff. They were given captain's uniforms, put up in luxury accommodation, driven to the front by military personnel and then subjected to heavy censorship. More often than not, such censorship was not necessary as newspapers were reluctant to publish accounts of slaughter and defeat, concentrating instead on optimistic stories that would maintain morale. "National" preceded public interest. The former "unilateral", Philip Gibbs, recalls that "in the later stages of the war I personally had no complaint against the censorship and wrote all that was good to write of the actions day by day, though I had to leave out something of the underlying horror of them all".[5] Gibbs was later knighted for his work as an official correspondent.

British press coverage of the First World War failed to highlight the savagery of trench warfare and the enormous number of casualties, mobilised public support for the war and publicised anti-German propaganda (much of which was later discredited). Not all of this can be blamed on reporting restrictions and censorship. One newspaper proprietor, Lord Rothermere, commented that: "We're telling lies, we know we're telling lies, we daren't tell the public the truth, that we're losing more officers than the Germans, and that it's impossible to get through on the Western Front."[6] Self-censorship, as much as official controls, was crucial. Sir Edward Cook, head of the Press Bureau, commented after the war that "the Press did all that it possibly could, and often more from a strictly journalistic point of view might reasonably have been expected, to print everything that the [government] Departments desired to impart to the public".[7]

The Second World War saw the British and US governments use the same combination of overt censorship and appeals to the "national interest". Following a "People's Assembly" in London demanding a "peace neither of conquest nor capitulation", the Communist Party's *Daily Worker* was shut down by the Labour home secretary Herbert Morrison. The Ministry of Information and its censorship division could stifle any material it thought to be against the war effort. In the US, the Office of Censorship defied the free speech rules of the First Amendment by banning a vast number of "subversive" images: of the bloody death of US soldiers, of wounded soldiers looking happy to leave the battlefield, of questionable US treatment of the enemy, of US stockpiles of liquid mustard gas, and many more. George Roeder argues that "the US government rationed photographs of the American dead more stingily than scarce commodities such as sugar, leather shoes and rubber tires".[8]

Did the media rise up against this? Hardly. In both countries, editors exercised careful self-censorship so that there was little need for direct government intervention. According to Angus Calder, the "attitude of newspaper editors made the efforts of the Censorship Division remarkably easy ... Editors were generally amenable to suggestions that such and such a passage, although not trespassing against security, should be omitted out of regard for the 'national interest'."[9] In Britain, official press releases were reprinted and broadcast uncritically while American "newspapers and magazines loyally followed directives important to the war effort".[10]

Correspondents were accredited in much the same way as in the First World War, though this time there were many more of them

(558 were officially accredited for the D-Day landings). Unfortunately the increased number of reporters did not result in a more independent or critical form of journalism. Coverage of the retreat at Dunkirk was almost uniformly triumphalist (even though, as Knightley points out, no British correspondents were actually at Dunkirk) while the "dam-busters" raid in 1943 was exaggerated way beyond its real military importance.[11] On the other hand, some events were scarcely reported at the time, most notably the bombing of civilians at Dresden and Hiroshima in 1945.

All too often, accreditation slipped into assimilation: reporters became part of the armies they were supposed to report on. Correspondents covering the war in North Africa were deeply embedded into the forces and welcomed by General Montgomery as "an element of my staff". General Eisenhower described accredited correspondents as "quasi-staff officers" and some were even awarded military honours for "devotion to duty and fortitude" (if not to truth).[12] Of course, censorship and the sheer scale of the war made it difficult to report on events and battles but there are few signs that, even without these external constraints, mainstream coverage of the war would have been much different.

The most celebrated example of the "adversarial" conception of the journalist's role is US coverage of the Vietnam War where the uncensored and brutal portrayal of American casualties undermined public support and effectively "lost the war". Broadcast coverage of (US) corpses and critical comments about US involvement were argued to have transformed public opinion. Television pictures of Vietnam, according to President Nixon, "showed the terrible human suffering and sacrifice of war ... the result was a serious demoralization of the home front, raising the question whether America would ever again be able to fight an enemy abroad with unity and strength of purpose at home".[13]

In his detailed account of media coverage of the war, *The Uncensored War: The Media and Vietnam*, Daniel Hallin challenges the myth that a proactive and critical media corps deliberately sabotaged US military involvement. For example, in the early days of the war, the US temporarily halted its bombing of North Vietnam in a move that was designed more to win domestic and international favour than to secure peace. Hallin concludes that reporters abandoned any notion of "objective journalism" in disseminating the administration's view of events: the "television journalist presented himself, in this case, not as a disinterested observer, but as a patriot, a partisan of what he frequently referred to as 'our' peace offensive".[14] Even by the end of the war when US society was split over the question of Vietnam, "for the most part television was a follower rather than a leader: it was not until the collapse of consensus was well under way that television's coverage began to turn around; and when it did turn, it only turned so far".[15] News bulletins were prepared to criticise the conduct of the Vietnam War (along with millions of anti-war protestors), but they were never prepared to question why the US was there in the first place and the ambitions that lay behind the American war on Vietnam.

Even this limited amount of critical reporting was too much for US and British politicians who vowed to step up censorship and news management techniques for wars in the modern media age. Yet while this has led to increasing tension between reporters and government (witness the constant disputes since the Falklands War between the BBC and British governments), there is little evidence that editors and correspondents are prepared to question the right of governments to go to war or the efficacy of war as a means of achieving peace.

Of course some things have changed in the 150 years since the birth of "professional" war reporting. Correspondents are operating in a far more competitive climate in which the pressure to be "first" or to tell a different story may sometimes lead to damning indictments of particular aspects of war. Technological developments have also transformed war reporting making it easier to collect news and harder to stop its distribution. But the increase in size and influence of the news business means that politicians are more concerned to win favourable coverage and simultaneously more anxious to prevent critical coverage. Finally, reporters are no longer fringe participants in war-zones but are increasingly seen as targets making "unilateral" reporting all the more dangerous. This has a real impact on what can be reported. When the ITN unilateral Terry Lloyd was killed by US forces in Iraq in March 2003, his editor-in-chief reflected on the need for "independent teams" arguing that: "People who were embedded [in the 1991 Gulf War] were not able to file any meaningful reports" (*Guardian*, 24 March 2003), a condemnation of the coverage that we did not hear at the time.

The tradition of the "embed" is well established, from the earliest correspondents in the nineteenth century through to *The Times'* man in post-revolutionary Russia, Andrew Soutar, who wholeheartedly supported the efforts of the British army to crush the Bolsheviks, launching a newspaper for the troops, befriending the officers and becoming an honorary major.[16] The many "embeds" in the Second World War and Vietnam were followed by reporters like Max Hastings of the London *Evening Standard* who, though fiercely critical of military censors, "had an enormous affection for the British Army and the British forces. I felt my function [covering the Falklands War] was simply to identify totally with the interests and feelings of that force."[17]

In conclusion, while there have been many moments of tension between media and government in the reporting of war, their interests are not fundamentally opposed. Governments need sympathetic media coverage to legitimise and sustain war while, with very few honourable exceptions, editors and journalists share many of their government's ideological assumptions about war and are anxious not to undermine the "national interest". The consequence of this is that much of the British and American media has done a pretty poor job in reporting the horrific wars of the last century and a half. Although faced with real obstacles concerning censorship and access, they have mainly accepted the agendas and briefings of the politicians and generals. Reporters have criticised particular military operations often in the hope of facilitating military objectives rather than challenging them, of prosecuting war rather than questioning it. For every truly "unilateral" reporter, there have been many more all too eager to identify with the military, to bed themselves down in regiments and platoons, to reproduce the statements of military and political officials and to spread the idea that war is an acceptable or necessary part of modern life.

NOTES

1. Phillip Knightley, *The First Casualty*, London: Quartet, 1982, p. 17.
2. Philip Gibbs, *Realities of War*, London: Hutchinson and Co., 1929, p. 11.
3. Philip Gibbs, *The Pageant of Years: An Autobiography*, London: William Heinemann, 1946, pp. 98–9. Thanks to Maurice Walsh for drawing my attention to this material.
4. Cate Haste, *Keep the Home Fires Burning: Propaganda in the First World War*, London: Allen Lane, 1977, p. 68.
5. Gibbs, *Realities of War*, pp. 27–8.
6. Quoted in Haste, *Keep the Home Fires Burning*, p. 68.
7. Edward Cook, *The Press in War-Time*, London: Macmillan and Co., 1920, p. 51.
8. George Roeder Jr, *The Censored War*, London: Yale University Press, 1993, p. 7.

9. Angus Calder, *The People's War: Britain 1939–1945*, London: Pimlico, 1992, pp. 507–8.
10. Roeder, *The Censored War*, p. 12.
11. Knightley, *The First Casualty*.
12. Ibid., pp. 289–300.
13. Daniel Hallin, *The Uncensored War: The Media and Vietnam*, Oxford: Oxford University Press, 1986, p. 3.
14. Ibid., p. 116.
15. Ibid., p. 163.
16. Knightley, *The First Casualty*, p. 148.
17. Robert Harris, *Gotcha! The Media, the Government and the Falklands Crisis*, London: Faber & Faber, 1983, p. 135.

9
Psychological Warfare Against the Public: Iraq and Beyond

Mark Curtis

Since late 2002 the British public has been subject to a government propaganda campaign of perhaps unprecedented heights in the post-war world. Clare Short, after resigning her position as International Development Secretary, told a parliamentary enquiry of "a series of half-truths, exaggerations and reassurances that were not the case to get us into conflict [with Iraq] by the spring".[1] In this chapter, I will review briefly some elements of this propaganda campaign.

Before turning to Iraq, however, let us consider an extraordinary document freely available on the Ministry of Defence website well before the invasion of Iraq. This document, called "The Future Strategic Context for Defence" notes that "we need to be aware of the ways in which public attitudes might shape and constrain military activity". It continues:

> Increasing emotional attachment to the outside world, fuelled by immediate and graphic media coverage, and a public desire to see the UK act as a force for good, is likely to lead to public support, and possibly public demand, for operations prompted by humanitarian motives.

Therefore, "public support will be vital to the conduct of military interventions". In future, "more effort will be required to ensure that such public debate is properly informed".[2]

The meaning of this appears to be: first, government propaganda is key to attaining objectives and we should expect a lot more of it; second, this propaganda will tell us that the government is acting from humanitarian, rather than baser, motives. It is interesting to see a government openly committing itself to a strategy of propaganda, especially in its concern to emphasise "humanitarian motives", precisely what occurred over Iraq. Even before the invasion, and certainly now, there were no excuses for journalists simply to report government statements or opinions at face value, without ridicule.

The propaganda campaign in the pre-war phase was therefore entirely to be expected. It was seriously funny watching the clique around Tony Blair try to work through various pretexts for attacking Iraq. It appears that the population is regarded as a giant focus group to test each new argument, simply a hurdle to be overcome by anything that enables elites to achieve their objectives.

Initially in 2002, ministers were mainly seizing on the argument about making Iraq comply with UN resolutions; however, the problem here was that too many people saw little or no similar pressure being applied to Israel and other allies. Then, Saddam's human rights record was tried; however, the problem was that this appalling record was comparable to that of many regimes supported by Britain and that London had anyway backed Saddam through-out the period of the worst atrocities in the 1980s. So by early 2003, the two favourite pretexts for a full onslaught against Iraq became the regime's alleged development of weapons of mass destruction (WMD) and a supposed "link" between it and al-Qaeda. Only once these two had been tried (and largely failed) did Blair hit on his bottom line, asserting the "morality" of a war against Iraq.

The biggest problem to overcome was the fact that Iraq presented no threat. Reporting to the UN Security Council in June, after the invasion, chief weapons inspector Hans Blix stated that his weapons inspections commission, UNMOVIC, "has not at any time during the inspections in Iraq found evidence of the continuation or resumption of programmes of weapons of mass destruction or signifi-cant quantities of proscribed items – whether from pre-1991 or later". He continued by saying that "this does not necessarily mean that such items could not exist. They might – there remain long lists of items unaccounted for – but it is not justified to jump to the conclusion that something exists just because it is unaccounted for."[3]

Earlier statements by Blix and the director of the International Atomic Energy Agency, Mohamed El Baradei, repeated this conclusion. Baradei said on 7 March 2003, for example, that "after three months of intrusive inspections, we have found no evidence or plausible indication of the revival of a nuclear weapon programme in Iraq". On the same day, Blix told the Security Council that Iraq was taking "numerous initiatives ... with a view to resolving longstand-ing open disarmament issues" and that "this can be seen as 'active', or even 'proactive' cooperation".[4]

Indeed, it appears that the lack of threat posed by Iraq was also the conclusion of the British and US intelligence agencies, and was dismissed as the wrong line by political leaders committed to war. According to a report in the *Independent* (9 June 2003), No.10 suppressed a six-page report from the Joint Intelligence Committee saying there was no evidence the Saddam regime posed a significantly greater threat than in 1991. The report was written in March 2003, the same month as Alastair Campbell, Blair's then Director of Communications (i.e., head of propaganda), was briefing journalists that the government would present evidence in the next two weeks asserting that the regime was building weapons of mass destruction.[5]

The lack of a credible threat was also evidenced in a report from the Pentagon's Defense Intelligence Agency, leaked to the media in June. A summary obtained by CNN said that "there is no reliable information on whether Iraq is producing and stockpiling chemical weapons or where Iraq has or will establish its chemical warfare agent production facilities". This report was produced in September 2002, the same month as the British dossier appeared alleging all manner of threats from Iraq (see below).[6]

Former Foreign Secretary Robin Cook told the Foreign Affairs Committee that by 2001 the government was

fairly confident that Saddam did not have a nuclear weapons capability, did not have a long-range missile capability and, indeed, at one point in the late 1990s, we were willing to consider closing those files and moving from inspection on to monitoring and verification.

Cook added that "I was surprised to see allegations of a nuclear programme resurfacing." He also said after the invasion that "Frankly, I doubt whether there is a single senior figure in the intelligence services who is surprised at the difficulty in finding a weapon of mass destruction in working order."[7]

Clare Short said that "the suggestion that there was the risk of chemical and biological weapons being weaponised and threatening us in the short time was spin. That didn't come from the security services." When asked by a parliamentary enquiry whether she thought that ministers had exaggerated the use of intelligence material, she replied: "that is my suggestion, yes". This was done in order "to make it [the threat] more immediate, more imminent, requiring urgent action".[8]

The *Guardian* reported that "senior officials in the security and intelligence services made it clear that the threat posed by Saddam Hussein's Iraq was not as great as ministers suggested". This battle within the elite provoked the chiefs of MI6 and MI5 to seek the government's assurance that it will never again pass off as official intelligence information which does not come from them, according to the *Guardian*. One source was quoted as saying that "there were anxieties about the casual use of intelligence" and that "it must not be doctored".

Disagreements occurred between the security services and No.10 on the September 2002 dossier alleging the threat from Iraq. A government memo showed that Alastair Campbell agreed to MI6 demands to drop a conclusion he wanted included, describing the imminent threat posed by Iraq, in exchange for an introduction written by Blair claiming Saddam was "a serious threat to UK interests". Friction increased when, despite this deal, Campbell proceeded to brief journalists in the same terms as the removed conclusion.[9]

This September 2002 dossier – the key plank of the British government's case against Iraq – was striking in two respects. First, it provided no actual evidence of a threat from Iraq (not surprisingly, since there was none). Robin Cook later noted that "there is a striking absence of any recent and alarming and confirmed intelligence". The *Guardian* reported that "British government officials have privately admitted that they do not have any 'killer evidence' about weapons of mass destruction. If they had, they would have already passed it to the inspectors." On the day before Blair announced that the dossier would soon be published, a Whitehall source was quoted as saying that the dossier was based on information found up to 1998, when the inspectors withdrew from Iraq, and that there was "very little new to put into it".[10]

Second, the specific claims in the dossier were riddled with deceptions. Glen Rangwala, of Cambridge University, notes five key aspects: the sites mentioned as places where Iraq might be developing weapons of mass destruction have not been found by the inspectors to contain any; some claims in the dossier have subsequently been shown to be false (for example, the allegation that Iraq was seeking to procure uranium from Niger, which was based on forged documents, and that Iraq possessed WMD capable of being ready to use within 45 minutes; see below); claims about prohibited weapons that it was highly unlikely that Iraq had (ballistic missiles with a range of up to 650 km); the claim that Iraq had retained stockpiles of weapons from before 1990, which was highly unlikely; and the Prime Minister's foreword, stating that Iraq had "beyond doubt" continued to produce WMD, was an exaggeration and contradicted by the chief weapons inspectors.[11]

A second government report released in February 2003 has become known as the "dodgy dossier", though it hardly seems more or less dodgy than the first. Blair explicitly passed this report off as the work of the intelligence services only for it to be revealed that much of the document had been directly copied from a source on the internet. The "authors" of the report in government were close to Alastair Campbell, who oversaw the project, which was intended mainly as a briefing for the media. The dossier exaggerates from the original text in a number of places, changing, for example, Iraq's "aiding opposition groups in hostile regimes" to "supporting terrorist organisations in hostile regimes".[12]

The most stark assertion by the government, included in the September dossier, was that Iraq's "military planning allows for some of the WMD to be ready within 45 minutes of an order to use them". The government later acknowledged this claim came from a single source, a senior Iraqi army officer. But it had already been contradicted by Blair himself who said, four months before in May, that "there is no doubt in my mind" that Iraq had concealed its weapons and that it would be "far more difficult for them to reconstitute that material to use in a situation of conflict". Clare Short also told the parliamentary enquiry that in the numerous personal and written briefings she received from the intelligence services, the 45 minutes allegation was never a feature.[13]

After the invasion, the pretext of an Iraqi threat having served its purpose, ministers tried to in effect disassociate themselves from the deception. Foreign Secretary Jack Straw told a parliamentary enquiry that "I do not happen to regard the 45 minute statement having the significance which has been attached to it" – a preposterous assertion in light of Blair's emphasis on it in the foreword to the dossier and associated media briefings. Straw was also asked whether he still stood by the claim. Rather than simply replying yes, Straw first said "it was not my claim. I stand by the integrity of the JIC [Joint Intelligence Committee]", supposedly the original source. The most he could say was "I accept the claim but did not make it."[14]

The failure to find weapons of mass destruction in Iraq after the war has completely given the game away as to the government's claims. So the Foreign Secretary produced an intriguing response to this dilemma, by saying that this (i.e., the whole pretext on which the war was waged) didn't matter. Straw said in a radio interview in May 2003 that it was "not crucially important" to find WMD because the evidence of Iraqi wrongdoing was overwhelming.[15] Now that the pretext has served its purpose, it can be dropped.

Similarly, US Deputy Defense Secretary Paul Wolfowitz told *Vanity Fair* magazine that WMD was chosen for reasons of political expediency: "The truth is that for reasons that have a lot to do with the US government bureaucracy, we settled on the one issue that everyone could agree on – which was weapons of mass destruction – as the core reason." A "huge" outcome of the war, he noted, was the opportunity for the US to pull troops out of Saudi Arabia.[16]

After the US/British task had been completed, Straw also downplayed the threat posed by Saddam. In the parliamentary enquiry, he said that neither he nor Blair "had ever used the words 'immediate or imminent' threat" to describe Iraq, but that they had talked of "'a current and serious threat', which is very different". Straw added: "Impending, soon to happen, as it were, about to happen today or tomorrow, we did not use that because plainly the evidence did not justify that."[17] So, we could have waited for inspections, avoiding the deaths of thousands of people: surely a retrospective acceptance of criminal guilt. This has been largely ignored in the mainstream media in favour of more marginal issues such as the intra-elite spat between Alastair Campbell and the BBC.

A further desperate claim by the government was of Iraq's links with al-Qaeda, which began to be asserted towards the end of 2002. A truly comic episode then began. Planners were unable to present any evidence of this link whatsoever. In October 2002, before the government appeared to formally seize on the new pretext, the *Guardian* quoted a well-placed source who, when asked whether Saddam had any links with al-Qaeda, said "quite the opposite". The paper noted that "the clear message from British intelligence" is that far from allying itself with al-Qaeda, the Iraqi regime was distancing itself from it. This was the interpretation of the murder in Baghdad of the Palestinian terrorist, Abu Nidal, in August 2002.[18] Indeed, the Iraqi regime had been consistently opposed to Islamic fundamentalist groups (unlike London and Washington, incidentally, who can count many as allies, notably the ruling family of Saudi Arabia, the world's most fundamentalist state).

Planners then hit on a variant of the new formula: "Terrorism and rogue regimes are part of the same picture," Jack Straw started saying around the turn of the year. The reason was that "the most likely sources of technology and know-how for such terrorist organisations are rogue regimes". Then, in speech after speech the same message was delivered. The assertion is plainly false since the record shows that the spread of WMD technology is likely to come as much from NATO countries as anywhere else (Germany, for example, probably provided the biggest aid to developing Iraq's WMD). But this mere truth is of course not the issue; simply asserting the link is. The media largely took their cue, generally reporting government assertions as serious, even if with some criticism and, most importantly, failing to ridicule them as simply propaganda.

After the alleged "link" was hit upon, all sorts of imminent terrorist threats to Britain arose in the media, apparently the result of the "security services" leaking unattributable stories. Examples are the supposed London Underground nerve gas attack, reported threats to cross-Channel ferries and the story of traces of the poison ricin found in the flat of a group of Algerians, together with numerous high-profile arrests. Much of the media have dutifully covered these stories, with some papers adding racist diatribes against asylum seekers now conveniently lumped into the camp of official terrorist threats. As noted by Mike Berry of the Glasgow University Media Group, Britain's foremost body critically analysing media reporting, these operations usually result in arrests, but few charges or convictions, but by then they "have already served their purpose in helping to generate a climate of pervasive fear across the country".[19] The message the public was meant to get loud and clear was that removing Saddam would also remove a terrorist threat to us.

Clare Short also said following her resignation that the "search for a diplomatic solution" to the crisis over Iraq was a charade, a further deception. While Blair was assuring her of a commitment to secure a second Security Council resolution, Short noted that three "extremely senior people in the Whitehall system" said that the Prime Minister had already agreed with President Bush the "previous summer" to invade Iraq the following February (later extended to March because of Turkey's refusal to accept US troops). "I think the US wanted to go to war in the Spring and the UK, I now think, had pre-committed to that timetable," Short noted. "We never found out whether Blix could be more successful" because "I think Britain was never on that route."

Short also said the effort was made to go through the UN "for the sake of international public opinion" and that "they wanted to be free to act, having tried the UN, when they wanted to act". Crucially, she also stated that even worse than being personally misled was that "this way of making the decision led to the lack of proper preparation for afterwards and I think that a lot of the chaos, disorder and mess in Iraq flowed from not having made the decision properly and made the preparations properly".[20]

The wider context of ongoing state propaganda is critical to understand and little-known. Judging from the abyss between its rhetoric and the reality of policy, the Blair government may have broken all post-war British records in state propaganda on its foreign policy, and is recognised as a global leader in this area. Everyone knows about "spin", but this term is itself spin, while the media has only reported some aspects of it: the extent of state propaganda goes much deeper.

The Ministry of Defence has a new name for state propaganda. It used to call it "psychological operations" but New Labour renamed it "information support" (a change Orwell would have understood). "But", the House of Commons Defence Committee has said, "the concept has changed little from the traditional objective of influencing the perceptions of selected target audiences." The aim of these operations in Britain is "to mobilise and sustain support for a particular policy and interpretation of events".

In the war against Yugoslavia in 1999, the MoD identified four target audiences, according to the Defence Committee: the British public, Milosevic and his supporters, NATO allies, and Kosovo Albanians. Thus the government identified the British public and Milosevic as targets: both are enemies, albeit in different ways. The Defence Committee commented that with the British public "the prime task was to mobilise and to keep on-side public and political support for the campaign". It said that "the whole campaign was designed with one and a half eyes on media perceptions" and concluded approvingly that:

> Ministers could not be accused of neglecting the media aspects of the battle. From the top-down, the UK government committed its considerable media operations resources to the campaign and to the task of mobilising international and British public opinion.

Just before the bombing campaign against Yugoslavia was launched, NATO quadrupled the size of its media operation in Brussels on the advice of Alastair Campbell. The number of ethnic Albanians killed by Milosevic's forces in Kosovo was exaggerated, with the Foreign Office claiming 10,000 at the time, later revising the figure to 2,000. The bombing of Yugoslavia proceeded with an array of propaganda about good versus evil, a moral test for the future and government acting from the deepest humanitarian values (largely taken seriously, and actively promoted, by a willing media).

"The campaign directed against home audiences was fairly successful," the Defence Committee noted approvingly. It outlined Britain's role as NATO's chief propagandist, saying that the "UK was rightly seen as the most proficient member of a generally under-performing Alliance" in media operations. It also noted that "if anything, the UK's contribution to the war of perceptions was of more significance than its strictly military contribution". But "if anything, the UK's efforts to shape perceptions were less efficient than they could have been".[21]

So, an all-party group of MPs supported a government strategy to deceive the public, even saying it didn't go far enough – a nice illustration, perhaps, of the degree to which elected elites serve the public.

Who is the real enemy here? It is quite clearly the public. A former MI6 officer has said that the purpose of MI6's psychological warfare section is "massaging public opinion into accepting controversial foreign policy decisions". Blair, Campbell and others are proving their commitment to the same end. We are clearly in an era of systematic government psychological warfare against the public.

NOTES

1. Clare Short, evidence to the House of Commons Foreign Affairs Committee, 17 June 2003, Q63, <http://www.publications.parliament.uk/pa/cm200203>.
2. Ministry of Defence, "The Future Strategic Context for Defence", <http://www.mod.uk/issues/strategic_context>.
3. Hans Blix, Notes for the briefing of the Security Council on the 13th quarterly report of UNMOVIC, UN News Centre, 5 June 2003.
4. Cited in Glen Rangwala, "Iraq's Weapons of Mass Destruction: the assessment of the British government – Problems, contradictions, falsehoods", undated, and "Misled into War", 21 March 2003, both at <http://www.middleeastreference.org.uk>.
5. Marie Woolf and David Usbourne, "MPs Press Blair and Campbell to Explain WMD Report", *Independent*, 9 June 2003.
6. "I was shocked by poor weapons intelligence – Blix", *Guardian*, 7 June 2003.

7. Robin Cook, evidence to the House of Commons Foreign Affairs Committee, 17 June 2003, Q3, <http://www.publications.parliament.uk/pa/cm200203>; Richard Norton-Taylor, "An Insult to British Intelligence", *Guardian*, 30 April 2003.

8. "Blair: I have secret proof of weapons", *Observer*, 1 June 2003; Clare Short evidence, Q89, 94.

9. "Intelligence Chiefs Tell Blair: No more spin, no more stunts", *Guardian*, 6 June 2003; "Blair: I have secret proof of weapons", *Observer*, 1 June 2003.

10. Robin Cook evidence, Q9; "Iraq Hits Back with CIA Offer", *Guardian*, 23 December 2003; "Secret of Saddam's Hidden Arsenal", *Guardian*, 5 September 2002.

11. Cited in Glen Rangwala, "Iraq's Weapons of Mass Destruction".

12. Glen Rangwala, "Paper Written for the Foreign Affairs Committee", <http://www.middleeastreference.org.uk>.

13. Cited in Rangwala, "Iraq's Weapons of Mass Destruction"; Clare Short evidence, Q103–4.

14. Jack Straw, evidence to the Foreign Affairs Committee, 24 June 2003, Q737, 845–6, <http://www.publications.parliament.uk/pa/cm200203>.

15. Nicholas Watt, "Straw Retreats on Finding Banned Weapons", *Guardian*, 15 May 2003.

16. Julian Borger, "Intelligence Was Wrong, Admits General", *Guardian*, 31 May 2003.

17. Jack Straw evidence, Q735.

18. Richard Norton-Taylor, "UK Spies Reject Al Qaida link", *Guardian*, 10 October 2002.

19. Letter to the *Guardian*, 22 January 2003.

20. Clare Short evidence, Q64, 83, 124, 129.

21. House of Commons, Defence Committee, *Fourteenth Report*, Session 1999/2000, paras 254–7, <http://www.publications.parliament.uk/pa/cm199900>.

10
The Propaganda Machine

David Miller

Since 11 September 2001 both the US and UK governments have comprehensively overhauled their internal and external propaganda apparatus. These have been globally co-ordinated as never before to justify the "war on terror" including the attacks on Afghanistan and Iraq and the assault on civil liberties at home. To win the war on Iraq the US and UK governments evidently believed that they could not rely on the media to report consistently in conformity with the official line. Consequently there has been serious investment in an extensive machinery of propaganda.

There is very little public debate on the propaganda apparatus and very few people know of the extensive machinery which has been built up in the past two years. The UK Foreign Office public diplomacy operation alone costs £340 million annually for operations taking place in London and not including work done in embassies around the world.[1] In the US the Pentagon has its own machinery and the State Department has the Office of Public Diplomacy. The latter tries to win hearts and minds in the Arab world and operates with a budget in excess of $1 billion.[2] The overall cost of the propaganda campaigns to justify the "war on terror" and the attack on Afghanistan and Iraq is a secret, but it must run into billions of dollars in the US and hundreds of millions of pounds in the UK.

The machinery has a number of parallel elements in the US and UK and the efforts are also co-ordinated globally between the US and UK. In the US the White House has the Office of Global Communications (OGC) which sits at the top of the global pyramid. The OGC was set up by the Bush White House based on the experience of the Coalition Information Centers (CIC) operated during the Kosovo and Afghanistan adventures. These drew on the propaganda expertise of the British government and are reported to have been the idea of Alastair Campbell, the former No.10 Press Secretary.[3] The CIC was set up in October 2001 for the Afghanistan campaign with offices in Washington, London and Islamabad to co-ordinate across time-zones. According to reports it was this initiative which sparked information sharing to ensure that the US and UK (and other governments) "sang from the same hymn sheet".[4] The CIC was made permanent under the auspices of the White House with the creation of the OGC in July 2002. It was the OGC which fed out the lies about the threat posed by the Hussein regime including the faked and spun intelligence information supplied by the UK and by the secret Pentagon intelligence operation, the Office of Special Plans. This was set up by Rumsfeld to bypass the CIA, which was reluctant to go along with some of the lies.[5]

According to Suzy DeFrancis, deputy assistant to President Bush for communications, the aim during the attack on Iraq was to ensure information dominance by constant feeding of the official line:

> When Americans wake up in the morning, they will first hear from the [Persian Gulf] region, maybe from General Tommy Franks ... Then later in the day, they'll hear from the Pentagon, then the State Department, then later on the White House will brief.

The day's message was set "with an early-morning conference call to British counterpart Alastair Campbell, White House communications director Dan Bartlett, State Department spokesman Richard Boucher, Pentagon spokesperson Torie Clarke, and White House Office of Global Communication (OGC) director Tucker Eskew – a routine that mirrors procedure during the conflict in Afghanistan".[6] The OGC produces each day's "talking points". "[C]ivilian and military personnel, for example are told to refer to the invasion of Iraq as a 'war of liberation'. Iraqi paramilitary forces are to be called 'death squads'."[7]

From the White House the message is cascaded down to the rest of the propaganda apparatus. In the US, the State Department Office of Public Diplomacy is responsible for overseas propaganda. It also underwent a reorganisation and appointed a new director after 11 September. According to the new director Charlotte Beers, a former ad agency executive (and who lasted only until March 2003), the Office's 800 staff in the US link into some 16,000 embassy staff globally. "We reach them through web, through e-mail, through cable, and our own American Embassy television channel. They can take our products and activate them locally in ways that we in Washington cannot."[8] Every night the Office sends an email bulletin known as the "Global Messenger" "containing talking points and ready-to-use quotes".[9]

In the UK there is a parallel apparatus. The Ministry of Defence and the Foreign Office have the biggest propaganda operations of any UK government departments and their efforts are co-ordinated with Downing Street. The co-ordination was accomplished by means of a cross-departmental committee known as the Communication and Information Centre, later changed back to the Coalition Information Centre as it had been in the Afghan campaign. It is administratively based in the Foreign Office Information Directorate, yet, was chaired by Alastair Campbell and run from Downing Street.[10] Campbell also chaired a further cross-departmental committee at No.10 – the Iraq Communication Group.[11] It was from here that the campaign to mislead the media about the existence of weapons of mass destruction (WMD) was directed. In particular it oversaw the September dossier on WMD and the second "dodgy" dossier of February 2003 which was quickly exposed as plagiarised and spun. In another parallel with the US, Downing Street has "exasperated" the Foreign Office by setting up an alternative diplomatic policy centre in No.10 which is linked straight in to the centres of power in Washington, particularly via Sir David Manning, the most senior diplomat in No.10, who regularly speaks on the phone with his "friend" Condoleezza Rice. In the Foreign Office the parallel machinery is known as the "cosa nostra".[12]

The propaganda apparatus below this had four main elements. First was the external system of propaganda run by the Foreign Office and co-ordinated by the Public Diplomacy Policy Department. Second was internal propaganda focused on the alleged "terrorist threat" co-ordinated out of the Cabinet Office by the newly established Civil Contingencies Secretariat. Third and very much subordinate to the command and control propaganda systems in Washington and London was the operation "in theatre" – the stage for the crushing of Iraq. This was Centcom in Doha, Qatar, the Forward Press Information Centre in Kuwait and the embedded reporters with their military minders. Lastly, there were the US and UK military psychological operations teams undertaking overt and covert operations inside Iraq which are said only to target enemy opinion to break resistance. All of these operations have their own contribution to make to the attack on Iraq although most public debate has focused on the Centcom/embed system and latterly (in the UK) on the Downing Street operation overseen by Campbell.

CHANGING PERCEPTIONS: THE FOREIGN OFFICE

The Foreign Office has undergone a major review of all its propaganda work "using", as an internal report puts it, "the events of 11 September as a peg". Following the US example the Foreign Office "re-branded" its propaganda work as "public diplomacy" in the late 1990s. The review of public diplomacy has brought together all Foreign Office activity in this area including the BBC World Service and the cultural propaganda outfit the British Council. The review concluded that the government needed an "overarching public diplomacy strategy"[13] which would shape the "core messages that we wish to put across to our target audiences".[14] To oversee this propaganda effort a strategy board was appointed.

Mark Leonard of the Foreign Policy Centre, a think-tank set up by Blair and then Foreign Secretary, Robin Cook, has written extensively on public diplomacy. His view on honesty and openness in communication is that neither should be an obstacle to government propaganda: "If a message will engender distrust simply because it is coming from a foreign government then the government should hide that fact as much as possible."[15] One can guess how much this reflects official thinking by the fact that Leonard is now one of the members of the Public Diplomacy Strategy Board which oversees Foreign and Commonwealth Office (FCO) propaganda.

The Foreign Office has a long history of covert and semi-covert propaganda operations via the secret Information Research Department, closed down in 1978, and its successor the Information Department which continued the tradition of "grey" propaganda in the production of briefings, news stories, radio and TV items which were planted in news outlets around the world. The Foreign Office was historically rather coy about the fact that these were produced by the British government.[16] Today the tradition continues. Four "grey" propaganda operations run by the FCO are the London Press Service, the London Radio Service, the London Television Service and the relatively new British Satellite News. These provide pro-British news and information free of charge and copyright to news organisations across the world. There is little indication in the material itself that it is produced by the British government and it is then published in international media as if it was genuine news.[17] The response to 11 September has been to step up such material and reshape the entire information apparatus with renewed emphasis on managing perceptions overseas.

A favoured tactic is to conduct trips for journalists. The Foreign Office departmental report brags about the success of one to Afghanistan in 2002. According to FCO propaganda official, David Dearnley, the journalists from Islamic media were shown "what Britain and the British-led forces were doing to help rebuild Afghanistan". The journalists were also taken "through some of the most devastated parts of [Kabul] to a recently refurbished school where many girls and young women were eagerly taking the opportunity to catch up on their education". Little is shown of the truth of the situation in Afghanistan which by July 2003 was described as follows: "More than 18 months after the collapse of the Taliban regime, there is a remarkable consensus among aid workers, NGOs and UN officials that the situation is deteriorating. There is a further point of consensus: that the deterioration is a direct consequence of 'coalition' policy."[18] Instead, as the Foreign Office blushingly tells us: "The journalists subsequently published many articles giving positive coverage of Britain's work in Afghanistan."[19]

The attack on Afghanistan in 2001 also occasioned the creation of a unit within the Foreign Office tasked specifically with dealing with the Islamic media such as Al Jazeera and Abu Dhabi TV. It was made permanent in 2002. As the attack on Iraq loomed, the rare UK media mentions of the unit painted it as a traditional example of plucky yet genteel British propaganda. The head of the unit, Gerard Russell, is described as "Britain's lone crusader" or as "almost single-handedly responsible" for putting the British case in the Arab world.[20] This picture fails to take account of the fact that the Islamic Media Unit, which Russell heads, has eight staff[21] and is tapped into the rest of the extensive apparatus of public diplomacy, including work with the London Correspondents Unit which arranges visits to Britain for journalists from the Arab world, and British Satellite News which beams slanted news coverage into the Middle East with both English and Arabic scripts. Russell says "a lot of my job is demolishing myths" and countering the "emotive enunciations of extreme views on Arab television".[22] Among the myths are the notion that US and UK imperialism are alive and well today. According to Russell: "I have to be very careful when I talk about democracy that they understand this means power of the people, and not imposing western ways of life or undermining Arab identity."[23]

The strategy of the FCO is to fundamentally misrepresent the British role as consisting of benevolence and a respect for human rights. UK "public diplomacy" campaigns are not propaganda but the truth. The public diplomacy strategy of the government is available on the web, but has caused no major headlines in the media. The "core narrative" of the strategy includes maintaining that the UK is

> principled and professional as shown in our: ...
> – reliability, straight dealing and trustworthiness in business and international affairs.
> – Commitment to justice, human rights, the rule of law and international security.[24]

This statement was written and posted on the internet in May 2003 just after the attack on Iraq – in breach of international law and after the systematic deception about the threat from Iraq had started to unravel in the media. A clear illustration of the parallel universe inhabited by the UK government's propagandists.

UK RESILIENCE AND THE CIVIL CONTINGENCIES SECRETARIAT

Without attracting front page attention the Blair government has quietly presided over a revolution in internal propaganda systems for dealing with national emergencies. The overhaul was set in train in July 2001 as a result of the foot and mouth crisis and drawing on the experience of the floods of winter 2000 and the fuel protests. The Civil Contingencies Secretariat (CSS) is based in the Cabinet Office and was overseen initially by the most senior propaganda official in the civil service, the head of the Government Information and Communication Service (GICS), Mike Granatt. It works closely with another new body, the Health Protection Agency which encompasses parts of the Department of Health disease surveillance operation and the MoD's chemical and biological labs at Porton Down. Under the rather chilling website branding of "UK Resilience", this network of organisations also works closely with the Special Branch and MI5. They tap straight into the CIC, formerly chaired by Alastair Campbell. The aim of the CSS is said to be to improve the UK's "resilience" to "disruptive challenge".[25] It has already seen action in the firefighters dispute – an indication of the orientation of the CCS towards state rather than public service agendas. It was centrally involved in circulating information on the alleged "threat" from Islamic "terrorism".

The CCS houses a 24-hour monitoring spin operation called the News Co-ordination Centre (NCC) which stands ready for use in the event of the next emergency. It has also (in the wake of 11 September) established a wide-ranging review of information handling in an emergency situation undertaken by a working party involving government press officers and senior media executives together with police and local authority crisis planners. The Media Emergency Forum has produced a long report which the CCS claims "reflects a more productive relationship" with the media.[26] The approach taken by the CCS is more sophisticated than previous emergency planning responses which allow the government simply to take over the broadcast media. That system is still in place. According to Mike Granatt, then Director General of the GICS, "we've got a system that was put in place for nuclear war. We could press the button and pre-empt every transmitter in this country." But this would be counter-productive. "Voluntary" agreements with the media are seen as more effective. Granatt says "we need a credible, active, sceptical – rather than cynical – system of news reporting ... Anything we do to subvert the process of giving trust in that is wrong ... If the BBC or ITN ... said we think you should do this because the government says so, we would be lost."[27] So productive has this been that it has occasioned little attention in the media.

It was the new propaganda apparatus that oversaw the release of the information on the alleged discovery of ricin in January 2003 and which ordered the tanks to Heathrow in late 2002, following an intelligence tip-off, reported as a surface-to-air missile attack on the airport. In the case of Heathrow Granatt has noted:

I will now confess to you. I sat at all the meetings that decided to do that, and I have seen agony cross their face before ... Ministers actually considering putting tanks at our biggest economic asset ... after what I sat and heard, doing it was absolutely necessary and I can't tell you more – I'm very sorry about it but that's the fact. But I can tell you first hand there was no lack of sincerity and nobody does that because it's going to make some propaganda point for a war that at that point, wasn't entirely certain anyway.[28]

What Granatt and others sat and heard was the intelligence assessment of the threat. Whether or not the threat was genuine, or just more dodgy "intelligence", no one was arrested and no surface-to-air missiles were found. Militarily it is not clear what the effectiveness of light armoured vehicles at Heathrow with a top speed of 30-odd miles an hour would be against a missile attack, launched at some distance from the airport. But according to senior sources involved in the decision: "You don't catch rockets in an armoured vehicle. That is not the point. Part of the point of these things may be deterrence. So visibility is another part of the game." Visibility – otherwise known as propaganda.

In the ricin case, the information was released, after deliberation in the Civil Contingencies Secretariat, under the name of the then deputy chief medical officer Dr Pat Troop.[29] She conducted a joint briefing at Scotland Yard with the police. Troop has maintained that the information that ricin had been found was released because "what we didn't know when we started was whether or not we were then going to find lots more ricin somewhere else and therefore it was felt the public had the legitimate right to know".[30] According to a senior source involved, "the broadcasters' response was very positive. They told us afterwards it enabled them to go straight to air ... because they were talking to people they believed were trustworthy and experts in their fields."[31] The CCS released the information in the knowledge that it would potentially prejudice the trial of the people arrested in connection with the find. As Mike Granatt noted, prejudicing a trial comes way down the list of priorities after "public safety".[32]

The claim that the information was released for public health reasons ushers in a new era or threat warning and assessment where the threat of terrorist attack is whipped up on shaky evidence for our own good – a very New Labour propaganda solution. The "threat" from ricin in the "environment" was clearly very small. The poison has to be ingested, inhaled or injected. Even if we suppose that the warning was genuinely given by civil servants operating in good faith, the information on which the warnings are based depends on the "intelligence" services. Their collective lack of understanding of Islamic activists together with their own overhauled spin apparatus makes it difficult to discern whether the information was based on "genuine" if misinterpreted intelligence or deliberate fabrication, as in the case of the MI5 leak that a planned gas attack on the London Tube had been foiled.[33]

Either way the UK Resilience apparatus appears credible to journalists and ensures effective wall to wall coverage for stories based on dubious sources which played very nicely into the propaganda campaign to take the UK to war and legitimates government assaults on civil liberties.

NO NEWS IS NEWS AT CENTCOM

In the 1991 Gulf War, the pool system has been the main means of control of journalists. In 2003 the Pentagon got more sophisticated and more determined to eliminate the possibility of independent reporting. They pressured journalists to leave Baghdad and by 18 March about half of the 300 there had left, including many of the key UK and US journalists.[34] They also threatened independent journalists and killed an unprecedented number (as discussed elsewhere in this book). The threats are all part of the PR strategy along with which goes the Forward Press Information Centre in Kuwait, the million dollar press room in Doha, Qatar, and the system of "embedding" journalists with military units.

The Doha Centre (Centcom) operated much like in previous wars and there were many complaints about the lack of information which flowed from it and from the Forward Press Information Centre. The grumbling came to a head when Michael Wolff asked the obvious question: "I mean no disrespect, but what is the value proposition of these briefings. Why are we here? Why should we stay? What's the value of what we're learning at this million dollar press centre?" As Wolff notes: "It was the question to sour the dinner party. It was also, because I used the words value proposition, a condescending and annoying question – a provocation."[35]

In response to the question, and the spontaneous round of applause from the assembled reporters,

> General Brooks said that I was here of my own volition and, if it wasn't satisfactory to me, I should go home, this was far from a statement of policy. The last thing the Pentagon wanted was for the media to go home. Indeed, Centcom refused to confirm or deny what everyone could see for themselves: that chairs were being removed from the briefing every day (in one day alone, six chairs were removed) so that, as numbers dwindled, empty seats would not be shown to the world. This was a serious problem. What if you gave a war and the media didn't come?

The problem for Centcom apart from the instinctive secrecy of the military, was that it lacked the ability to issue information without approval and it was bypassed by the footage supplied by embedded journalists. As one reporter in Doha noted,

> At General Tommy Franks's headquarters, it is easy to work out whether the day's news is good or bad. When there are positive developments, press officers prowl the corridors of the press centre dispensing upbeat reports from pre-prepared scripts, declaring Iraqi towns have been liberated and that humanitarian aid is about to be delivered. Yet if American and British troops have suffered any sort of battlefield reverse, the spin doctors retreat into their offices at press centre and await instructions from London and Washington.[36]

When the instructions came the important thing was to ensure consistency. When the questions arose about the inability of the US to find Saddam Hussein, US spokespersons "from the White House to the Pentagon to the Central command in Qatar – simultaneously insisted that the war was 'not about one man'".[37]

Centcom was certainly not the resounding success that the system of embedding proved. The success of embedding was its co-option of journalists which ensured that the military could trust them – in the words of the BBC's first director general John Reith – "not to be really impartial".

EMBED WITH THE MILITARY

Embedded journalists were the greatest PR coup of the war. Dreamt up by the Pentagon and Donald Rumsfeld the "embeds", as they were now routinely described, were almost completely controlled by the military. Embeds agreed to give up most of their autonomy in exchange for access to the fighting on military terms. Most importantly, embeds were afforded protection from physical harm by the military.

Each embedded reporter had to sign a contract with the military – a significant departure from previous conflicts. They were also governed by a 50-point plan issued by the Pentagon detailing what they could and could not report. The list of what they could report is significantly shorter than the list of what they could not.[38] The rules were presented as voluntary and appeared to some to offer "unprecedented freedom to report the facts". But on closer inspection, a number of clauses buried in the text indicate the iron fist in the velvet glove. While the rules state that there is "no general review process" of reports, a later section notes that "if media are inadvertently exposed to sensitive information they should be briefed after exposure on what information they should avoid covering". A security review also becomes compulsory if any sensitive information is released deliberately by the military. In a classic passage attempting to present strict censorship rules as voluntary, the Pentagon notes that "agreement to security review in exchange for this type of access must be strictly voluntary and if the reporter does not agree, the access may not be granted".[39] In all the debate in seminars after the fall of Baghdad, on both sides of the Atlantic, the contract and the guidelines have barely even been mentioned by the embeds or their editors. In a rare exception to this, ITN reporter Juliet Bremner has disclosed that the British military "wanted the right to vet every piece that we put out before it went on air. If we didn't sign up to this we couldn't go. So of course we did [sign up]."[40]

The PR genius of the embed system was that it allowed unprecedented access to the fighting and, also, unprecedented identification by the reporters with the military. British minister of Defence Geoff Hoon has claimed: "I think the coverage ... is more graphic, more real, than any other coverage we have ever seen of a conflict in our history. For the first time it is possible with technology for journalists to report in real time on events in the battlefield."[41] It is certainly true to say that it is new to see footage of war so up-close, but, it is a key part of the propaganda war to claim that this makes it "real". In fact, the aim of the embedding system is to control what is reported by encouraging journalists to identify with their units. To eat and drink together, to risk danger and to share the same values.

The embed system was hailed as a great success by all sides. From the Falklands via Grenada, Panama and the Gulf in 1991, there has never been such a collective love-in about the reporting of war.[42] Some journalists couldn't get enough of cheerleading while others worried about being used. The kind of criticism faced in previous conflicts and evident in relation to Centcom was much more muted and marginal. Why? Those most comfortable with the system tended to argue that they had "total freedom" to cover "virtually everything we wanted to cover" in the words of NBC's Chip Reid.[43] Or in the words of Gavin Hewitt of the BBC: "there was an incredible amount of freedom". Hewitt was one journalist who evidently came to identify closely with the troops. He describes the evolution of the relationship with the military:

Initially they were cautious and I could tell the captain was having briefings and we were excluded … By the time we got to Baghdad that relationship had changed. We had been in battle with them. I felt my safety was dependent on them, which it was. They felt we had been through a lot together, so the relationship had become much closer.[44]

So close in fact, that Hewitt ended up picking out targets for the military. At a public meeting in London Hewitt recounted how he had spotted a truck through his binoculars. "I had an absolute instinct that not only the unit would come under attack, because I was travelling with it, that I would come under attack," he said. So:

I shouted across to the Captain "that truck over there – I think these guys are going to attack us." I thought the Captain would have sent one of the tanks to try and investigate. Within seconds a Bradley fighting vehicle was opening up – tracers were flying across the field… eventually the truck went up – boom – like this. And I was absolutely horrified. I thought for a moment that these could have been innocent civilians. I could have made a mistake and at that moment I thought "are we getting too close to this?" … Then there was a secondary and tertiary explosion and this truck was full of grenades. And of course all the unit were delighted. From then on the bonding grew tighter.[45]

What is so noteworthy is that Hewitt felt able to volunteer the information (at an event on World Press Freedom day no less) and that his only qualm appeared to be that he might have made a "mistake" by identifying civilians. When journalists so identify with their military unit that they pick out targets, they have moved from being reporters, straight through propagandists to become active combatants in war. There have been no calls for Hewitt to be sacked by the BBC. Presumably acting as an accessory to murder (which is what the killing of combatants in an illegal war amounts to) is seen as a less serious offence than Andrew Gilligan's alleged crime of mis-reporting a source.

There are two or three examples of critical coverage of the coalition forces resulting from embed reporting. So why were the military so happy with the system? The key to this from the official point of view is precisely that the debate on embedding has been so muted. According to Peter Kovach, a US propagandist in the Office of Public

Diplomacy, the beauty of the system was that it prevented journalists complaining about lack of access while securing overwhelmingly positive coverage for the coalition:

> I remember that the opaqueness of the US government and its spokespersons became the story [in 1991] ... embedding from our point of view was a risk. It carried risks that bad behaviour on our [US military] part might be caught on camera ... But I have to say as a consumer of news I think there has been a very high reward ... I think the benefits of that have been very great.[46]

The success of the embedding system in other words is that it co-opts journalists so that they become advocates for the system of control.

PSYOPS

Psyops or psychological operations are an important yet hidden element of the information apparatus. On the rare occasions where their work does surface in the mainstream media, the propaganda line that they engage only in "white" operations involving radio broadcasts and leaflet drops which are targeted only at enemy opinion (i.e., Iraqi forces) in order to save lives is scrupulously maintained. As Major Harry Taylor, the head of 42 Commando Royal Marines psyops unit puts it: "The main thing is that we are trying to save these peoples lives."[47]

In the UK psyops has been renamed "Information Support" a decidely Orwellian name change. Thousands of British soldiers have passed through the psyops course run by the military at Chicksands, the Defence Intelligence and Security Centre in Bedfordshire. The US psyops teams in Iraq were the largest of any conflict, including eleven companies and almost 1,000 personnel in Iraq or in support roles in the US, according to Lt Col. Glenn Ayers, commander of the 9th Psychological Operations Battalion.[48]

After the war, commanders at the US psyops HQ at Fort Bragg, were so proud of their achievements that they invited the media into their new $8.1 million centre and showed them round the facilities said to be capable of producing 1 million leaflets an hour. More than 150 million leaflets have been produced at Fort Bragg and distributed throughout Afghanistan and Iraq since September 2001. According to the commander of the 4th Psychological Operations Group, Col. James Treadwell, the staff at the complex support the work of nearly 900 psyops troops in 13 countries. Of course no attention was drawn to the hidden part of their work which has remained largely unreported.[49]

It almost goes without saying that the content of the psyops material is mendacious. According to Major Taylor one of the messages in Iraq is that the UK and US will not "plunder the country". Both the US and UK have run "white" radio operations inside Iraq including "Information Radio" broadcast by the US and Radio Nahran (Two Rivers Radio) run by the British in Basra during the war.[50] According to some reports "grey" operations are continuing in Iraq with one Baghdad weekly printing articles supplied by Fort Bragg, "most of which don't appear to come from a US or military source". In exchange the US buys and distributes 70,000 copies.[51] The day after the fall of Baghdad UK and US psyops operatives launched their first television channel. Broadcast on the frequency formerly occupied by Iraqi TV, *Towards Freedom* featured messages from Bush and Blair. The channel was the idea of a UK government information working group and was commissioned by the FCO, paid for by the British Ministry of Defence and transmitted via the US 4th Psychological Operations Group (airborne) at Fort Bragg for eventual broadcast to Iraq from Kuwait, from the US psyops plane known as Commando Solo and from SOMS-B (Special Operations Media System-B) inside Iraq. The programmes are outsourced to World Television News, the private company which already runs the UK grey propaganda operation known as British Satellite News.[52]

Still, it is clear that psyops does continue to include "black" propaganda operations, including radio stations which disguise their sponsors and media disinformation. But their covert work does leave some traces. For example, one "elaborate disinformation operation" was conducted even before the bombs began to fall on 19 March 2003.[53] The UK Foreign Office confirmed that it was "investigating rumours" that the Deputy Prime Minister of Iraq had defected.[54] This prompted Tariq Aziz into making a live media appearance to deny the story. According to reports, Aziz was then "tracked ... to a bunker at a presidential palace where they expected him to report to Saddam", leading to the "decapitation strike" on 20 March.[55] As with much of the "intelligence" surrounding Iraq this turned out to be a botched job and neither Aziz nor Hussein were killed.

Another "black" operation was Radio Tikrit which launched in early February 2003. "It appeared to be just another regime-run station. It mocked the US and ... praised 'Saddam Hussein's Iraq'." By late February the tone had changed and according to BBC monitoring it started to call on the Republican Guard to desert their posts "before it is too late".[56]

This is the kind of approach which psyops and government present as an attempt to save the lives of combatants and it is similar to the messages aimed at the civilian population to keep away from military installations. This version of their work is itself spin since what they are aiming to do is terrorise the population by threatening their lives. As Christopher Simpson, author of an authoritative study of psyops in the US, argues psyops "are premised on violence and they're premised on terror. That's why they work, to the extent that they work at all."[57] As if to underline this statement Major Taylor of the Royal Marines gives this account of the work of British army psyops:

> We use tactical and strategic methods. Tactically, on the first stage, we target the military by dropping leaflets stating the inevitability of their defeat, telling them they will not be destroyed if they play our game and exactly how they can surrender. On the second wave we show them pictures of Iraqi officers who complied. On the third wave we show them pictures of those people who did not.[58]

In other words – co-operate or we will try to kill you. This effort is a co-ordinated part of the overall propaganda push. All psyops material is "signed off right at the very top, by General Tommy Franks", according to Taylor. And the co-ordination is also evident in the wider role which psyops has, but tries to keep under wraps. This is the fact that it also contributes to the battle for hearts and minds internationally and at home as well as targeting "enemy" opinion. As Lt Col. Jerry Broeckert a US Marine Corps public affairs officer acknowledged, the use of the media "blurs the line between public relations and psychological operations".[59] As the attack on Iraq became bogged down at the end of the first week, a Russian website with links to Russian intelligence reported an intercepted report from the US Psychological Operations Tactical Group for the Special Ground Forces Command. The report was concerned about the development of a "resistance ideology" in Iraq. Its solution: "A more active use of the Iraqi opposition was suggested for propaganda work … The same opposition members will be used to create video footage of the 'repented' Iraqi POWs and footage of the local [Iraqi] population 'opposing Saddam'."[60] As the US tanks rolled into Baghdad eleven days later, footage of Iraqis celebrating as the statue of the dictator was toppled outside the Palestine Hotel, where the international media were based, was indeed transmitted around the world. Other sources have suggested that among the celebrants were members of the Iraqi opposition Iraqi National Congress. The toppling of the statue was a propaganda triumph for the US and UK governments. The involvement of psyops in the photo opportunity indicates both the co-ordinated nature of "coalition" propaganda and that psyops operatives spend at least some of their time managing media operations which impact on domestic opinion.

FINALLY

Since 11 September 2001 both the UK and US have systematically overhauled their propaganda operations. This has put in place a very significant operation with global reach which seems to have no precedent (possibly even including the 1939–45 war).

The propaganda operation is entirely outside of democratic control and appears not to be constrained by adhering to any significant standards of truthfulness. It seems instead to operate on the basis that anything goes so long as it is calculated that it can be got away with. The centralisation of propaganda control in the White House, the Pentagon and Downing Street and the unprecedented co-ordination indicates the determination of the clique around Bush and Blair to pursue their project. Overall the operation shows a great deal of contempt for the process of democracy, since the lies are constructed to misinform and persuade – in part – the electorate of the US and UK as well as world opinion. Some will argue that the apparatus is not successful in its attempts to mould media coverage and popular opinion.

It is certainly true that there is some scope for dissent in the mainstream media although this is without doubt limited. It is also true that in the UK a large majority of the public opinion saw through many of the lies and opposed the war. In the US the picture is less clear and public opinion has – under a media onslaught – been more favourable to war.

But the most important questions to ask here are not whether the public believed the lies. The cabal which runs the US and UK care little for public opinion and belief and they will only take note when their interests and strategies are thwarted. This happens in two ways: first, when the public takes action in demonstrations and other political activity and, second, when parts of the elite political system start to feel the pressure which popular opposition generates. A key reason why the propaganda continues and why the media are seen as important is not because public opinion is important but because elite differences can hamper war making. When the House of Commons and the US Congress ratified war, this was the last obstacle to be surmounted and it was a key target of the propaganda. In the end propaganda succeeds if it allows political elites to carry out their plans. In the case of Iraq it was not an unqualified success – as the fallout over the WMD fabrications shows to some extent – but it was a success nevertheless.

NOTES

1. Foreign and Commonwealth Office, *Changing Perceptions: Review of Public Diplomacy (The Wilton Review)*, 22 March 2002.
2. Independent Task Force Report, *Public Diplomacy: A Strategy for Reform*, A Report of an Independent Task Force on Public Diplomacy Sponsored by the Council on Foreign Relations, <http://www.cfr.org/PublicDiplomacy_TF.html>.
3. Foreign Affairs Select Committee, Ninth Report *The Decision to go to War in Iraq*, 7 July 2003, Report, together with formal minutes, HC 813-I, "The February dossier", <http://www.parliament.the-stationery-office.co.uk/pa/cm200203/cmselect/cmfaff/813/81308.htm>.
4. Julia Day, "US Steps Up Global PR Drive", *Guardian*, 30 July 2002, <http://media.guardian.co.uk/attack/story/0,1301,765637,00.html>.
5. John Pilger, "War on Truth", *New Statesman*, 4 August 2003, pp. 14–15.
6. Douglas Quenqua, "White House Prepares to Feed 24-hour News Cycle", *PR Week*, 24 March 2003, <http://www.prweek.com/news/news_story.cfm?ID=174751&site=3>.
7. Bob Kemper, "Agency Wages Media Battle", *Chicago Tribune*, 7 April 2003, <http://www.chicagotribune.com/news/chi-0304070189apr07,1,438283.story>.
8. Charlotte L. Beers, Under-Secretary for Public Diplomacy and Public Affairs United States Department of State Hearing on American Public Diplomacy and Islam, Thursday 27 February 2003, Committee on Foreign Relations, United States Senate, <http://foreign.senate.gov/hearings/BeersTestimony030227.pdf>.
9. Quenqua, "White House Prepares".
10. *Hansard*, Written Answers, "Iraq" 9 Jul 2003 : Column 818W. <http://www.parliament.the-stationery-office.co.uk/pa/cm200203/cmhansrd/cm030709/text/30709w09.htm>.
11. Foreign Affairs Select Committee, Ninth Report *The Decision to go to War in Iraq*.
12. Anthony Sampson, "Hijacked by that mob at No. 10", *Observer*, 8 June 2003, p. 29.

13. Foreign and Commonwealth Office, *Departmental Report 2003* Chapter 8, Influence worldwide, p. 83, <http://www.fco.gov.uk/Files/kfile/ 08_InfluenceWorldwide.pdf>.

14. FCO, *Changing Perceptions*.

15. Mark Leonard, "Diplomacy By Other Means", *Foreign Policy*, Sept/Oct 2002, <http://www.foreignpolicy.com>, cited in Mark Curtis, *Web of Deceit*, London: Vintage, 2003.

16. On IRD see P. Lashmar and J. Oliver, *Britain's Secret Propaganda War 1948–1977*, Stroud: Sutton Publishing, 1998. On the Information Department see David Miller, *Don't Mention the War: Northern Ireland, Propaganda and the Media*, London: Pluto Press, 1994.

17. <http://www.lrs.co.uk/user/default.cfm>; <http://www.londontv.com/>; <http://www.bsn.org.uk/>.

18. Isabel Hilton, "Now We Pay the Warlords to Tyrannise the Afghan People", *Guardian*, Thursday 31 July 2003, <http://politics.guardian.co.uk/ comment/story/0,9115,1009505,00.html>.

19. FCO, Departmental Report 2003, p. 84.

20. Julia Day, "FO Goes on Offensive in Media War", *Guardian*, 17 June 2002, <http://media.guardian.co.uk/attack/story/0,1301,739032,00.html>; Christina Lamb, "Our Man in the Land of Zam Zam Cola", *New Statesman*, 16–30 December 2002, p. 32, <http://www.newstatesman. co.uk/iraqdossier/clamb.htm>; Anton La Guardia, "British Spokesman Assumes Star Status in Middle East", *Daily Telegraph*, 1 April 2003, <http://www.telegraph.co.uk/news/main.jhtml?xml=/news/2003/04/01/ nmed101.xml>.

21. Tom Baldwin, *The Times*, 16 January 2002, <http://www.timesonline. co.uk/article/0,,129–178198,00.html>.

22. Lamb, "Our Man in the Land of Zam Zam Cola".

23. Ibid.

24. Public Diplomacy Strategy Board, *Public Diplomacy Strategy*, London: FCO, <http://www.fco.gov.uk/Files/KFile/PUBLICDIPLOMACYSTRATEGY_May 2003.pdf>.

25. <http://www.ukresilience.info/role.htm>.

26. <http://www.ukresilience.info/mefreport.htm>.

27. Mike Granatt, address to the Communicating the War on Terror conference, the Royal Institution, London, 5 June 2003.

28. Ibid.

29. From: Dr Pat Troop, Deputy Chief Medical Officer, Department of Health "CONCERN OVER RICIN POISON IN THE ENVIRONMENT" 7th January 2003, Reference: CEM/CMO/2003/1, joint statement from the Metropolitan Police and the Deputy Chief Medical Officer, <http:// 199.228.212.132/doh/embroadcast.nsf/0/2344372825A05AFC80256CA7 005727CE?OpenDocument>.

30. Pat Troop, address to Communicating the War on Terror conference, the Royal Institution, London, 5 June 2003.

31. Interview with the author, the Cabinet Office, 17 July 2003.

32. Granatt, Comunicating the War on Terror conference.

33. See David Miller, "'They Were All Asylum Seekers': The Propaganda Campaign to Link Iraq to Terrorism at the Expense of Refugees", *Scoop*,

Thursday 27 March 2003, <http://www.scoop.co.nz/mason/stories/HL0303/S00262.htm>.

34. Ciar Byrne, "Media Mull Iraq Evacuation", *Guardian*, Tuesday 18 March 2003, <http://media.guardian.co.uk/broadcast/story/0,7493,916727,00.html>.

35. Michael Wolff, "I Was Only Asking", *Guardian*, 14 April 2003, <http://media.guardian.co.uk/mediaguardian/story/0,7558,936087,00.html>.

36. Tim Ripley, "Good News, No News and the Infamous Fog of War", *The Scotsman*, Wednesday 26 March 2003, <http://www.thescotsman.co.uk/international.cfm?id=360422003>.

37. Kemper, "Agency Wages Media Battle".

38. PUBLIC AFFAIRS GUIDANCE (PAG) ON EMBEDDING MEDIA DURING POSSIBLE FUTURE OPERATIONS/DEPLOYMENTS IN THE U.S. CENTRAL COMMAND'S (CENTCOM) AREA OF RESPONSIBILITY (AOR). February 2003, <http://www.militarycity.com/iraq/1631270.html>.

39. Patrick Barrett, "US Reporters Condemn Pentagon Press Controls", *Guardian*, Thursday 27 February 2003, <http://media.guardian.co.uk/presspublishing/story/0,7495,903552,00.html>.

40. Juliet Bremner, address to conference to mark World Press Freedom day, City University, London, 2 May 2003.

41. *Question Time*, 27 March 2003, BBC1.

42. For a discussion of the propaganda lessons learned from previous conflicts see David Miller, "War Journalism Guided with Military Precision", *Al Jazeera*, 24 March 2003, <http://english.aljazeera.net/topics/article.asp?cu_no=1&item_no=820&version=1&template_id=282&parent_id=258>.

43. David Bauder, "Iraq Embed Program Hailed as a Success', *Optimum Online*, 20 April 2003, <http://devlc.optonline.net/Article/Feeds/0,4003,channel%3D31&article%3D6626042,00.html>.

44. Gavin Hewitt speaking on *Breakfast With Frost*, 20 April 2003, BBC1.

45. Gavin Hewitt address to conference to mark World Press Freedom day, City University, London, 2 May 2003.

46. David Demers, "Did Embedded Journalists Sell Their Souls to the Bush Administration?", *Global Media News*, Summer 2003, 5(3), pp. 1, 6–7.

47. Richard Edwards, "The Propaganda War in Iraq" *Guardian*, 26 March 2003, <http://media.guardian.co.uk/broadcast/story/0,7493,921764,00.html>.

48. Jim Krane, "US Units Try to Win Iraqi Hearts and Minds", *Kvue.com*, 5 June 2003, <http://www.kvue.com/sharedcontent/iraq/military/060503cciraqhearts.8d028054.html>.

49. Associated Press, "Army Gives Psychological Operations Unit New Base of Operation", *The Herald Sun*, 1 July 2003, <http://www.heraldsun.com/state/6–367297.html>.

50. "Iraq Media Dossier: Psychological Warfare against Iraq', *Radio Netherlands*, <http://www.rnl.nl/realradio/features/html/iraq-psywar.html>.

51. Krane, "US Units Try to Win Iraqi Hearts and Minds".

52. "Iraq Media Dossier".

53. Chris McLaughlin, "Under Fire: Spy Trick Led Us to Saddam", *Sunday Mirror*, 23 March 2003, p. 4.

54. Press Association, "Mystery Surrounds Fate of Saddam's Deputy", *Independent*, 19 March 2003, <http://news.independent.co.uk/world/middle_east/story.jsp?story=388761>.

55. McLaughlin, "Under Fire".

56. Brian Whitaker, "Wargames Open with Clandestine Broadcasts: Psychological Assault Led by 'Radio Tikrit'", *Guardian*, 25 February 2003, <http://www.guardian.co.uk/Print/0,3858,4612747,00.html>.

57. Leslie MacKinnon, "Reality Check: Psychological Operations – Cheaper than Blood", *CBC News Online*, 26 March 2003, <http://www.cbc.ca/news/iraq/issues_analysis>.

58. Edwards, "The Propaganda War in Iraq".

59. J. Broeckert, "Loose Lips Float Ships! How the Military Uses the Media Today", *Rake Magazine*, April 2003, <http://www.rakemag.com/features/detail.asp?catID=46&itemID=2136>.

60. <http://www.aeronautics.ru>, 29 March 2003, 0924hrs MSK (GMT +4 DST).

11
History or Bunkum?

Phillip Knightley

The Pentagon made it clear from the beginning of the war against Iraq that there would be no censorship. What it failed to say was that war correspondents might well find themselves in a situation similar to that in Korea in 1950. This was described by one American correspondent as the military saying: "You can write what you like – but if we don't like it we'll shoot you." The figures in Iraq tell a terrible story. Fifteen media people dead, with two missing, presumed dead. If you consider how short the campaign was, Iraq will be notorious as the most dangerous war for journalists ever. This is bad enough. But – and here we tread on delicate ground – it is a fact that the largest single group of them appear to have been killed by the American military.

We know that the Americans do not target journalists. Brigadier General Vince Brooks, deputy director of operations, has told us so. But some war correspondents do not believe him, and Spanish journalists have demonstrated outside the US embassy in Madrid shouting "murderers". What is going on? I believe that the traditional relationship between the military and the media – one of restrained hostility – has broken down, and that the US administration, in keeping with its new foreign policy, has decided that its attitude to war correspondents is the same as that set out by President Bush when declaring war on terrorists: "You're either with us or you're against us."

Those journalists prepared to get on side – and that means 100 per cent on side – will become "embeds" and receive every assistance. Those who try to follow an objective, independent path, the so-called "unilaterals", will be shunned. And those who report from the enemy side will risk being shot. If you don't like all this, they won't give a damn. Welcome to the new and highly dangerous world of the war correspondent in the twenty-first century.

The media should have seen it coming. Last year the BBC sent one of its top reporters, Nik Gowing, to Washington to try to find out how it was that its correspondent, William Reeve, who had just re-opened the Corporation's studio in Kabul and was giving a live, down-the-line TV interview for BBC World, was suddenly blown out of his seat by an American smart missile. Coincidentally, four hours later, a few blocks away, the office and residential compound of the Arab TV network Al Jazeera was hit by two more American missiles.

The BBC, Al Jazeera, and the US Committee to Protect Journalists thought it prudent to find out from the Pentagon what had gone wrong and what steps they could take to protect their correspondents if war came to Iraq. The Pentagon, in the figure of Rear Admiral Craig Quigley, deputy assistant defence secretary for public affairs, was frank. Nothing had gone wrong. Quigley said that the Pentagon was indifferent to media activity in territory controlled by the enemy, and that the Al Jazeera compound in Kabul was considered a legitimate target because it had "repeatedly been the location of significant al-Qaeda activity". It turned out that this activity was interviews with Taliban officials, something that Al Jazeera had hitherto thought to be normal journalism.

FOOLHARDY AND DANGEROUS

All three organisations concluded that the Pentagon was determined to deter western correspondents from reporting any war from the "enemy" side, would view such journalism in Iraq as activity of "military significance", and might well bomb the area. This view was reinforced in the early days of the war in Iraq when the Pentagon wrote officially to Al Jazeera asking it to remove its correspondents from Baghdad. Downing Street made the same request to the BBC. In the United States a Pentagon official called media bosses to a meeting in Washington to tell them how foolhardy and dangerous it was to have correspondents in the Iraqi capital. But no one realised that it might also be dangerous to work outside the system the Pentagon had devised for allowing war correspondents to cover the war – embedding.

Six hundred correspondents, including about 150 from foreign media, and even one from the music network MTV, accepted the Pentagon's offer to be embedded with military units: to live, eat, sleep and travel with troops in the field, be protected by them, run the same risks as they did, have the honorary rank of major and, apart from military information that might be of use to the enemy, to write what they liked. The idea was copied from the British system in the First World War, when six correspondents embedded with the army on the Western front produced the worst reporting of just about any war and were all knighted for their services. One of them, Sir Philip Gibbs, had the honesty, when the war was over, to write: "We identified ourselves absolutely with the armies in the field." The modern embeds, too, soon lost all distinction between warrior and correspondent and wrote and talked about "we" with boring repetition.

I was able to find only one instance of an embedded correspondent who wrote a story highly critical of the behaviour of US troops and which went against the official account of what had occurred. On 31 March, US soldiers opened fire on a civilian van which had failed to stop at a checkpoint, and killed seven Iraqi women and children. US officials said that the driver of the car failed to stop after warning shots and that troops had fired at the passenger cabin as "a last resort". But William Branigin, of the *Washington Post*, embedded with the 3rd Infantry, witnessed the shooting, and reported that no warning shots were fired and that ten people, not seven, were killed. It will be interesting to see what becomes of Branigin's relations with the US military. For the rest of the embeds, the considered conclusion of that old-fashioned correspondent, Sydney H. Schanberg (the former *New York Times* man whose reporting from Cambodia in the 1970s was featured in the film *The Killing Fields*), sums up their dilemma: "Embedded means you're there," he said. "It also means you're stuck."

But that is what the Pentagon wanted, and after the death of ITN reporter Terry Lloyd, and the probable deaths of two of his team (they remain "missing") who had been operating as "unilaterals", the coalition commander, General Tommy Franks, pointed out that no embedded correspondent had been killed. What General Franks did not reveal was exactly how Lloyd died. At the time of writing, more than a month after Lloyd's death, neither the Ministry of Defence nor the Pentagon has told ITN what the investigation into his death has revealed. He appears to have been killed by American marines who shot at his car, or – the American version – "caught in crossfire". However unlikely, it may turn out that it was an unfortunate accident, another "friendly fire" incident in a war in which they were common. But what happened at the Palestine Hotel was a different matter.

On 8 April, three war correspondents were killed by Americans at locations that were known to the Pentagon to be housing media. Reuters cameraman Taras Protsyuk was killed when an American tank fired a shell at the Reuters suite on the 15th floor of the Palestine

Hotel. Jose Couso, a cameraman for the Spanish TV channel Telecino, was wounded in the same attack and died later in hospital. And Tariq Ayyoub, a cameraman for Al Jazeera, was killed when a US plane bombed the channel's office in Baghdad. American forces also opened fire on the offices of Abu Dhabi TV, whose identity is spelled out in large blue letters on the roof. There was no love lost between the coalition forces and Al Jazeera. The Pentagon has never forgiven Al Jazeera for broadcasting Osama bin Laden tapes around the world from its Kabul office during the war in Afghanistan. In this war it has regarded Al Jazeera as an enemy propaganda station, putting out devastating accounts of Iraqi civilian casualties to a vast Arab audience, thus fuelling anti-American sentiments. Al Jazeera was apprehensive about American reaction and repeatedly informed the US military of the exact co-ordinates of its Baghdad office so that if it were hit, the Pentagon could not offer the excuse that it was an accident. It was a waste of time. The Pentagon has offered neither explanation nor apology.

CONTRADICTORY ACCOUNTS

It might have tried the same "silence" tactic over the Palestine Hotel attack. In fact it did. When the news of the attack first came, the American command said nothing – until it emerged that the French TV channel, France 3, had filmed the tank aiming and firing. Then the coalition put out a series of contradictory accounts. Colonel David Perkins, commander of the 3rd Infantry Division's 2nd Brigade, said Iraqis in front of the hotel were firing rocket-propelled grenades at the tank. Then the Division's commander, General Bouford Blount, issued a statement saying that the tank had come under sniper fire from the hotel's roof and had fired at the source of the shooting which had then stopped.

Correspondents in the Palestine Hotel insisted that there had been no grenades and no sniper fire. Sky's correspondent David Chater said he had not heard a single shot. The BBC's Rageh Omaar said that none of the other journalists in the hotel heard any sniper fire. But the most telling evidence that the tank fired without provocation is that France 3's cameraman had started filming some minutes before the tank opened fire, and his camera's sound track records no shots whatsoever.

More puzzling was an official Spanish government statement about the death of Jose Couso. The Defence Minister, Frederico Trillo, announced that the coalition had actually declared the Palestine Hotel a military objective 48 hours before it was attacked and that the correspondents should have left. This was news to the correspondents, all of whom denied any knowledge of any warning. "Journalists", a watchdog group that defends press freedoms, demanded an investigation and in a letter to the US Defense Secretary, Donald Rumsfeld, said it believed that the attacks on correspondents violated the Geneva Conventions.

My own view is that there will be no investigation, no explanation, no apology. I am convinced that in the light of all the foregoing evidence the Pentagon is determined that there will be no more reporting from the enemy side, and that a few deaths among correspondents who do so will deter others. To that end I believe that the occasional shots fired at "media sites" are not accidental and that war correspondents may now be targets, some more than others. And the Pentagon's policy will work. Al Jazeera seriously considered pulling all of its correspondents out of Iraq because it could not guarantee their safety. Arab TV and British media bosses will think twice in any future war of sending staff reporters to the enemy side – not least because insurers will refuse to underwrite the risk. I think the Pentagon is not concerned in the slightest about public unease over its attacks on journalists because it is convinced that the public, especially the American public, will support its view and its actions.

Consider the difference in the way the war has been reported on the two sides of the Atlantic. It is as if you are looking at two different wars. For the Americans the war has been essentially a military story and a sanitised one at that. With five out of ten Americans believing that most of the terrorists who carried out the attack on 9/11 were Iraqis, the American media decided that its readers and viewers were not interested in the plight of Iraqi victims of the war. The *New York Times* said it aimed to capture the true nature of the war but avoided "the gratuitous use of images simply for shock value". Steve Capus, executive editor of NBC Nightly News, complained: "You watch some Arab coverage and you get the sense there is a blood bath at the hand of the US military. That is not my take on it."

The biggest radio group in the United States, Clear Channel, used its stations to organise pro-war rallies. McVay Media, one of America's largest communications consulting companies, advised its radio clients to play "patriotic music that makes you cry, salute and get cold chills" and under no circumstances cover war protests because they will "hurt your bottom line". When *New York Magazine* writer

Michael Wolff broke ranks at the coalition's daily press conference at Qatar and asked General Brooks: "Why are we here? Why should we stay? What's the value of what we're learning at this million dollar press centre?" he soon had an answer. Fox TV attacked him for lack of patriotism, and right-wing commentator Rush Limbaugh gave out Wolff's email address – in one day he received 3,000 hate emails. Finally, a mysterious civilian in army uniform took him aside and told him: "This is a fucking war, asshole. No more questions for you."

Wolff realised that the press conferences were not for the benefit of the correspondents. How could they be? What correspondent worth his salt would be content with repeating to camera what he had just been told by some general when the question and answer had already been televised? The correspondents were merely extras in a piece of theatre. The system was designed not to illuminate journalists but to play over their heads towards an international TV audience, which soon accorded the briefing officers the status of soap stars. The whole farce could not have taken place if the correspondents had packed up and gone home, but given the competitive nature of war reporting, there was no danger of that. The military did worry about it, though. As Wolff said: "What if they gave a war and the media didn't come?"

£22 MILLION EXTRA SPEND

The main problem with the British coverage was that there was so much of it, more than any brain could absorb. Anyone so inclined could have spent 24 hours a day immersed in war news. British news networks on TV extended their budgets by a combined £22 million. There were more live pictures from the battlefield than has been the case in any previous war. Split screens, feeds from every front, crosses to Washington, then to coalition headquarters in Qatar, then to Downing Street, then back to a real-time firefight near Basra, some pretty pictures of missiles leaving a warship somewhere in the Gulf (but not of their arrival in a market place in Baghdad), interview after interview (often one journalist interviewing another), back to the expert in the studio, then back to breaking news which is breaking yet again about a town that has finally fallen – even though it fell two days ago. And over it all, echoing out of the all-pervasive fog of war, a tone of barely suppressed hysteria. It took a confused *Guardian* reader to sum it up: "Despite scouring two national newspapers every day, listening to the radio, surfing the web and watching the TV news, I have absolutely no clue how the war is going." Join the club.

It was the recognition that perhaps more was not really better that provoked British news executives into an unseemly race to declare who had had the better war. The headline "Rageh Omaar Wins It for BBC in Baghdad" brought David Mannion, editor of ITV News, rushing into print to plug the achievements of ITV correspondents John Irvine, Neil Connery and Julian Manyon: "Expert observers ... believe that the ITV News coverage of Baghdad was the finest, boldest and most comprehensive in the world." A few days later, Richard Sambrook, the BBC's director of News, quoted a survey showing that "the BBC – uniquely out of the broadcasters analysed – was even-handed in its reporting of the U.S. military action and in reporting of casualties". This is one battle of the war that will rumble on.

Let's finish with a look at the image that everyone will still remember when the debate and all these issues are long forgotten. As seen on television and on the front pages of newspapers around the world, cheering Iraqis attach a rope and a chain to Saddam's neck then call on the services of an American vehicle to haul him down. The statue hesitates, bends at the knees and topples into the dust. In an information war heavy with symbolism, this marked the end of Saddam Hussein and the coalition's victory.

But, like Robert Capa's moment of death, this image was not quite what it seemed. The statue was pulled down by American troops using American equipment – the Iraqis on their own would not have been able to do it. Although there were lots of other statues, the toppling of this one conveniently took place just opposite the Palestine Hotel, where most members of the international media were still staying. Without the media, the event would have meant nothing. Long-distance shots show that the Iraqis who helped topple the statue and later celebrated its fall numbered no more than 100 (early BBC reports suggested even fewer and some unkind commentators joked that the correspondents outnumbered the celebrating Iraqis). The square was cordoned off by US tanks and marines but they allowed these Iraqis through.

So who were they? At least one website, NYC IndyMedia, says they were members of the Free Iraqi Forces, headed by Iraqi National Congress founder, Ahmed Chalabi, the Pentagon's favourite to head a new Iraqi government. It produces evidence to support this claim – one of Chalabi's lieutenants, photographed as the Pentagon flew him and his boss into the southern Iraq city of Nasiriyah, is the same man shown on film in Firdos Square dancing on Saddam's statute. So what happened? Was it as portrayed – a spontaneous outpouring of joy by ordinary Iraqis delighted at being liberated and determined to show their contempt for their former leader? Or was it a photo opportunity, a staged event in the theatre of propaganda? Excited TV presenters told their viewers they were witnessing history. But whose history?

12
Spies and Lies

Stephen Dorril

When journalists write about intelligence matters and reach for a cliché, inevitably it is that intelligence is "a wilderness of mirrors". Rarely used is James Angleton's other dictum that "disinformation might be the chief job of an intelligence agency". The latter is a more accurate statement of what has been appearing in the media since the events of 11 September.

Most journalists appear to confuse "information" with "intelligence" when they are two separate concepts. The truth is, they are very different. Agencies collect information that is collated, processed, analysed and then, more often than not, spun into intelligence. Raw, unmediated intelligence is rarely available to the media, though it is worth recalling that during the Cuban Missile Crisis the Kennedy administration did release ultra-secret U-2 high-altitude surveillance photographs of the Soviet missile sites on Cuba to the United Nations and then the press.

In the weeks following 9 September 2001, we were liberally dosed with hasty, unverifiable and often contradictory intelligence (Osama bin Laden is worth $400 million: he is broke; he is a friend of Algeria and Iraq: he hates Algerians and Iraqis), little of which can be regarded as reliable. The working practices of investigative journalists on the *Washington Post* of *All the President's Men* era, when no fact was published without three separate sources to verify it, seems a distant dream.

Ministers, who are often entranced by the magic word "secrecy", hide behind the phrase "intelligence sources and methods" to curtail debate and scrutiny. The reality is that sources can be obscured and blacked-out in documents, while methods have not really changed, except for technical details, in decades. Bugs are planted, telephones, fax machines, mobile phones, websites, internet communications are tapped. All this is common knowledge.

Bin Laden knows this all too well, which is why some reports claim that he never uses these forms of communication. Which, of course, makes his alleged telephone call to his mother just before 11

September, all the more intriguing. Did he make it? His stepfather naturally rebuts the claim but adds: "Osama has not used a telephone since he discovered that his conversations were being monitored by the United States" (*Sunday Times*, 7 October 2001).

The point here is, why not release the original tape of the conversation? Did he use the phrase "massive events"? Is it a correct translation? Robert Fisk, whose sceptical reporting has been a beacon of good journalistic practice, has noted (*Independent*, 29 September 2001) previous "serious textual errors" made by CIA translators.

The British government's 21-page dossier laying out the case for bin Laden's orchestration of the events of 11 September is not particularly impressive. In fact, it is at best flimsy, with little new material of any substance. Chris Blackhurst (*Independent on Sunday*, 7 October 2001) called it "a report of conjecture, supposition and unsubstantiated assertions of fact", which is about right. Clearly, the Americans thought the same because the CIA decided two days later to "leak" further information in an attempt to shore up the case. Bin Laden may indeed be guilty of the crime but there was little evidence to prove it in the dossier.

In 1951 Prime Minister Clement Attlee was warned of intelligence fears that Russian agents had suitcases with kits to construct an atomic bomb. Attlee was not unduly concerned. The same scenario appeared in the early 1970s. Then it was Soviet special forces. It surfaced again in the mid-1990s, when stories appeared about weapons-grade plutonium disappearing from Soviet states.

Intelligence agencies continually create alarmist disinformation. Who now recalls "Red Mercury", the mysterious substance that was a source of cheap nuclear weapons for terrorists; the "white-coated mercenaries", the demobbed Soviet scientists selling their knowledge of weapons of mass destruction to Libya and Iraq; the nuclear artillery shells which went missing from Soviet southern states; the "Islamic bomb" which terrorists were building to be in use by 1995; and the cheap and easily assembled "dirty bomb".

Since 11 September the intelligence agencies with the aid of gullible journalists, editors desperate for endless copy and politicians on a crusade have constructed a truly global conspiracy theory. At the top is the mastermind from every Ian Fleming fantasy, Osama bin Laden, who has a "golden domino" theory of regional domination in the Middle East, controlling a vast network, al-Qaeda, of thousands of terrorists across the globe, now asleep but with access to millions of dollars, and all awaiting the call to murder us in our beds.

Al-Qaeda, according to the press, has so far attempted to buy uranium from the Russian mafia; attempted to manufacture chemical and biological weapons, including anthrax and the plague; planned attacks on European gas and oil pipelines; plotted to blow up the US embassy in Paris; planned to kill President Bush at the G8 summit at Genoa; made a huge profit from share dealing immediately prior to the attack in America; plotted a Belgium attack; and is planning another 30 attacks against the west in London, Washington, European capitals and the Vatican.

If James Angleton was alive he might have added a third quote: The function of an intelligence agency is to create fear. Occasionally, of course, they get their analysis absolutely right.

In 1993 British intelligence put together a paper, "Islamic Fundamentalism in the Middle East". It noted that it thrived on the failure to resolve economic and social problems, corruption in government and the bankruptcy of political ideologies of all kinds. The report said that

> fundamentalist groups advocating violence and revolution are in a minority. Nevertheless ... Western, particularly American, culture and materialism are seen as a threat to Islamic values [but] fundamentalism does not present a coherent and monolithic threat to Western interests in the way that Communism once did. It is not supported by a superpower. Its appeal in Western countries is confined to Muslim minorities and the threat of subversion is, in the UK at least, minimal. Dealings with extreme fundamentalist regimes would be highly unpredictable but not necessarily unmanageable.

The essential message was that the west had to deal with the underlying problems rather than fundamentalism itself. Unfortunately, the message was not heeded and it continues to get lost in the mix of poor intelligence, political spin and disinformation that proves to be so attractive to the media.

SPOOKS AND HACKS

Shortly after the release of the government's intelligence dossier on Iraq (in September 2002), the doyen of government-watchers, Peter Hennessy, told a group of intelligence writers and specialists that this was a unique and significant event. For the first time the government had allowed a Joint Intelligence Committee assessment to be made public. An enthused Hennessy thought that we would see more similar initiatives in the future.

Alas, this may turn out to be the last such occasion the spooks surface. The dossier proved to be an embarrassing mixture of long out-of-date material, wild suppositions and, now we know, reliance on forgeries which contained, UN inspectors revealed, "laughable and childlike errors" about the non-existent export of uranium from Niger to Iraq. The infamous aluminium tubes turned out not to have a nuclear purpose. Jack Straw's claim that Iraq was "weeks" away from building a nuclear bomb was simply untrue.

In the UN Security Council, the two chief weapons inspectors calmly, and deliberately, pulled apart the intelligence which had been given to them by the Americans and British. An inspector on the ground in Iraq described the intelligence as "rubbish". This was before the second Cabinet "intelligence" dossier was exposed for its plagiarism.

The majority of the scoops and insider stories which the press have lapped up at the end of 2002 on Iraq's nuclear capability, mobile biological weapons laboratories, links with al-Qaeda, and so on, have simply disintegrated.

Two important points emerge: one, the intelligence has been, as former Foreign Secretary Geoffrey Howe once said, "not even cornflakes in the wind'; two, the most gullible people in the world are journalists.

As the range and reach of the media expands, the world of intelligence has become a vital arm of government propaganda. Most political stories are so minutely picked over that even the best efforts of the spin doctors can only delay the appearance of the inside story. Intelligence, however, is different. Governments hide behind the walls of secrecy, safe in the knowledge that reference to the refrain that "ministers do not discuss intelligence" or "we cannot discuss operational matters" or "we need to protect those carrying out these tasks" will stop in their tracks the journalists' traditional response that "this bastard is lying".

At a Royal United Services Institute (RUSI) conference on the post-11 September world, the secretary of the parliamentary committee on intelligence put the blame on journalists for the misuse of intelligence and their reference to "secret sources". In effect, journalists just made it all up. If only that was the case.

The reality is that intelligence is the area in which ministers, and the MI6 Information Operations (I/Ops) staff behind them, can say anything they like and get away with it. Intelligence with its psychological invite to a secret world, and with its unique avoidance of verification, is the ideal means for flattering and deceiving journalists. Journalists will be given secret briefings or access to Iraqi defectors and take them at their word, even though defectors are the most unreliable of all sources. Ministers know that journalists will simply lap it up and editors will splash it on their front pages. They know that journalists do not have the high-level intelligence contacts to check on the "facts". In Britain there is no equivalent of Bob Woodward. But the stories keep on coming – the three giant cargo ships said to be carrying Iraqi weapons of mass destruction (*Independent*, 19 February 2003); "Saddam 'killed missile chief' to thwart UN team" (*Sunday Telegraph*, 2 March 2003); and "Saddam's Thai gem spree hints at getaway plan" (*Sunday Times*, 9 March 2003). These are just three of numerous stories which rely on little more than a nod and a wink from some "official" or leaked document. What ever happened to the investigative journalists' standard of three separate sources? Even one would be good. The intelligence services have not shared Hennessy's enthusiasm for the public light shone on their intelligence-gathering. MI6 officers have briefed journalists angry at the way their material has been used by the spin doctors whilst CIA officers have gone public, "distressed at the politicisation of intelligence".

The real point is, however, that MI6 and the CIA simply do not have reliable intelligence. There is no "smoking gun", there is no "Adlai Stevenson moment" because, despite the billions spent, they have simply been unable to penetrate a totalitarian regime. It was the same with the Soviet Union. There is no mystery about this: intelligence agencies are not very good. The only mystery is why journalists have not treated them with the same derision and contempt they generally reserve for politicians. Maybe, hopefully, the row over the plagiarised Cabinet dossier will change our view.

INTELLIGENCE FAILURE

The news that the 75th Exploitation Task Force, having found no weapons of mass destruction, is leaving Iraq is proof of one of the great intelligence disasters of the last 50 years. Despite the CIA and MI6 spending hundreds of millions of pounds targeting intelligence-gathering efforts on Saddam and the massive media campaign on WMD, not a single weapon has been discovered.

The media response to this disaster has been, surprisingly, not to blame the intelligence services but to accuse the politicians of spin. The idea that the politicians "over-hyped" the intelligence and forced the services to "politicise" their intelligence has become the standard and accepted explanation – see Rachel Sylvester (not a journalist normally connected with intelligence stories) in the *Telegraph* (29 April 2003), "Spies want to be allowed to spy – not to spin for politicians", and in the *Guardian* (30 April 2003), "An insult to British intelligence". This is, however, another intelligence line-a defence to pre-empt the possibility of an official inquiry into this intelligence debacle.

This line of defence first surfaced when the Joint Intelligence Committee-sanctioned dossier on WMD was released into the public domain against the wishes of MI6, but at the insistence of Tony Blair and Jack Straw. Senior MI6 figures made it known to correspondents that they viewed the dossier as being "politically motivated". They had been unwilling to release material which, they argued, might identify the original source. The evidence suggests, however, that the reason for their reticence in releasing intelligence-derived material was that the services knew that it was, at best, weak.

The story began shortly after the election of New Labour to government in 1997. The Paddy Ashdown diaries include an intriguing entry. Blair told Ashdown, a former MI6 officer, that he had seen "intelligence about Saddam and what has happened to these weapons. I can tell you, it's so scary I can't believe it." He added: "I don't understand why the French don't get it." Clearly, MI6 had presented its own dossier and Blair had swallowed it whole.

At the end of 1997, with divisions on the UN Security Council over sanctions on Iraq and the hindering by Baghdad of the weapons inspectors, MI6, according to Seymour Hersh (*New Yorker*, April 2003) "resorted to spreading false information about Iraq" through its I/Ops unit. An agent within the UN inspection team funnelled to MI6, "intelligence that was crap". This was subsequently planted on MI6's media contacts and outlets throughout the world.

Some of this disinformation was obvious at the time. There was a flood of articles, particularly about the transfer of nuclear material and weapons to Iraq, and also to al-Qaeda. According to George Jones in the *Daily Telegraph* (19 April 2003), throughout 1998 Blair was in receipt of more intelligence which fuelled his worries about WMD.

Even before 11 September, Blair was warning the Americans about the dangers of the "marriage" between terrorists and rogue states with WMD. Iraq was identified as a state developing a ballistic missile capability which could be weaponised with WMD.

The reality is that MI6 had been pushing the WMD agenda for a number of years, partly to persuade the UN, and particularly the French, to do something about Iraq. They used intelligence which they knew to be "crap" and some of which was undoubtedly forged, as in the case of the Niger documents on nuclear supplies to Iraq. They used the testimony of Iraqi defectors which was tainted and unreliable, and falsified the intelligence from other defectors who stated that Saddam ordered the destruction of WMD warheads some years previously (see Hersh, *New Yorker*, May 2003).

Politicians certainly spin and pushed the intelligence services to provide the evidence of WMD in Iraq, but the services had already been spinning their tales for years before 11 September. The untangling of the origins of the war on Iraq begin with the election of Tony Blair and in the trail of disinformation which followed in the newspapers and other MI6 I/Ops outlets.

13
No Blood for Oil?

Andy Rowell

In November 2002, Tony Blair was interviewed on the Arabic service of Monte Carlo Radio – a radio station that No.10 believed Saddam Hussein listened to. But Blair's main message was to the Iraqi people. One aim was to dispel the persistent feeling throughout the Arab world that any forthcoming conflict was about oil not weapons of mass destruction. "The idea that this is about oil for us is absurd. If all we wanted was greater oil supplies we could probably do a deal with Iraq or any other country on that basis," said Blair.[1]

The US administration was equally dismissive about oil in the build-up to the war. "The only interest the United States has in the region is furthering the cause of peace and stability, not [Iraq's] ability to generate oil," contended President Bush's spokesman, Ari Fleischer.[2] Speaking a month after the Blair radio broadcast, Donald Rumsfeld was asked whether the war was about oil: "It just isn't," he replied. "There – there – there are certain things like that, myths that are floating around. I'm glad you asked. I – it has nothing to do with oil, literally nothing to do with oil."[3] It was a line that was reiterated by the American right-wing think-tanks that have fuelled the Bush administration's intellectual agenda. "The United States is not fighting for oil in Iraq," wrote David Frum, a former speechwriter for President Bush, from the American Enterprise Institute the same month in December 2002.[4]

A month later, in January, Tony Blair went further still:

Let me first of all deal with the conspiracy theory idea that this has somehow to do with oil. There is no way whatever, if oil were the issue, that it would not be infinitely simpler to cut a deal with Saddam, who I'm sure will be delighted to give us access to as much oil as we wanted, if he could carry on building weapons of mass destruction.[5]

The denials started to come thick and fast. That month, Blair dismissed the oil/conspiracy theory at a meeting of Labour backbenchers and in parliamentary questions.[6] The Foreign Secretary, Jack Straw, also dismissed the idea that oil had anything to do with it.[7] The following month Blair derided the "oil conspiracy theory" in front of a live British TV audience.[8] A document put out on the No.10 website about Myths and Facts over Iraq asked whether the conflict was about oil. The response was unambiguous. "This is 100 per cent not the case."[9]

Michael Renner, a senior researcher at the respected World Watch Institute in Washington, calls the remarks like Fleischer's that mirrored Blair's "a disingenuous, if not downright deceptive, statement".[10]

To deny that oil is even in the equation of Middle Eastern politics represents nothing more than a denial of history itself. Oil may not have been the only factor in the 2003 invasion, but it was clearly in the equation. Even establishment energy experts, such as Daniel Yergin, author of the Pulitzer winning book *The Prize – The Epic Quest for Oil, Money, and Power*, although denying the war was "all about oil", said there "is a clear energy dimension to the confrontation".[11]

Others connected to the oil industry went further. One leading oil and gas analyst interviewed by *The Middle East Journal* said:

> The US administration keeps talking about weapons of mass destruction, about a rogue regime bent on arming terrorists with biological or bacterial weapons, but ask any oil executive in Texas about the real reason for Bush and Cheney's determination to overthrow Saddam Hussein and they will laugh. Oil, oil, oil is the reason, weapons of mass destruction are just a smokescreen.[12]

Larry Goldstein, president of the Petroleum Industry Research Foundation told the *Wall Street Journal*, "If we go to war, it's not about oil. But the day the war ends, it has everything to do with oil."[13]

The global economy has everything to do with oil, and it cannot survive without Middle East oil. As *The Middle East Journal* put it, "Oil literally forms the bedrock of the Middle East ... When you think of oil, you think of the Middle East."[14] Or put another way you cannot talk about Middle Eastern politics without oil. The two are so intricately linked they are inseparable. "It is so obvious that oil was a major motivation in this war," says Steve Kretzmann, from the Institute for Policy Studies in the US.

The burden of proof that it wasn't should have been on the Bush administration. But the way that they flatly denied that it was and shifted the burden of proof to the critics, it was very difficult to prove that it was about oil. Common sense dictates that of course oil was a major factor and everyone knows that.[15]

For most of the last century, the geopolitics of the vast oil reserves of the Middle East have dominated the political landscape of the region from the old colonial days to the recent resurgence of Arab nationalism. The colonising powers have sought to control the reserves, since just under a hundred years ago they realised that coal's dominance was declining as a fuel to power the military. But during the first half of the twentieth century it was the British that were the driving colonial power. During the First World War, in 1917, British forces took Baghdad. Soon after, Sir Maurice Hankey, the powerful secretary of the British War Cabinet wrote that the Persian and Mesopotamian oil reserves that lie under modern-day Iraq were crucial and therefore "control over these oil supplies becomes a first-class British war aim". In August 1918, the then British Foreign Secretary said simply "I do not care under what system we keep the oil, but I am clear it is all-important for us that the oil should be available."[16]

By 1925, such a system was in place when the Iraqi government was forced to sign an agreement with the forerunner of the Iraq Petroleum Company (IPC) – that would dominate oil exploration in Iraq for 50 years – granting a concession to explore for oil until 2000. It decreed that the company would remain British and its chairman would remain British. The fact that Iraqis were going to just receive royalties for their oil and not own it sowed the seeds of bitterness against the colonial powers for decades to come.[17] The IPC had four major shareholders: BP, Shell, Exxon/Mobil and Total Fina Elf – holding a 23.75 per cent stake each. The remaining 5 per cent belonged to Calouse Gulbenkian, who was known in the industry as "Mr five per cent", due to his share. But in 1928 came the "most remarkable carve-up in oil history" called the "Red Line Agreement".[18] This essentially monopolised oil exploration and production for the IPC's partners over a vast area of the Middle East, from Turkey in the north to Yemen in the south, including Saudi Arabia and Iraq, but not Kuwait and Iran, then known as Persia. The agreement also became a source of bitter conflict amongst the shareholders and with the Iraqis and other governments for decades.[19]

Finally in 1961, after the failure of protracted negotiations, the Iraqis passed Law 80 that expropriated 99.5 per cent of the IPC's concession area. The Iraqis considered the law an act of "self-defence", the companies as a "violation of international law".[20] British government documents from the time show that the companies still wanted to monopolise Iraqi oil and that "oil companies other than the IPC would not in practice be allowed to operate within Iraq".[21] The British government, who believed "our interests and those of the companies march together", worried that Iraqi leaders had become "unhinged" and that "an ugly rush" of foreign firms might ensue if the negotiations failed.[22]

Nearly a decade of wrangling later, the deadlock in the negotiations was broken by the Iraqis nationalising the whole oil industry in 1972. It was forced by the "desire to eliminate injustice" and the "robbery and exhaustion practised by the monopolistic oil companies" that had made the oil industry in Iraq suffer "from weakness, stagnation and backwardness", according to Iraqi documents.[23]

The Arab Ba'ath Socialist Party, that Saddam Hussein headed, considered "liberating oil from the clutches of monopolistic companies" a "top priority".[24] Such was its importance that nationalisation was celebrated every year.

But other events happened in the early 1970s that shook the world. In 1973 the Saudis stopped supplying the US with oil due to its support of Israel and the price of oil rocketed. The world faced an energy crisis, whose effects have preoccupied strategic planners in western governments ever since. The US strategy to secure long-term stable oil supplies could be construed to be twofold: one, to try to reduce dependence on Middle Eastern oil whilst, two, doing everything to gain control over it. Exploration and production of alternative oil sources, such as Venezuela, the Gulf of Mexico, Alaska, the North Sea, Russia and the Caspian are still all encouraged, but the US is totally dependent on Middle Eastern oil.

In January 1980, the fallout from the Saudi action was still being felt by the US together with new issues such as the Iranian Revolution and the Soviet invasion of Afghanistan. In his last year as President, Jimmy Carter said that any "attempt by an outside force to gain control of the Persian Gulf region will be regarded as an assault on the vital interests of the United States". He pledged to defend that interest by "any means necessary, including military force".[25]

Carter was soon gone, to be followed by the hard-line Reagan administration. In the early 1980s some of the architects of the current war worked for Reagan. One of those was Donald Rumsfeld. In the middle of the Iran–Iraq war, just before Christmas in 1983, Rumsfeld met Saddam to talk about building a pipeline that would offer a secure route for Iraqi oil from Iraq to the Gulf of Aqaba in Jordan. It would be built by the US company Bechtel. Rumsfeld impressed upon Saddam the US desire to help increase exports, but failed to criticise the regime for recently using chemical weapons against Iranian troops. After two years of negotiations, Iraq turned down the pipeline signalling "a turn in US–Iraq relations".[26] The relationship has soured ever since, with Saddam becoming a hated figure by the American right, long before 11 September. The problem for America was that Saddam sat on the world's second largest oil reserves and then threatened his neighbours such as Kuwait and Saudi Arabia which also sat on large reserves.

The reason oil is so important is that America uses more oil than any other nation – needing 20 million barrels of crude a day to survive. It is a nation badly dependent on imports – over 60 per cent of its oil. Because of this, it is a nation dependent on the Middle East, which holds two-thirds of the world's oil reserves.

"The Bush energy policy is predicated on growing consumption of oil, preferably cheap oil," argues Michael Renner, from the World Watch Institute. In early 2003 the US Department of Energy warned that America would have to increase its oil imports sharply in the next 25 years to meet rising domestic demand. Thirty years ago, the United States was virtually self-sufficient in oil, but it now imports 60 per cent of its needs, and by 2025 it will be 70 per cent. "The bulk of future supplies will have to come from the Gulf region," says Renner.[27] The region holds some 680 billion barrels of proven oil reserves – again, some two-thirds of the world total – and nearly 2,000 trillion cubic feet of gas – or just over a third of world reserves. Over 90 per cent of excess global oil production lies in the region, mainly in Saudi Arabia,[28] closely followed by Iraq. For the US, which has long been able to rely on its allies in Saudi Arabia, post-11 September there are serious questions to be raised about the kingdom's political stability and uncertainties about the future of the Saudi royal family.[29]

It is well known that Iraq holds vast reserves of oil that could rival Saudi Arabia's. Current estimates are around 112 billion barrels. Its western desert could contain a further 108 billion barrels, but other analysts say reserves could eventually rival those of Saudi Arabia, whose reserves are some 262 billion barrels.[30] Iraq's oil is also the cheapest in the world to extract. "Iraq has the lowest lifting costs in the world," says Fadhil Chalabi, ex-Iraqi Ministry and now executive director of the Centre for Global Energy Studies in London. "I estimate it at below $1 a barrel, compared with Saudi Arabia, which is around $2.50 a barrel." In the Gulf of Mexico or the North Sea the comparable figure is $3 to $4. In other parts of the US it's $10.[31] Only 15 out of Iraq's 73 fields have been developed.[32] To many of the western oil companies, who are being forced into ever more remote regions to find oil, and who are beginning to alarm city investors by missing production targets, Iraq offers the last great oil boom. To America, more importantly, it means energy security, in an age post-11 September of increasing insecurity.

The war had everything to do with America's global domination, a domination that is fuelled by oil, a domination that has to control oil, a domination that has to have energy security. To have security for its economy, America has to have a secure source of oil. America is the new colonising power of the twenty-first century – the new empire that vastly eclipses the British at the height of their power.

"The only precedent to what is shaping up now is the Roman Empire," argues Michael Klare, a professor of peace and world security studies at Hampshire College. "There is only one power. I don't think Britain, France or Spain even came close in other centuries to the United States today. If the United States controls Persian Gulf oil fields, it will have a stranglehold on the world economy."[33] It is a dream pushed by the American military. In 1999, General Anthony C. Zinni, commander in chief of US Central Command, testified before Congress that the Gulf region, with its huge oil reserves, was a "vital interest" of "long standing" for the United States and that the US "must have free access to the region's resources".[34]

In December 2002, James Paul, the executive director of the Global Policy Forum that monitors policy making at the United Nations, wrote that "For all the talk about terrorism, weapons of mass destruction and human rights violations by Saddam Hussein, these are not the core issues driving US policy. Rather, it is 'free access' to Iraqi oil and the ultimate control over that oil by US and UK companies that raises the stakes high enough to set US forces on the move and risk the stakes of global empire".[35] This "free access" gives "strategic security". "Our next war in the Gulf will mark a historical tipping point – the moment when Washington takes real ownership of strategic security in the age of globalization," argues Thomas Barnett, a professor of warfare analysis at the US Naval War College and adviser to the US Secretary of Defense.[36]

But more importantly it is a dream pursued religiously by the American right, now known as neo-conservatives, who form the backbone of the Bush administration, and who are intricately linked to the oil industry. On 26 January 1998, the Project for the New American Century formed by hawkish right-wingers like Dick Cheney, Donald Rumsfeld and Paul Wolfowitz,[37] who would all take up senior positions in the Bush government, wrote to the then President Bill Clinton, urging "the removal of Saddam Hussein's regime from power". If Clinton failed to act, "the safety of American troops in the region, of our friends and allies like Israel and the moderate Arab states, and a significant portion of the world's supply of oil will all be put at hazard".[38] In May, they sent a further letter to Newt Gingrich – who was then Speaker of the House – warning that failure to act could mean that "our friends and allies in the Middle East and Europe will soon be subject to forms of intimidation by an Iraqi government bent on dominating the Middle East and its oil reserves". To avoid this they argued that "we should establish and maintain a strong US military presence in the region, and be prepared to use that force to protect our vital interests in the Gulf – and, if necessary, to help remove Saddam from power".[39] Three years before the terrorist attacks of 11 September, Saddam was already a marked man.

By 2001, a report sponsored by the right-wing James A. Baker III Institute for Public Policy of Rice University and the Council on Foreign Relations concluded that:

> As the 21st century opens, the energy sector is in critical condition. A crisis could erupt at any time from any number of factors and would inevitably affect every country in today's globalized world. While the origins of a crisis are hard to pinpoint, it is clear that energy disruptions could have a potentially enormous impact on the U.S. and the world economy, and would affect U.S. national security and foreign policy in dramatic ways.[40]

So, asked the critics, was US national security, not weapons of mass destruction the real reason for war? Other evidence began to build highlighting oil as an issue. Before the invasion happened, leaked

State Department documents stressed that protection of the oilfields was "issue number one".[41]

Hours into the invasion, US forces seized two important offshore terminals that transfer 2 million barrels of oil to tankers as well as the vital southern Rumaila oilfield. When the Americans entered Baghdad, according to *Time* magazine

> they headed straight for the Oil Ministry building and threw up a protective shield around it. While other government buildings, ranging from the Ministry of Religious Affairs to the National Museum of Antiquities, were looted and pillaged, while hospitals were stripped of medicine and basic equipment, Iraq's oil records were safe and secure, guarded by the US military. General Richard Myers, Chairman of the Joint Chiefs of Staff, had an explanation: "I think it's, as much as anything else, a matter of priorities".[42]

Then came Bechtel, the company that had tried to build the pipeline in the 1980s. It won the $680 million contract to rebuild Iraq.[43] Then came the man to run Iraq's oil in the short term – Philip Carroll, the ex-head of Shell Oil, the US arm of Royal Dutch/Shell. Part of Carroll's responsibility will be to look at privatising the Iraqi oil industry,[44] something the US right-wing have long called for. Once Iraq is privatised, the rest of OPEC could follow. "If successful, Iraq's privatizations of its oil sector, refining capacity, and pipeline infrastructure could serve as a model for privatizations by other OPEC members, thereby weakening the cartel's domination of the energy markets," argued an article in the right-wing US *National Review*.[45]

So that is the neo-conservative vision. A US with unlimited access to Middle Eastern oil, a world with a weak OPEC. US energy security would be nearly complete. To fit the final piece of the jigsaw in place for total energy security, other areas need to be secured by the US military. The first stage of this final strategy was indicated a month after the war, with the US military planning to move troops to other parts of the world, where America has key oil interests. In June 2003 the Pentagon announced that is was "to significantly shrink the U.S. force of 70,000 troops in Germany, a military stronghold for half a century, and put far more American forces in Africa and the Caucasus region". The move was "driven by the increasing importance that the U.S. is placing on protecting key oil reserves in Africa and the Caucasus region near the Caspian Sea, as well as addressing concerns about combating terrorism".

According to the *Wall Street Journal*, "U.S. officials said that a key mission for U.S. forces would be to ensure that Nigeria's oil fields, which in the future could account for as much as 25 per cent of all U.S. oil imports, are secure." Another region singled out for strategic security was the Caspian. "In the Caspian Sea you have large mineral reserves," said General Charles Wald, deputy commander of US European Command. "We want to be able to assure the long-term viability of those resources."[46]

So was the 2003 Gulf war part of the US military/neo-conservative vision to "assure the long-term viability" of oil in Iraq? "The Bush administration, not to mention the Blair government, were at great pains to say that the war was about weapons of mass destruction that no one has been able to find," said Steve Kretzmann from the Institute for Policy Studies in Washington in June 2003. "The critics are simply saying that the war had everything to do with what everyone knows Iraq does have – the world's second largest reserves of oil."[47]

NOTES

1. S. Jeffery, "We Don't Want Your Oil, Blair Tells Iraqis", *Guardian*, 15 November 2002.
2. M. Renner, "Blood and Oil Alternatives to War in Iraq", World Watch Institute, Washington, 22 November 2002.
3. CBS, *60 Minutes*, 15 December 2002.
4. D. Frum, "The Curse of Oil Dependence", *Jerusalem Post*, 22 December 2002; <http://www.aei.org/news/newsID.14766,filter./news_detail.asp>.
5. Australian Broadcasting Corporation, "Oil No Consideration in Iraq War, says Blair", *ABC Radio*, 16 January 2003, 6pm.
6. M. Tempest, "Blair: Iraq Oil Claim is 'Conspiracy Theory'", *Guardian*, 15 January 2003.
7. <http://www.number-10.gov.uk/output/page1809.asp>.
8. M. White, and B. Whitaker, "Blair: We Will Not Be Put Off By UN, PM Faces Critics and Makes the Case for War", *Guardian*, 7 February 2003.
9. <http://www.number-10.gov.uk/output/page3189.asp>.
10. Renner, "Blood and Oil Alternatives to War in Iraq".
11. D. Yergin, "A Crude View of the Crisis in Iraq", *Washington Post*, 8 December 2002.
12. N. Vesely, "It's All About Oil", *The Middle East Journal*, November 2002, p. 19.
13. T. Herrick, "Oil Firms Gauge Potential in Iraq – Host of Opportunity Awaits Should War Topple Hussein, Starting with Restoration", *Wall Street Journal*, 13 January 2003.
14. N. Ford, "Optimistic Outlook for Regional Oil and Gas", *The Middle East Journal*, June 2002, p. 37.

15. S. Kretzmann, interview with author, 5 June 2002.
16. D. Yergin, *The Prize – The Epic Quest for Oil, Money, and Power*, New York: Simon and Schuster, 1991, pp. 188–9.
17. A. Sampson, *The Seven Sisters – The Great Oil Companies and the World They Shaped*, London: Coronet, 1976, pp. 83–4.
18. Ibid., p. 84.
19. Ibid., pp. 84–5.
20. INOC, *The Legitimate Steps Behind the Nationalization of Iraqi Oil*, Press Information, 7 July 1972; Basrah Petroleum Company, Press release, 6 April 1972.
21. Archive Editions Limited, *Records of Iraq 1914–1966*, Vol. 15, 2001, p. 437.
22. Ibid., Vol. 14, p. 528; Vol. 15, pp. 443, 447.
23. Ministry of Oil, *Nationalization of Iraqi Oil and its Economic Dimensions; The Nationalization in Iraq is the Genuine Model for the Liberation of Oil Wealth*, 1975, p. 4.
24. *Iraq Oil News*, 16th Anniversary News, May 1988.
25. S. Kretzmann, "Oil, Security, War – The Geopolitics of U.S. Energy Planning, The Business of War", *Multinational Monitor*, Vol. 24, Jan/Feb 2003.
26. J. Vallette, S. Kretzmann and D. Wysham (2003) *Crude Vision – How Oil Interests Obscured US Government Focus on Chemical Weapons Use By Saddam Hussein*, Sustainable Energy & Economy Network, Institute for Policy Studies, March 2003.
27. M. Renner, "Post-Saddam Energy Visions", *International Herald Tribune*, 17 January 2003; Yergin, *The Prize*, pp. 204–5.
28. Ford, "Optimistic Outlook for Regional Oil and Gas", p. 37.
29. CBS, *60 Minutes*, 15 December 2002.
30. Deutsche Bank, *Baghdad Bazaar – Big Oil in Iraq?* 21 October 2002; Renner, "Blood and Oil Alternatives to War in Iraq".
31. P. Klebnikov, "Hitting OPEC by Way of Baghdad", *Forbes Magazine*, 28 October 2002; D. Barlett and J. Steele, "Iraq's Crude Awakening", *Time Magazine*, 19 May 2003.
32. Arab Press Service, "The Future of Iraq", *APS Review Oil Market Trends*, Vol. 59, No. 22, 25 November 2001/ 2 December 2002; Klebnikov, "Hitting OPEC by Way of Baghdad"; Barlett and Steele, "Iraq's Crude Awakening".
33. L. Diebel, "Oil War: 23 Years in the Making", *Toronto Star*, 9 March 2003.
34. A. Zinni, "Testimony to the Senate Armed Services Committee", 13 April 1999, quoted by J. Paul, *Iraq: the Struggle for Oil*, Global Policy Forum, December 2002.
35. Ibid.
36. T. Barnett, "The Pentagon's New Map – It Explains Why We're Going to War, and Why We'll Keep Going to War", *Esquire Magazine*, March 2003, <http://www.nwc.navy.mil/newrulesets/ThePentagonsNewMap.htm>.
37. <http://www.newamericancentury.org/statementofprinciples.htm>.
38. <http://www.newamericancentury.org/iraqclintonletter.htm>.
39. <http://www.newamericancentury.org/iraqletter1998.htm>.
40. *Strategic Energy Policy Challenges for the 21st Century*, Report of an Independent Task Force, Sponsored by the James A. Baker III Institute

for Public Policy of Rice University and the Council on Foreign Relations, New York, 2001, p. 8.

41. P. Paton Walsh, J. Borger, T. Macalister and E. MacAskill (2003) "US Begins Secret Talks to Secure Iraq's Oilfields", *Guardian*, 23 January 2003.

42. Barlett and Steele, "Iraq's Crude Awakening".

43. C. Hirst, "The World's at Bechtel's Beck and Call", *Independent on Sunday*, 20 April 2003, Business p. 5.

44. Associated Press, "Iraq Restarts Flow of Northern Oil Crude to Fuel Country's Power Plants", Doha, Qatar, 25 April 2003.

45. A. Cohen and G. O'Driscoll, "Privatize Iraqi Oil, Post-war Planning", *National Review*, 11 December 2002, <http://www.nationalreview.com/cohen/cohen121102.asp>.

46. G. Jaffe, "In a Massive Shift, US Plans To Reduce Troops in Germany", *Wall Street Journal*, 10 June 2003.

47. S. Kretzmann, interview with author, 5 June 2002.

Part 3
Misreporting War

Live from Baghdad

WAR ON
Iraq   BREAKING NEWS
Poorly sourced rumour elevated to status of major news event

...insignificant development presented out of context... irrelevant de

14

The Minute It's Made Up
You'll Hear About It

Mark Steel

3 April 2003

You expect lies, but usually they're found out once a war is over. But in this war the lying is so inept that it gets rumbled the next day. So the news starts "Oh, apparently that uprising we yelled about all through yesterday didn't happen" or "Ah, yes, that chemical weapons factory turned out to be an all-night petrol garage."

The military briefings must be given by one of those pathological liars you get in pubs. One day the press conference from Washington will begin: "Guess what, I won an Olympic swimming medal once. I had to swim underwater so no one could see me because I was in the secret service."

The presenters who front this bilge should say: "We're here to bring you 24-hour rolling cack that's been made up. The minute it's made up, you'll hear about it. And there's some breaking cack being made up right now, apparently Saddam has filled some clouds with anthrax and he's forcing giants in the Republican Guard to blow them towards Bournemouth. We'll bring you more as soon as it's made up."

One of the sickest examples is the squirming over how 55 civilians came to be killed in a market. Their investigations are going on, they tell us. Because it's a great mystery how, in a city in which 300 cruise missiles a night are exploding with "shock and awe", anyone might have been blown up. Working that out must be like living through an episode of *Inspector Morse*.

The most likely explanation, says Jack Straw, is that the Iraqis did it themselves, and the exploded missile with an American serial number found at the site was probably put there by wily Iraqis. Or maybe the Iraqis have built a replica Baghdad somewhere in the desert, where Saddam is forcing his people to blow themselves up so it can be filmed to make the Americans look bad.

Another persistent myth is that, as one report told us, "the main objective of the coalition forces is to get food and medicine into Basra". If the reporter is asked why, despite this generosity, the Iraqi people still don't seem to trust us, he'll probably say: "I expect it's because most people in Basra are, at the moment, on a diet. And they may resent the coalition for putting temptation in their way." I suppose that the Americans are hoping that eventually the people of Basra will come round and say: "They might have blown my mate's leg off, but credit where it's due, once they got here they gave him some very soothing cream for his stump."

On Tuesday night, a news report told us that anti-war protests had "melted away". To prove this, the reporter announced: "One night before the war Parliament Square was packed with protesters, but now there's just one lone man with a wet banner." Did it really not occur to this reporter that the reason there were no demonstrators was because on Tuesday night there was no demonstration? Perhaps he does sports reports where he says: "Support for Manchester United has melted away. On Saturday afternoon there were 60,000 people at Old Trafford, but the following morning there were just a couple of cleaners."

The terrifying thing is that the people who seem to fall for the propaganda most of all are the governments who make it up in the first place. The result is that the first two weeks of this war can appear like the first four years of Vietnam with the film speeded up. They expected to be welcomed, and when they weren't, they almost pleaded: "Can't you see? We're here to liberate you." So when civilians oppose them the generals declare they must be "Republican Guard" in civilian clothing. So the whole population becomes a potential enemy, the troops get edgy and fire on women and children. And, as in Vietnam when Kissinger bombed Laos and Cambodia, the Americans are already threatening Syria and Iran.

So I don't follow the line that "We must support the war to back our troops." If teenagers run off to join the mafia, you don't say: "I was against them going but now they're there we can't undermine them by saying they should come home." The only consistent way to support the troops' safety is to demand that they come home and go back to starting fights in pubs in Colchester as normal.

Because when the Stars and Stripes flies in Baghdad, that isn't the end. Millions of Arabs won't walk away like a football manager after losing a match, muttering, "Well our defence let us down but good luck to Donald Rumsfeld in the next round." Because the country will be under the control of the President who, as he was about to announce the war had begun, threw his arms into the air and yelped: "I feel good."

Who knows how nutty he'll be next time? The war on Iran will begin with George Bush announcing: "Fellow Americans, get on up like a sex machine. We will not rest until I've been taken to the bridge."

15
Reporting the War
on British Television

Justin Lewis and Rod Brookes

There has been much debate about the British television coverage of the 2003 war in Iraq. In a very public row, the government attacked the BBC for, allegedly, having an anti-war bias. Critics of the war, meanwhile, argued that once battle commenced, broadcasters closed ranks with the government and were far less questioning or analytical than they should have been.

We conducted a detailed analysis of British television coverage during the war to test these competing claims.[1] We were particularly interested in looking at how television reported the government's case for war, both in terms of the overall messages and of the reporting of specific claims. We chose to focus on three of the main propositions central to the government's case: first, the idea that Iraq possessed "weapons of mass destruction"; second, the desire of ordinary Iraqis to be liberated from the Saddam Hussein regime; and third, the evil nature of that regime. The first of these constituted the legal basis for war, and all three were pivotal in gaining public support for the war.[2]

Our sample consisted of 1,534 news reports[3] about the Iraq war during the war (all weekdays from 20 March to 11 April inclusive) on the main evening news bulletins on BBC1, ITV News, Channel 4 News and Sky.[4] From this sample, we coded and analysed every reference to "weapons of mass destruction", all references to the Iraqi people (including reports of casualties and looting), and all references to the evil or decadent nature of the regime. Just over half the news reports contained a reference to one of these themes, by far the most common one being references to the Iraqi people – referred to in a total of 383 reports, or in 25 per cent of all the reports in the sample. We found 127 reports with references to weapons of mass destruction (8 per cent of the sample) and 110 reports referring to the evil/decadent nature of the regime (7 per cent of the sample).

Apart from getting a sense of how the war was reported, our aim was to establish how far television coverage of these themes fitted the government version of events. Alternatively, we wanted to determine whether coverage may have supported critics of the war, who argued that the threat of weapons of mass destruction was exaggerated, and that most Iraqis would regard US/British action as an invasion rather than a liberation. While few disputed the brutality of Saddam Hussein, critics of the war argued his most bloody period was as a US and British ally, and that, since the containment period after the war of 1991, Iraq was no more brutal than many other repressive regimes around the world.

THE SOURCE OF CLAIMS

Most references to these themes were made during reports by studio anchors (23 per cent) or by correspondents compiling reports from available footage (29 per cent), although a high number came from reports by journalists embedded with US/UK forces (17 per cent) or in Baghdad (13 per cent). In this war, information was less likely to come from reporters based with US/UK military headquarters in Qatar or Kuwait (3 per cent) or from experts (3 per cent). Broadcasters therefore exploited their ability to get frontline footage (from their own reporters or elsewhere) – notably from embedded reporters or reporters in Baghdad, and the coverage was dominated less by briefings than by action footage.

The source of these claims usually came from the media themselves – generally from an assertion made by a correspondent (47 per cent) or an anchor (17 per cent), and these would sometimes be accompanied by actual footage providing visual evidence for the claim (pictures of Iraqis welcoming US forces, for example). Most of the non-media sources were US/UK government or military (16.5 per cent) or official Iraqi sources (10.3 per cent), with comparatively few other sources (such as the Red Cross) being used (only 7 per cent of non-media sources were non-military/governmental, and almost half of these – 3 per cent – were Iraqi citizens). Those who might have shed light on events – whether NGOs, weapons inspectors, academics or experts on and in the Arab world – therefore played very little part in the story told by television news. The coverage was thus about the process and progress of war, rather than the broader issues raised by the war itself.

This is not an incidental point: with the onset of war, the narrative shifted away from claims about the efficacy of war and towards claims about its outcome. Simply put, how long would it take for US/British forces to win, and at what cost? A relatively short war without major civilian casualties, would, in this context, be regarded as a successful outcome. The debate thus narrowed in the government's favour, since they could claim vindication in victory – even though (a few doom-mongers aside) few of those who argued against war did so because they thought US/British forces would lose. This was perhaps best demonstrated when the BBC's political editor, Andrew Marr, caught up in the moment of triumph when US forces took control of Baghdad, suggested that the Prime Minister had been "proved right".

Although many journalists – including Marr – regained their critical faculties in the rather messy aftermath, the fact that such a claim could be made is testimony to the way in which the change in focus made, in itself, many of the arguments against war seem irrelevant.

WEAPONS OF MASS DESTRUCTION?

While there was much discussion of the failure to find any evidence of weapons of mass destruction in Iraq after the US and British forces took control, the assumption behind most media reports during the war was to accept the government's line that such weapons existed and might be – or indeed were – deployed. While this assumption had been seriously questioned beforehand – notably by Robin Cook in his resignation speech – it appeared to be undented during the war itself. This often took the form of US/UK forces or journalists using gas masks to protect themselves against potential chemical/biological attacks, or the discovery of Iraqi gas masks (with the implication that these would be used during attacks rather than for defensive purposes).

Since no such weapons were either used or discovered, most references to this issue were speculative – either about capability or possible use (such as reports of a line around Baghdad which, once breached, would trigger the use of chemical weapons). This speculation generally assumed the existence of such weaponry rather than questioning that assumption (as many have done since). Indeed, when we compared the number of reports that suggested the presence (or possible deployment) of chemical/biological weapons to those that indicated their absence, we found the coverage very clearly erred on the side of the former. Overall, 86 per cent of the reports we examined that referred to weapons of mass destruction suggested Iraq had such weapons, and only 14 per cent raised doubts about their existence or possible use. Again, the coverage here was more likely to support the government's case than undermine it. Indeed, we found only one reference that flatly suggested there *were* no weapons of mass destruction – a notable absence given that none have been found to date.

INVASION OR LIBERATION?

To what extent did TV news portray the Iraqi people as welcoming the invasion? Overall, the Iraqi people were roughly twice as likely to be portrayed as pro-invasion than anti-invasion. Of references to the Iraqi people, 26 per cent showed or suggested the Iraqi people welcoming the invasion or the overthrow of Saddam Hussein,[5] compared with only 14 per cent of references to Iraqis being unhappy, angry, upset or merely suspicious about the invasion. The ratio was rather higher on Sky (29 per cent to 12 per cent), with only Channel 4 showing "liberated" and "invaded" Iraqis in roughly equal number (20 per cent to 17 per cent).[6]

This is not to say that TV news ignored the negative effects of war on the Iraqi people – 37 per cent of reports about Iraqi people concerned the injury or death of Iraqi citizens. Channel 4 was, again, the most likely news bulletin to refer to Iraqi casualties (46 per cent of its reports on Iraqis mentioned casualties). It would be a mistake to assume, however, that such news was automatically a problem for the government's case. On the contrary, since the numbers reported in these cases were usually quite small, they could be interpreted as supporting the idea that casualties were minimal.[7]

Other references to the Iraqi people covered a range of ideologically more ambiguous images – we saw, for example, Iraqis going about their everyday lives (7 per cent), Iraqis looting (13 per cent), and Iraqis reported as being intimidated by the Saddam Hussein regime (3 per cent).

Overall, since we were much more likely to see or hear about Iraqis feeling liberated rather than invaded, it seems that the weight of coverage of the Iraqi people was more likely to support the government's case than undermine it. And since much of the pro-invasion imagery happened towards the end of the war, it could be argued that the lasting impression was of a people happy to be free of Saddam Hussein, and less of a people disgruntled about being invaded and occupied.

THE EVIL REGIME

Reminders of Saddam Hussein's brutality was scarcely news, but from the government's point of view, such reminders bolstered their case. Hence, for example, the Prime Minister's rather too hasty condemnation of the "execution" of two British soldiers – as he put it, "If anyone needed further evidence of the depravity of Saddam's regime, this atrocity provides it."

Although this was the least referred to of the government's themes, 7 per cent of the reports in our sample contained references to evidence suggesting the evil nature of the regime. Nearly two-thirds of these were either about the mistreatment of US/UK POWs (30 per cent), or the manipulative nature of Iraqi propaganda (30 per cent). A number of reports (18 per cent) referred to the decadent nature of the regime – usually signified by journalists discovering the opulence of Saddam Hussein's palaces – 14 per cent involved the discovery of torture or surveillance facilities, 18 per cent involved and 8 per cent were reports of atrocities committed against Iraqi people.

While most of these reports contained evidence that was unremarkable for a dictatorial regime (indeed, since Britain has one of the wealthiest monarchies and one of the highest levels of inequality in Europe, the charges of decadence were particularly curious), we found no reports that made this point, or put them in an international context. These reports thus served to highlight the brutality of the regime and thereby bolster the government's case that the Iraqi regime was exceptional in its abuse of human rights.

REPORTING MISINFORMATION: "WE ARE IN A POSITION TO DO NOTHING MORE THAN BELIEVE WHAT THEY SAY"

In order to get a more qualitative sense of how official government and military sources were treated, we looked in detail at the way the four channels treated stories in which initial reports – usually coming from government or military sources – proved to be unreliable. There were a number of these, and while they were often dismissed as part of the "fog of war", many of them involved *claims that favoured the US or British government's version of events*. Some of these were simply trumpeting successes (such as the many premature reports of the fall of Umm Qasr), some implied the brutality of the Iraqi side (such as reports of the execution of two British POWs) and the procedural correctness of the US/UK forces (such as Pentagon claims that civilians killed at a US army checkpoint ignored warning shots), some implied Iraqi use of banned weapons (such as Iraq's reported use of Scud missiles) and some fitted the idea that Iraqis were simply waiting for the opportunity to rise up against Saddam Hussein (such as reports of the Basra uprising). In short, to what extent did broadcasters treat these claims with circumspection, and offer clear retractions when they proved to be unfounded?

Overall, we found that most of these stories were generally given more credence than they should have been, and considerably more time was given to the original stories than to any subsequent retractions (if any retractions were made). While a number of reporters were careful in their use of language (to identify, for example, that there were "reports" that something had happened), other were not. Moreover, the use of a phrase such as "we're getting reports that …" often implied that such reports were reliable.

Overall, we found that Sky News at 10pm was the most likely programme to treat such reports as fact, although both BBC and ITV news tended to do so. Channel 4 News was consistently the exception here, offering the most cautious and interrogative coverage, taking care to use and report on conflicting information. By this measure alone (and we cannot assume this applies across the board), Channel 4 News provided the most technically accurate picture of events.

The one story that, while given prominence, *did* receive more cautionary treatment on all four channels was the claim, made by Tony Blair, that two British soldiers had been executed. This story was also unusual because it was one of the few we found in which a subsequent retraction was also widely reported. This may be indicative of a greater journalistic suspicion of news coming from politicians, while claims coming from military sources appear to be given more credence. So while British journalists often adopt a sceptical posture towards politicians, we found that, despite the long history of military propaganda, broadcasters often got the story wrong because they placed too much faith in military sources.

SCUDS OR DUDS?

So, for example, on 20 March, it was widely reported that Iraq had fired Scud missiles (which they claimed not to possess) into Kuwait. This claim came from US and British forces, was denied by Iraq and was not independently confirmed. Subsequent evidence suggests no Scuds were fired.

We found 27 references to the Iraqi Scuds incident on the four channels during the war. Of these, most assumed that the Scud claim was true and simply reported it as fact without attribution: for example:

> You just don't know when these Scud missiles come in whether they've got chemical or biological warheads on them ... there's a Scud shelter just to my left ... we've only just come out of it ... after the eighth time. (Ben Brown, 20 March 2003, 6pm, BBC1)

> Iraq responded to the raid on Baghdad by firing several Scud missiles into Kuwait. Two were shot down, none had chemical or biological warheads. They did however, spark gas alerts. (Mark Austin, 20 March 2003, 6.30pm, ITV)

> Iraq's response to the first wave of attacks was swift ... It launched a series of missile attacks sending Scuds over the border into Kuwait towards US troops and local people. (Anna Boting, 20 March 2003, 10pm, Sky News)

Of the 19 references on 20 March on ITV, BBC and Sky, only one was attributed to a named source. The exception here was contained in a report on Sky, in which reporter Mike McCarthy, speaking over a large graphic stating that Iraq had fired "SCUD MISSILES ON TARGETS INSIDE KUWAIT", reported that: "One broadcaster in the Middle East showed footage which it said depicted that aftermath of an Iraqi Scud intercepted by a patriot missile above the Kuwait desert."

Channel 4 was conspicuously more circumspect than the other three channels. Anchor Jon Snow made three references to the Scud claim: one referred to "the firing of three Scud-like missiles", another that "Iraqi forces have fired at least three missiles into Kuwait but Iraqis have denied reports that at least one is a banned Scud missile." The third reference took the form of a question to reporter Alex Thompson, who had just made two statements referring to Scud attacks:

Jon Snow: The Iraqis have been very adamant that they have fired no Scuds today, that whatever they fired were not Scuds. Why are the people at your end so convinced that they were?

Alex Thompson: Because various American forces went to examine the debris where the missile fell ... they know which breed of missile they are looking at ... they saw what was lying on the ground and they told us it was a Scud ... we are in a position to do nothing more than believe what they say.

This exchange was notable in that it revealed the source of the claim, as well as, interestingly, the level of trust many journalists had in military sources.

The only other references in our sample which injected any doubt came on Sky over a week later on 1 April, when Will Owen was asked: "Have we ever discovered whether Scuds were fired over towards Kuwait to the camps or even towards the city or was it a different sort of missile that was fired?" Owen replied that: "there's still considerable debate as to whether any of the attacks on Kuwait were conducted by a Scud". This was the closest any of the news reports we examined came to a retraction of the original story.

THE BASRA UPRISING

We found a similar willingness to accept information coming from military sources on 25 March, when British forces claimed that there had been a popular uprising against Saddam Hussein in Basra – reports which were later revealed (notably by Al Jazeera inside the city) to be untrue. Unlike the Scud story, on BBC and ITN most of the statements in support of the story did imply that the story had a source, although in most cases this was simply to refer to "reports", as in:

Reports from Basra of an uprising against Saddam backed by British troops. (George Alagiah, 25 March 2003, 6pm, BBC1)

Uprising in Basra, reports that the Iraqi army is killing civilians. (Katie Derham, 25 March 2003, 6.30pm, ITV)

While this language is *technically* cautious – the use of the term "reports" implying the need for confirmation – the general tone here implies that such reports are highly plausible, rather than the rumours they turned out to be.

Details were then given by embedded reporters Ben Brown and Juliet Bremner, who both referred to specific sources, but implied that these "confirmed" the story:

> We have just been talking to senior British commanders at field headquarters ... they are confirming to us that some sort of popular uprising does appear to be underway in Basra at the moment ... British commanders are delighted and relieved that some sort of uprising is underway ... they couldn't quite understand why it hasn't happened before this ... they'd really been banking on an uprising. (Ben Brown, 25 March 2003, 6pm, BBC1)

> I've just had it confirmed by British commanders at our base that they have been seeing crowds of people on the street in Basra, up to 40–50 at various locations ... that might be some kind of popular mood to get the ruling party out of power. (Juliet Bremner, 25 March 2003, 6.30pm, ITV)

The BBC made more of the story, commenting on its political implications, although towards the end of the broadcast, Nicholas Witchell did add: "A degree of caution ... the reports from Basra are clearly very confused. They want to know here are these claims real and if so, on what scale? ... Potentially, if it is correct, it is very significant." Both the BBC and ITN then modified or retracted the story the following day, although not unequivocally, as Ben Brown put it: "While British commanders believe there was a small uprising there last night, it was not enough to count."

Unlike the BBC and ITN, Sky's coverage made few references to "reports" or any other language to imply the story needed confirmation. Even though Sky's news at 10pm had more time to check the story, seven of the ten references to the uprising on the 25th simply reported it as fact, as in

> It happened during a battle west of Basra where there has since been an uprising against Saddam Hussein. (Anna Boting, 25 March 2003, 10pm, Sky News)

Let's take a look at what happened in Basra today ... it began with a popular uprising against the Ba'ath party. (Chris Roberts, 25 March 2003, 10pm, Sky News)

There was a popular uprising. (Richard Gaisford, 25 March 2003, 10pm, Sky News)

While Sky may have retracted the story in other bulletins, the first reference to a retraction on their 10pm news programme did not come until 2 April.

Channel 4 was, once again, the most cautious of the four channels. The following statement by Alex Thompson is fairly typical:

Late in the day we suddenly had these reports coming out unconfirmed that there was a civilian uprising going on. Now I've just had an update on that from the military briefers here, they say perhaps scaling down ... they think there are some reports of something happening along those lines in the city, it's no more strongly put than that ... we have to be cautious before we get concrete evidence on what is going on in the city. (Alex Thompson, 25 March 2003, Channel 4 News)

Similarly, Jon Snow ended the broadcast with the statement that: "It is still not clear if there has indeed been any uprising there." The story was firmly retracted on Channel 4 the following night.

THE EXECUTION OF BRITISH SOLDIERS

If the Scud and Basra stories suggest that three of the four broadcasters relied too heavily on the veracity of military sources, the treatment of non-military government sources was sometimes more careful. In particular, on 27 March, when Tony Blair claimed that two British POWs had been executed by the Iraqis, broadcasters reacted with a degree of caution.

While the Prime Minister's claim got considerable coverage (his statement that "If anyone needed further evidence of the depravity of Saddam's regime, this atrocity provides it" was shown on all four channels) only the BBC 6pm news failed to examine the (lack of) evidence to support it. The other three news programmes all included journalists who (rightly, as it turned out) pointed to the lack of clear evidence to support the PM's assertion:

A real show of anger, Tony Blair on what he alleged was the execution of two British soldiers ... he can't give the evidence for that ... But I think what it is evidence of is a little panic, they no longer have the pictures they'd hoped for, pictures of liberated Iraqis ... instead they are having to make the British population angry to get them to back this war. (Nick Robinson, 27 March 2003, 6.30pm, ITV)

On the basis of the evidence offered so far by the British government, the suspicion of execution is no more than that ... what the British are saying is that two members of the Desert Rats were missing in action on Sunday, they believe those are the bodies that have been identified now. But they are saying that on the basis that they were not wearing their body armour and their helmets, and one of them appears to have been shot in the chest, that they were executed. Well that is certainly at the best, very circumstantial evidence. (Adam Boulton, 27 March 2003, 10pm, Sky News)

When a relative of one of the soldiers was subsequently reported as being outraged by the claim – since it appeared the soldiers had been killed in combat – the government were forced to climb down. This was reported on both ITN and Channel 4 News the following evening.

CONCLUSION

While British broadcasters clearly did not submit to the kind of cheerleading that characterised much of the US network coverage, our research suggests that the wartime coverage was generally sympathetic to the government's case. This manifested itself in various ways, notably: the focus on the progress of war to the exclusion of other issues and non-military or governmental sources; the tendency to portray the Iraqi people as liberated rather than invaded; the failure to question the claim that Iraq possessed weapons of mass destruction; and the focus on the brutality or decadence of the regime without putting this evidence in context.

This is not to say that all the coverage was sympathetic – the coverage given to looting, for example, or the questioning of Tony Blair's unfounded claims about executions was not in the government's interest. But we can see how the *overall weight* of the coverage might have encouraged some hitherto unconvinced people to support the war – thus explaining the shift in opinion polls. In terms of the quality of journalism, perhaps the most abiding issue in this context is the trust accrued to military sources. Our study suggests that the broadcaster that treated these sources most cautiously – Channel 4 – was also the one least prone to the spate of misinformed stories that punctuated the war coverage. The issue here is therefore not simply one of impartiality and journalistic independence, but of getting the story right.

NOTES

1. This research was conducted with the assistance of Kirsten Brander.
2. Although public support rarely rose above 60 per cent in most polls, the fact that the war had majority support while it was being conducted was obviously important for its perceived legitimacy.
3. A report, in this context, refers to a discrete and identifiable segment in the news bulletin, including a news anchor's summary reports.
4. We chose BBC News at 6pm; ITV News at 6.30pm; Channel 4 News at 7pm and Sky News at 10pm. The early evening news programmes on BBC and ITV were chosen because they were more consistent in terms of time slot and length throughout the war.
5. These two things are, of course, quite separate, although they tended to get lumped together in much of the coverage.
6. It was, of course, difficult to know how most Iraqis felt – the first survey to test Iraqi opinion post-war by YouGov for Channel 4 in Baghdad suggested a very mixed picture, with people happy to see the end of Saddam but unhappy about the US occupation and cynical about its motives.
7. We did get a sense that there were many thousands of civilian casualties, which most independent reports after the war have suggested.

16
9/11, Spectacles of Terror, and Media Manipulation

Douglas Kellner

The 11 September 2001 terror attacks on the World Trade Center in New York and on the Pentagon near Washington DC were shocking global media events that dominated public attention and provoked reams of discourse, reflection and writing. These media spectacles were intended to terrorise the US, to attack symbolic targets, and to unfold a terror-spectacle jihad against the west, as well as to undermine the US and global economy. The World Trade Center is an apt symbol of global capitalism in the heart of the New York financial district, while the Pentagon stands as an icon and centre of US military power.

The 9/11 terror spectacle unfolded in a city that was one of the most media-saturated in the world and that played out a deadly drama live on television. The images of the planes hitting the World Trade Center towers and their collapse were played repeatedly, as if repetition were necessary to master a highly traumatic event.

The 11 September terror attacks in New York were claimed to be "the most documented event in history" in a May 2002 HBO film *In Memorium*, which itself provided a collage of images assembled from professional news crews, documentary film-makers, and amateur videographers and photographers who in some cases risked their lives to document the event. As with other major media spectacles, the 11 September terror spectacle took over TV programming.

For several days, US television suspended broadcasting of advertising and TV entertainment and focused solely on the momentous events of 11 September. In the following analysis, I want to suggest that the images and discourses of the US television networks framed the terrorist attacks to whip up war hysteria, while failing to provide a coherent account of what happened, why it happened, and what would count as responsible responses. The mainstream media in the United States privileged the "clash of civilisation" model, established a binary dualism between Islamic terrorism and civilisation, and largely circulated war fever and retaliatory feelings and discourses that called for and supported a form of military intervention. Such one-dimensional militarism could arguably make the current crisis worse, rather than providing solutions to the problem of global terrorism. Thus, while the media in a democracy should critically debate urgent questions facing the nation, in the terror crisis the mainstream US corporate media, especially television, overwhelmingly promoted military solutions to the problem of global terrorism.

BUSH FAMILY MEDIA SPECTACLES

War itself has become a media spectacle in which successive US regimes have used military spectacle to promote their agendas. The Reagan administration repeatedly used military spectacle to deflect attention from its foreign policy and economic problems. Two Bush administrations and the Clinton administration famously "wagged the dog", using military spectacle to deflect attention from embarrassing domestic or foreign policy blunders, or in Clinton's case, a sex scandal that threatened him with impeachment.[1]

The Gulf War of 1990–91 was the major media spectacle of its era, captivating global audiences, and seeming to save the first Bush presidency, before the war's ambiguous outcome and a declining economy helped defeat the Bush presidential campaign of 1992. In the summer of 1990, the elder Bush's popularity was declining; he had promised "no new taxes" and then raised taxes, and it appeared that he would not be re-elected. Bush senior's salvation seemed to appear in the figure of Saddam Hussein. Bush and the Reagan administration had supported Hussein during the Iran–Iraq war of 1980–88 and Bush senior continued to provide loans and programmes that enabled Hussein to build up his military during his presidency.[2]

When Iraq invaded Kuwait in August 1990, Bush mobilised an international coalition to wage war to oust the Iraqis from its neighbouring oil emirate, demonising Hussein as "another Hitler" and a major threat to world peace and the global economy. Bush refused serious diplomatic efforts to induce Iraq to leave Kuwait, constantly insulting the Iraqi leader rather than pursuing diplomatic mediation. Instead, Bush appeared to want a war to increase US power in the region, to promote US military clout as the dominant global police force, to save his own failing political fortunes, and to exert more US influence over oil supplies and policies.[3] The televised drama of the 1991 Gulf War provided exciting media spectacles that engrossed a global audience and that seemed to ensure Bush's re-election (he enjoyed 90 per cent popularity at the end of the war).

After the war, in an exuberant rush of enthusiasm, Bush senior and his national security adviser Brent Scowcroft proclaimed a "New World Order" in which US military power would be used to settle conflicts, solve problems, and assert the US as the hegemonic force in the world. Such a dream was not (yet) to be, however, as the post-war peace negotiations allowed Saddam Hussein to keep power and the US failed to aid Shi'ite forces in the south and Kurds in the north of Iraq to overthrow Hussein. Images of the slaughter of Kurds and Shi'ites throughout the global media provided negative images that helped code the 1991 Gulf War as a failure, or extremely limited success. Hence, the negative spectacle of a messy endgame to the war combined with a poor economy helped defeat the elder Bush in 1992.

At the time of the 11 September terror attacks, Bush junior faced the same failing prospects that his father confronted in the summer of 1990. The economy was suffering one of the worst declines in US history, and after ramming through a right-wing agenda on behalf of the corporations that had supported his 2000 election,[4] Bush lost control of the political agenda when a Republican senator, James Jeffords, defected to the Democrats in May 2001. But the 11 September terror attacks provided an opportunity for George W. Bush to re-seize political initiative and to boost his popularity.

The brief war against the Taliban and al-Qaeda in Afghanistan from early October through December 2001 appeared to be a military victory for the US. After a month of stalemate following relentless US bombing, the Taliban collapsed in the north of the country, abandoned the capital Kabul, and surrendered in its southern strong-holds.[5] Yet the Afghanistan Terror War, like the elder Bush's Gulf War, was ambiguous in its outcome. Although the Taliban regime which hosted Osama bin Laden and al-Qaeda collapsed under US military pressure, the top leaders and many militants of al-Qaeda and the Taliban escaped and the country remains dangerous and chaotic. Violent warlords that the US used to fight al-Qaeda exert oppressive power and generate hostile conditions, while sympathisers for al-Qaeda and the Taliban continue to wield power and destabilise the country. Because the US did not use ground troops or multilat-eral military forces, the top leaders of the Taliban and al-Qaeda escaped, Pakistan was allowed to send in planes that evacuated hundreds of Pakistanis and numerous top al-Qaeda militants, and Afghanistan remains a threatening and unruly territory.[6]

While the 1991 Gulf War produced spectacles of precision-bombs and missiles destroying Iraqi targets and the brief spectacle of the flight of the Iraqis from Kuwait and the liberation of Kuwait City, the Afghanistan war was more hidden in its unfolding and effects. Many of the images of Afghanistan that circulated through the global media were of civilian casualties caused by US bombing, and daily pictures of thousands of refugees from war and suffering of the Afghanistan people raised questions concerning the US strategy and intervention. Moreover, just as the survival of Saddam Hussein ultimately coded the first Gulf War as problematic, so do did the continued existence of Osama bin Laden and his top al-Qaeda leadership point to limitations of the younger Bush's leadership and policies.

Thus, by early 2002, George W. Bush faced a situation similar to that of his father after the 1991 Gulf War. Despite victory against the Taliban, the limited success of the war and a failing economy provided a situation that threatened W's re-election. Thus Bush Jr needed a dramatic media spectacle that would guarantee his election and once more Saddam Hussein provided a viable candidate. Consequently, in his 20 January 2002 State of the Union address, Bush made threatening remarks about an "axis of evil" confronting the US, including Iraq, Iran and North Korea.

As 2002 unfolded, the Bush administration intensified its ideological war against Iraq, advanced its doctrine of pre-emptive strikes, and provided military build-up for what now looks like inevitable war against Iraq. While the explicit war aims were to shut down Iraq's "weapons of mass destruction", and thus enforce UN resolutions which mandated that Iraq eliminate its offensive weapons, there were many hidden agendas in the Bush administration's offensive against Iraq. To be re-elected Bush obviously needed a major victory and symbolic triumph over terrorism in order to deflect from the failings of his regime both domestically and in the realm of foreign policy.

Indeed, in the global arena, Bush appears to be the most hated US president of modern times and anti-Americanism is on the rise throughout the world. Moreover, ideologues within the Bush administration want to legitimate a policy of pre-emptive strikes and a successful attack on Iraq could inaugurate and normalise this policy. Some of the same militarist unilateralists in the Bush administration envisage US world hegemony, the elder Bush's "New World Order", with the US as the reigning military power and world's policeman.[7] Increased control of the world's oil supplies provides a tempting prize for the former oil executives who maintain key roles in the Bush administration. And, finally, one might note the Oedipus Tex drama, where George W. Bush's desires to conclude his father's unfinished business and simultaneously defeat Evil to constitute himself as Good is driving him to war with the fervour of a religious crusade.

With all these agendas in play, war against Iraq was inevitable. Bush's 6 March 2003 press conference made it evident that he was ready to go to war against Iraq. His handlers told him to speak slowly and keep his big stick and Texas macho out of view, but he constantly threatened Iraq and evoked the rhetoric of good and evil that he used to justify his crusade against bin Laden and al-Qaeda. Bush repeated the words "Saddam Hussein" and "terrorism" incessantly, mentioning Iraq as a "threat" at least 16 times, which he attempted to link with the 11 September attacks and terrorism. He used the word "I" as in "I believe" countless times, and talked of "my government" as if he owned it, depicting a man lost in words and self-importance, positioning himself against the evil that he was preparing to wage war against. Unable to make an intelligent and objective case for a war against Iraq, Bush could only invoke fear and a moralistic rhetoric, attempting to present himself as a strong nationalist leader.

Bush's rhetoric, like that of fascism, deploys a mistrust and hatred of language, reducing it to manipulative speechifying, speaking in codes, repeating the same phrases over and over. This is grounded in anti-intellectualism and hatred of democracy and intellectuals. It is clearly evident in Bush's press conferences, responses to questions and general contempt for the whole procedure. It plays to anti-intellectual proclivities and tendencies in the extreme conservative and fundamentalist Christian constituencies who support him. It appears that Bush's press conference was orchestrated to shore up his base and prepare his supporters for a major political struggle rather than to marshal arguments to convince those opposed to go to war with Iraq that it was a good idea. He displayed, against his will, the complete poverty of his case to go to war against Iraq; he had no convincing arguments, nothing new to communicate and just repeated the same tired clichés over and over.

Bush's discourse also displayed Orwellian features of Doublethink where war against Iraq is for peace, the occupation of Iraq is its liberation, destroying its food and water supplies enables humanitarian action, and where the murder of countless Iraqis and destruction of the country will produce "freedom" and "democracy". In a pre-war summit with Tony Blair in the Azores and in his first talk after the bombing began, Bush went on and on about the "coalition of the willing" and how many countries were supporting and participating in the "allied" effort. In fact, however, it was a coalition of two, with the US and UK doing most of the fighting and with many of the countries that Bush claimed supported his war quickly backtracking and expressing reservations about the highly unpopular assault that was strongly opposed by most people and countries in the world.

On 19 March, the media spectacle of the war against Iraq unfolded with a dramatic attempt to "decapitate" the Iraqi regime. Large numbers of missiles were aimed at targets in Baghdad where Saddam Hussein and the Iraqi leadership were believed to be staying, and the tens of thousands of ground troops on the Kuwait–Iraq border poised for invasion entered Iraq in a blitzkrieg toward Baghdad. The media followed the Bush administration and Pentagon slogan of "shock and awe" and presented the war against Iraq as a great military spectacle, as triumphalism marked the opening days of the US bombing of Iraq and invasion.

The Al Jazeera network live coverage of the bombing of a palace belonging to the Hussein family was indeed shocking as loud explosions and blasts jolted viewers throughout the world. Whereas some western audiences experienced this bombing positively as a powerful assault on evil, for Arab audiences it was experienced as an attack on the body of the Arab and Muslim people, just as the 11 September terror attacks were experienced by Americans as assaults on the very body and symbols of the United States. While during the 1991 Gulf War, CNN was the only network live in Baghdad, and then throughout the war framed the images, discourses and spectacle, there were over 20 networks in Baghdad this time, including several Arab networks, and the different broadcasting companies presented the war quite diversely.

Al Jazeera and other Arab networks, as well as some European networks, talked of an "invasion" and an illegal US and British assault on Iraq. While US TV networks presented a "War in Iraq" or "Operation Iraqi Freedom" as the framing concepts, the Canadian CBC used as a frame the "War on Iraq", and Arab and other global networks spoke of an "invasion" and "occupation". While Donald Rumsfeld bragged that the bombings were the most precise in history and were aimed at military and not civilian targets, Arab and various global broadcasting networks focused on civilian casualties and presented painful spectacles of Iraqis suffering. Moreover, to the surprise of many, after a triumphant march across the Kuwaiti border and rush to Baghdad, the US and British forces began to take casualties, and during the weekend of 22–23 March, images of their POWs and dead bodies of their soldiers were shown throughout the world. Moreover, the Iraqis began fiercely resisting and rather than cheering for British and US forces to enter the southern city of Basra, there was fierce resistance throughout southern Iraq.

Soon after, an immense sandstorm slowed down the march on Baghdad and images of Iraqi civilians maimed or killed by US and British bombing, accounts of mishaps, stalled and overextended supply lines, and unexpected dangers to the invading forces created a tremendously dramatic story. The intensity and immediacy of the spectacle was multiplied by "embedded" reporters who were with the occupying US and British forces and who beamed back live pictures, first of the triumphant blitzkrieg through Iraq and then of the invading forces stalling and subject to perilous counterattack.

A great debate emerged around the embedded reporters and whether journalists who depended on the protection of the US and British military, lived with the troops, and signed papers agreeing to a rigorous set of restrictions on their reporting could be objective. From the beginning, it was clear that the embedded reporters were indeed "in bed" with military escorts and protectors and as the US and Britain stormed into Iraq the reporters presented exultant and triumphant accounts that trumped any paid propagandist. The embedded US network television reporters were gung-ho cheerleaders and spinners for the US and UK military and lost all veneer of objectivity. But as the blitzkrieg stalled, a sandstorm hit, and US and British forces came under attack, the embedded reporters reflected genuine fear, helped capture the chaos of war, provided often vivid accounts of the fighting, and occasionally, as I note below, deflated a propaganda lie of the US or UK military.

Indeed, US and British military discourse was exceptionally mendacious, as happens so often in recent wars that are as much for public opinion and political agendas as for military goals. British and US sources claimed in the first days into Iraq that the border port of Umm Qasr and major southern city of Basra were under coalition control, whereas TV images showed quite the opposite. When things went very badly for US and British forces on 23 March, a story originated from an embedded reporter with the *Jerusalem Post* that a "huge" chemical weapons production facility was found, a story allegedly confirmed by a Pentagon source to the Fox TV military correspondent who quickly spread it through the US media.[8]

When US officials denied that they were responsible for major civilian atrocities in two Baghdad bombings in the week of 24 March, reporters on the scene described witnesses to planes flying overhead and in one case found pieces of a missile with US markings and numbers on it. And after a suicide bombing killed four US troops at a checkpoint in late March, US soldiers fired on a vehicle that ran a checkpoint and killed seven civilians. The US military claimed that it had fired a warning shot, but a *Washington Post* reporter on the scene reported that a senior US military official had shouted to a younger soldier to fire a warning shot first and then yelled that "you [expletive] killed them" when he failed to do so. Embedded newspaper reporters also often provided more vivid accounts of "friendly fire" and other mishaps, getting their information from troops on the ground and on the site, instead of from military spinners.[9]

Hence, the embedded and other reporters on the site provided documentation of the more raw and brutal aspects of war and telling accounts that often put in question official versions of the events, as well as propaganda and military spin. But, it was the independent "unilateral" journalists who provided the most accurate account of the horrors of the war and the military mishaps. Thus, on the whole the embedded journalists were largely propagandists who often outdid the Pentagon and Bush administration in spinning the message of the moment.

Moreover, the US broadcast networks, on the whole, tended to be more embedded in the Pentagon and Bush administration than the reporters in the field and print journalists. The military commentators on all networks provided little more than the Pentagon spin of the moment and often repeated gross lies and propaganda. Entire networks like Fox and the NBC cable networks provided little but propaganda and one-sided patriotism, as did, for the most part CNN. All these 24/7 cable networks, as well as the big three US broadcasting networks, tended to provide highly sanitised views of the war, rarely showing Iraqi casualties, thus producing a view of the war totally different from that shown in other parts of the world.

The Fox network was especially gung-ho, militarist and aggressive, yet Fox footage shown on 5–6 April of the daring US incursion into Baghdad displayed a road strewn with destroyed Iraqi vehicles, burning buildings, and Iraqi corpses. This live footage, replayed for days, caught something of the carnage of the high-tech slaughter and destruction of Iraq that the US networks tended to neglect. And an Oliver North commentary to footage of a US warplane blasting away one Iraqi tank and armoured vehicle after another put on display the high-tech massacre of a completely asymmetrical war in which the Iraqi military had no chance whatsoever against the US war machine.

US military commanders claimed that in the initial foray into Baghdad 2,000–3,000 Iraqis were killed, which suggests that the broadcasting networks were not really showing the brutality and carnage of the war. Indeed, most of the bombing of Iraqi military forces was invisible and dead Iraqis were rarely shown. An embedded CNN reporter, Walter Rogers, later recounted that the one time his report showed a dead Iraqi the CNN switchboard "lit up like a Christmas tree" with angry viewers demanding that they do not show any dead bodies, as if the US audience wanted to be in denial concerning the human costs of the war.[10]

A 6 April interview on Fox with *Forbes* magazine publisher and former presidential candidate Steve Forbes made it clear that the US intended to get all the contracts on rebuilding Iraq for American firms, that Iraqi debts held by French and Russians should be cancelled, and that to the victors would go all the spoils of war. Such discourse put on display the arrogance and greed that drove the US effort and subverted all idealistic rhetoric about democracy and freedom for the Iraqis. The very brutality of Fox war pornography graphically displayed the horrors of war and the militarist, gloating and barbaric discourse that accompanied the slaughter of Iraqis and destruction of the country showed the New Barbarism that characterised the Bush era.[11]

Comparing American broadcasting networks with the British, Canadian and other outlets as I did during the opening weeks of the US war against Iraq showed two different wars being presented. The US networks tended to ignore Iraqi casualties, Arab outrage about the war, global anti-war and anti-US protests, and the negative features of the war, while the BBC and Canadian CBC more often presented these negative features. As noted, the war was framed very differently by various countries and networks, while analysts noted that in Arab countries the war was presented as an invasion of Iraq, slaughter of its peoples and destruction of the country.

On the whole, US broadcasting networks tended to present a sanitised view of the war while Canadian, British and other European, and Arab broadcasting did variously present copious images of civilian casualties and the horrors of war. US television coverage tended toward pro-military patriotism, propaganda, and technological fetishism, celebrating the weapons of war and military humanism, highlighting the achievements and heroism of the US military. Other global broadcasting networks, however, were highly critical of the US and UK military and often presented highly negative spectacles of the assault on Iraq and the "shock and awe" high-tech massacre.

In a sense, the US and UK war on Iraq found itself in a double bind. The more thoroughly they annihilated Iraqi troops and conquered the country, the more aggressive, bullying and imperialist they would appear to the rest of the world. Yet the dramatic pictures of civilian casualties and harrowing images of US bombing and destruction of Iraq made it imperative to end the war as soon as possible. An apparently failed attempt to kill Saddam Hussein and the Iraqi leadership on 7 April, that destroyed a civilian area and killed a number of people, followed by the killing of journalists in two separate episodes by the US military on 8 April, produced an extremely negative media spectacle of the war on Iraq, but the apparent collapse of the Iraqi regime on 9 April, where for the first time there were significant images of Iraqis celebrating the demise of Hussein, provided the material for a spectacle of victory.

Indeed, the destruction of a statue of Saddam Hussein on live global television provided precisely the images desired by the Pentagon and Bush administration. Closer analysis of this spectacle revealed, however, that rather than displaying a mass uprising of Iraqis against the Ba'ath regime, there were relatively few people assaulting the Hussein statue, including members of the US-supported Iraqi National Congress, one of whose members shown in the crowd attempted to pass himself off as the "mayor" of Baghdad, until US military forces sidelined him. Moreover, the few Iraqis attacking the statue were unable to destroy it, until some US soldiers on the scene used their tank and cable to pull it down. In a semiotic slip, one soldier briefly put a US flag on top of Hussein's head, providing an iconic image for Arab networks and others of a US occupation and take-over of Iraq.

Subsequent images of looting, anarchy and chaos throughout Iraq, however, including the looting of the National Museum, the National Archive that contained rare books and historical documents, and the Ministry for Religious Affairs, which contained rare religious material, created extremely negative impressions.[12] Likewise, growing Iraqi demonstrations over the US occupation and continued violence throughout the country put on view a highly uncertain situation in which the spectacle of victory and the triumph of Bush administration and Pentagon policy might be put into question, domestically as well as globally.

For weeks after the fall of the Iraqi regime negative images continued to circulate of clashes between Iraqis and the US forces, gigantic Shia demonstrations and celebrations that produced the spectre of the growth of radical Islamic power in the region, and the continued failure to produce security and stability. This negative spectacle suggests the limitations of a politics of the spectacle that can backfire, spiral out of control and generate unintended consequences.

Indeed, in the first Gulf War, Iraqi's flight from its occupation of Kuwait and the apparent military defeat of the Iraqi regime was followed by images of Shi'ite and Kurdish uprisings and their violent suppression by the Saddam Hussein regime, ultimately coding that Gulf war as ambiguous and contributing to George Bush Sr's defeat in 1992. Likewise, while the 11 September terror attacks on the US by the al-Qaeda network appeared to be a triumph of the Islamic radicals, worldwide revulsion against the attacks and the global and multilateral attempts to close down its networks ultimately appear to have seriously weakened the al-Qaeda forces. Politics of the spectacle are thus highly ambiguous and unstable, subject to multiple interpretations, and generate ambiguous and often unanticipated effects.

Media spectacles can backfire and are subject to dialectical reversal as positive images give way to negative ones. They are difficult to control and manage, and can be subject to different framings and interpretations, as when non-US broadcasting networks focus on civilian casualties, looting and chaos, and US military crimes against Iraqis rather than the US victory and the evils of Saddam Hussein. It is obviously too soon to determine the effects of Bush Jr's Iraq war but the consequences are likely to be complex and unforeseen, thus rendering claims that the adventure represents a great victory premature and possibly erroneous.

CONCLUDING COMMENTS

In a highly-saturated media environment, successful political projects require carefully planned and executed media spectacles. In this study, I have suggested that both the 11 September terror attacks and the Bush family's wars against Iraq were prime examples of such spectacles. Both al-Qaeda terrorists and the two Bush administrations have used media spectacles to promote their highly controversial agendas. Hence, during an era of Terror War, politics are increasingly mediated and constituted by the production of spectacular media events and the militaristic agenda of these producers.

In the US and much of the western world, the corporate media have followed the Bush administration in demonising bin Laden, Saddam Hussein and terrorism, while celebrating US military interventions. In a mediated world in which only a few – and increasingly, fewer – media corporations control the broadcasting and print media, the internet provides the best source of alternative information. It offers a wealth of opinion and debate, and a variety of sites that present material for a better-informed public and the organisation of political alternatives to the current US regime.[13] Although there is a frightening amount of misinformation and reactionary discourse on the internet, it also provides users the potential to become literate and informed on a variety of important topics. Indeed, the internet has played a key role in nurturing the anti-corporate globalisation and global justice movements, and is playing an important role in facilitating the development of a global anti-war movement.

Further, the global peace movement that has been constituting itself as a counter-spectacle to Islamic terrorism and Bush militarism signals a democratic alternative to war. The spectacle of millions demonstrating against an attack on Iraq in 2003, activists going to Iraq to serve as human shields against US and British bombing, and the daily protests erupting throughout everyday life present opposition to war and struggles for peace and democracy. On the eve of Bush Jr's assault on Iraq, a virtual protest sent millions of email and telephone calls to Washington to oppose an impending Iraq attack. The beginnings of a global peace movement numbering millions is evident. While the counter-spectacle for peace was not able to stop the Bush administration's rush to war, it empowered countries and global organisation to oppose the war and has mobilised constituencies that may eventually block the Bush administration's problematic attempt at global hegemony.

It is clear that Bush administration Terror War policy envisages an era of (endless) war against terrorism and the countries that support terror, a situation in which media spectacle will be used to promote policies of unilateral aggression. One hopes that counter-spectacles of peace and opposition to Terror War will grow in force and that new media like the internet will be used as democratic tools to prevent the unleashing of a totalising and hegemonic political vision

of "us versus them" and "good versus evil" that the Bush administration is promoting. For such perennial war truly portends historical
regression on a frightening scale and threatens the world with
genocide and an endless spectacle of violence and destruction.

NOTES

1. Douglas Kellner, *Media Spectacle*, London and New York: Routledge, 2003.
2. Douglas Kellner, *The Persian Gulf TV War*, Boulder, Co.: Westview Press, 1992.
3. Ibid.
4. Douglas Kellner, *Grand Theft 2000*, Boulder, Co.: Rowman and Littlefield, 2002.
5. Kellner, *Media Spectacle*.
6. Ibid.
7. Douglas Kellner, *From 9/11 to Terror War: Dangers of the Bush Legacy*, Boulder, Co.: Rowman and Littlefield, 2003.
8. Soon after, British and then US military sources affirmed that the site was not a chemical weapons production or storage facility. For a critique of a series of "smoking gun" discoveries of weapons of mass destruction facilities and their subsequent debunking, see Jake Tapper, "WMD, MIA?" *Salon*, 16 April 2003.
9. On the Baghdad bombings, see the reporting of Robert Fisk in the London *Independent*; for the story that questioned official US military accounts of the checkpoint shootings of a civilian family, see William Branigin, "A Gruesome Scene on Highway 9", *Washington Post*, 1 April 2003.
10. Rogers was interviewed on Howard Kurtz's poorly named CNN media review "Reliable Sources" on 27 April 2003.
11. For systematic analysis of the New Barbarism accompanying and in part generated by the Bush administration and their hard-right supporters, see Kellner, *From 9/11 to Terror War*. See Jim Rutenberg, "Cable's War Coverage Suggests a New 'Fox Effect' on Television", *New York Times*, 16 April 2003. Rutenberg provides examples of Fox's aggressively opinion-ated and biased discourse, as when anchor Neil Cavuto said of those who oppose the war on Iraq: "You were sickening then, you are sickening now." Fox's high ratings during the war influenced CNN and the NBC networks to be more patriotic and dismissive of those who criticised the war and its aftermath.
12. Evidently, the museum community thought it had an understanding with the US military of the need to preserve Iraqi national treasures which were allowed by the US military to be looted and destroyed while they protected the Petroleum Ministry; see <http://www.nytimes.com/2003/04/16/international/worldspecial/16MUSE.html>. On the looting of the Ministry for Religious Affairs, see <http://www.nytimes.com/2003/04/16/international/worldspecial/16BAGH.html>.
13. Kellner, *Grand Theft 2000*; Kellner, *From 9/11 to Terror War*.

17
"Look, I'm An American"
Norman Solomon

Five days after the Saddam Hussein statue fell in Baghdad's Firdos Square, television anchor Dan Rather appeared on the CNN programme *Larry King Live* and emphasised his professional allegiance. "Look, I'm an American," the CBS newsman said. "I never tried to kid anybody that I'm some internationalist or something. And when my country is at war, I want my country to win, whatever the definition of 'win' may be. Now, I can't and don't argue that that is coverage without a prejudice. About that I am prejudiced."

In that spirit, the US mainstream media were indeed prejudiced about the war on Iraq in spring 2003 – and bias clearly determined the news coverage. The media watch group FAIR conducted a study of the 1,617 on-camera sources who appeared on the evening newscasts of six US television networks during the three weeks beginning with the start of the war on 20 March:

> Nearly two-thirds of all sources, 64 percent, were pro-war, while 71 percent of U.S. guests favored the war. Anti-war voices were 10 percent of all sources, but just 6 percent of non-Iraqi sources and only 3 percent of U.S. sources. Thus viewers were more than six times as likely to see a pro-war source as one who was anti-war; counting only U.S. guests, the ratio increases to 25 to 1.[1]

Less than 1 per cent of the US sources were anti-war on Dan Rather's flagship programme, the *CBS Evening News*, during the war's first three weeks. Meanwhile, as FAIR's researchers commented wryly, public television's PBS *NewsHour* programme hosted by Jim Lehrer "also had a relatively low percentage of US anti-war voices – perhaps because the show less frequently features on-the-street interviews, to which critics of the war were usually relegated".[2] Once the war began, the major network studios were virtually off-limits to vehement American opponents of the war.

For the most part, major US networks sanitised their war coverage, which was wall-to-wall on cable. As always, the enthusiasm for war was rabid on Fox News Channel. After a pre-war makeover, the fashion was the same for MSNBC. At the other end of the narrow cable-news spectrum, CNN cranked up its own militaristic fervour.

There were instances of exceptional journalism in the mainstream US press. Some news magazines provided a number of grisly pictures. A few reporters, notably Anthony Shadid of the *Washington Post* and Ian Fisher of the *New York Times*, wrote vivid accounts of what the Pentagon's firepower did to Iraqi people on the ground; only a closed heart could be unmoved by those stories. But America remained largely numb.

Media depictions of human tragedies may have momentary impact, but the nation's anaesthetic flood of non-stop media encourages us to sense that we're somehow above or beyond the human fray: Some lives, including ours of course, matter a great deal. Others, while perhaps touching, are decidedly secondary. The official directives needn't be explicit to be well understood: *Do not let too much empathy move in unauthorised directions.*

In wartime, mainstream news outlets were more eager than ever to limit the range of discourse. Here's a small example: When US forces took former Iraqi Deputy Prime Minister Tariq Aziz into custody, the *Houston Chronicle* quoted two sentences from me in a 27 April editorial: "Aziz epitomized the urbanity of evil. He was articulate and deft at rationalizing government actions that caused enormous suffering." But the daily newspaper's editorial did not quote the next sentence of my statement, which had appeared in a news release from the Institute for Public Accuracy: "His similarities to top U.S. officials are much greater than we're comfortable acknowledging."

That sort of point was pretty much taboo in US mass media coverage, which sometimes included vehement tactical arguments about the Bush administration's war – but not about the prerogatives of Washington to intervene militarily around the world. A basic media assumption is that leaders in the United States are cut from entirely different cloth than the likes of Tariq Aziz. But in some respects, the terrible compromises made by Aziz are more explainable than the ones that are routine in US politics. Aziz had good reason to fear for his life – and the lives of loved ones – if he ran foul of Hussein. In contrast, many politicians and appointed officials in Washington have gone along with lethal policies merely because of fear that dissent might cost them re-election, prestige or power.

In US media coverage, carefully selective use of the word "terrorism" is routine. That selectivity reflects the political character of the term

– and the slanted angles of customary reportage. It is not the wanton cruelty or the magnitude of murderous actions that excites media condemnation so much as the political context of such actions.

On 19 May 2003, President George W. Bush denounced "killers who can't stand peace". (As the Prussian general Karl von Clausewitz remarked two centuries ago, "A conqueror is always a lover of peace.") In that particular instance, Bush was referring to people who had engaged in deadly attacks that took the lives of Israeli civilians. But the same description could be applied to Israeli government leaders, who often order attacks that predictably take the lives of Palestinian civilians. And while Bush had become fond of denouncing "killers" and "terrorists" – using those words righteously and interchangeably – the same terminology could be applied to him and other top officials in Washington. Such a harsh assessment would undoubtedly come from thousands of Iraqi people who lost their loved ones during the spring of 2003. What American journalists routinely decline to note – and what mainstream media will be the last to tell us – is that news coverage of terrorism is routinely subjective, even arbitrary. Those with the power to use and not use the "terrorism" label in mass media are glad to do so as they please.

Meanwhile, the US media fixation on some terrorism has been markedly out of proportion. In mid-May 2003, the internationally syndicated columnist Gwynne Dyer observed that the previous week had brought news reports of terrorist attacks in Chechnya, Saudi Arabia, Pakistan, Morocco and Israel, resulting in a total of 153 deaths. He observed:

> Last week was the worst for terrorist attacks since Sept. 11, 2001. … Yet there were no headlines last weekend saying "750 people dead of gunshot wounds in the U.S. since Monday" or "Weekly traffic death toll in India tops 2,000," and only small headlines that several thousand people had been massacred in the eastern Congolese town of Bunia.

Endeavouring to put post-9/11 media fixations on terrorism in perspective, Dyer wrote:

> There are several agendas running in the Bush administration, and the one on top at the moment is the hyper-ambitious Cheney–Rumsfeld project that uses the terrorist threat as a pretext for creating a global "pax Americana" based on the unilateral use

of American military power. But the project of the Islamic terrorists is still running too, and this strategy is playing straight into their hands.

I would push the analysis a bit further. Both sides are busily playing into each other's hands, and this is not mere happenstance. The propaganda necessity is to portray one side's attacks as righteous and the other's as evil. Right now, it's fair to say, each side is committed to large-scale killing. Yet their lethal capacities are vastly asymmetrical. The Pentagon has the power to dominate the world, while al-Qaeda can only hope to dominate the headlines. In the process, to exploit the evil of al-Qaeda's actions for its own purposes, the Bush team has been pleased to fuel the skewed media coverage.

By a two-to-one margin, Americans "use clearly positive words in their descriptions of the president", a polling outfit reported in early May of 2003. The Pew Research Center concluded that "there is little doubt ... the war in Iraq has improved the president's image" in the United States. Such assessments stood in sharp contrast to views overseas. Earlier in the same spring, the Pew Center released survey results showing that "US favourability ratings have plummeted in the past six months" – not only in "countries actively opposing war" but also in "countries that are part of the 'coalition of the willing'". The poll numbers indicating a "favourable view of the US" were low in one country after another – only 48 per cent in Britain, 31 per cent in France, 28 per cent in Russia, 25 per cent in Germany, 14 per cent in Spain and 12 per cent in Turkey.

To a large extent, the disparity between public opinion in the US and elsewhere in the world can be explained with one word: media. Overall, the American news media do a great job of cheerleading Uncle Sam's stride across the planet.

Soon after the 2003 invasion of Iraq ended, meticulous researchers at FAIR (where I'm an associate) pointed out that US news outlets "have been quick to declare the U.S. war against Iraq a success, but in-depth investigative reporting about the war's likely health and environmental consequences has been scarce". As reported by the London-based *Guardian*, during the war the Pentagon dropped 1,500 cluster bombs – horrific weaponry designed to fire small pieces of metal that slice through human bodies. Unexploded cluster bombs continued to detonate, sometimes in the hands of Iraqi children. In addition, as had occurred during the first Gulf War, the US government again fortified some munitions with depleted uranium, leaving behind fine-particle radioactive dust of the sort that has been linked to cancer and birth defects.

Those important stories – about cluster bombs and depleted uranium – became known to many news watchers on several continents. But not in the United States. Searching the comprehensive Nexis media database through 5 May 2003, the FAIR researchers found that "there have been no in-depth reports about cluster bombs" on the major US broadcast TV networks' nightly news programmes since the start of the war on 20 March. Those news shows provided just "a few passing mentions of cluster bombs". And the network evening news programmes did even worse on DU reportage. "Since the beginning of the year," FAIR discovered, "the words 'depleted uranium' have not been uttered once on ABC *World News Tonight*, *CBS Evening News* or *NBC Nightly News*, according to Nexis".[3]

Meanwhile, the deck of cards featuring 52 Iraqi villains (with Saddam Hussein as Ace of Spades) became one of the great PR innovations of the war on Iraq. By coincidence, on the same day that FAIR completed its research, five "Army intelligence specialists" – who designed the cards – stepped forward to take a bow in Washington. Although a spokesperson for Central Command conceded that there was "no word on the cards helping find anyone", the Pentagon's deck had turned out to be a stroke of media genius. It tapped into the American public's appetite for fun ways to identify bad guys to be hunted down.

Propaganda systems gain strength from offering bogus alternatives, and the limited spectrum of mass media in the United States is no exception. Millions of Americans tune into NPR News. During the war, that public radio network carried the reporting of correspondent Anne Garrels, who provided some outstanding eyewitness accounts from Baghdad – but her exceptional reports were hardly indicative of NPR's overall coverage, heavily dominated by reliance on an array of US government sources, claims and assumptions.

Consider the approach, in the midst of the war, when two of the network's mainstays held forth on Saturday morning's *Weekend Edition*. During a 5 April discussion with host Scott Simon, the NPR news analyst Daniel Schorr exclaimed: "It really is quite amazing, whether one likes the plan of the Pentagon or not, it certainly, as of now, has been a most roaring success." Simon replied:

And let's remind ourselves today, of course, there have been casualties. So far, according to NPR's estimate, 67 US troops have died, 16 are missing, seven captured; 27 British troops dead, none missing or captured. Recognising that these are all sacred souls that have been lost, at the same time the casualties seem to be standing a good deal lower than some people had projected.

The response from Schorr:

That's right. And, you know, an interesting thing is one of the great successes of the week is what has not happened. One is that there have not been very major casualties. Another is they have not been able to devastate the oilfields. Another is that they have not been able to cow the American Marines and the troops by sending in suicide bombers. They've managed to cope with that. There've been some unfortunate deaths of civilians there. But whatever was the strategy of resistance has not worked, and whatever is the strategy for marching to Baghdad seems to be working pretty well.

The back-and-forth between Schorr and Simon embodied the dominant tenor of the war coverage – the kind of media assessments that seem to be tacitly guided by the overarching PC sensibilities of Pentagon Correctness. The homage is to victory. Americans and their allies are the sacred people. And accolades go to iron fists in the White House.

"If real leadership means leading people where they don't want to go," Michael Kinsley wrote in the 21 April 2003 edition of *Time* magazine, "George W. Bush has shown himself to be a real leader." Militarism in America had become a runaway train on a death track. Kinsley commented: "The president's ability to decide when and where to use America's military power is now absolute. Congress cannot stop him. That's not what the Constitution says, and it's not what the War Powers Act says, but that's how it works in practice."

Mostly, it works that way in practice because countless journalists – whether they're flag-wavers at Fox News or liberal sophisticates at NPR News – keep letting authorities define the bounds of appropriate empathy and moral concern. I know of very few prominent American journalists who pointed out that President Bush had the blood of many Iraqi children on his hands after launching an aggressive war in violation of the UN Charter and the Nuremberg principles established more than half a century ago. During the 2003 invasion of Iraq, the avoidance certainly extended to NPR News. When I did a Nexis search to find out how often the word

"Nuremberg" had been mentioned on NPR from 1 January through 30 April, the word came up a total of four times – and none of the references had anything to do with raising any question about the US government's war on Iraq.

Despite such deafening media silences, the judgments at Nuremberg and precepts of international law forbid launching an aggressive war – an apt description of what the US government inflicted on Iraqi people in the spring of 2003. "We must make clear to the Germans that the wrong for which their fallen leaders are on trial is not that they lost the war, but that they started it," said Supreme Court Justice Robert L. Jackson, a US representative to the International Conference on Military Trials at the close of the Second World War. He added that "no grievances or policies will justify resort to aggressive war. It is utterly renounced and condemned as an instrument of policy".

When a country – particularly "a democracy" – goes to war, the passive consent of the governed lubricates the machinery of slaughter. Silence is a key form of co-operation, but the war-making system does not insist on quietude or agreement. Mere passivity or self-restraint will suffice to keep the missiles flying, the bombs exploding and the faraway people dying.

NOTES

1. "Amplifying Officials, Squelching Dissent: FAIR study finds democracy poorly served by war coverage", *EXTRA! Magazine*, May/June 2003, pp. 12–13, <http://www.fair.org/extra/0305/warstudy.html>.
2. Ibid., print version.
3. Action Alert: "TV Not Concerned by Cluster Bombs, DU: 'That's just the way life is in Iraq'", FAIR, 6 May 2003, <http://www.fair.org/activism/tv-cluster-du.html>.

18

"Let the Atrocious
Images Haunt Us"

Julian Petley

Contemporary media representations of warfare are marked by a glaring paradox: whilst modern media technology has the potential to permit us to see more details of warfare than ever before, and whilst fictional representations of warfare, and of violent acts in general, have become ever bloodier and more explicit, non-fictional ones (at least in the British and US mainstream media) have become increasingly restrained and sanitised.

Never was this more apparent than in the 1991 Gulf War in which, due to a combination of rigid media management by the military and the fact that much of the action was waged from the air, the representation of the war was reduced to the level of a video game, with "clean" images from "smart" weapons complementing the emptying of language of any connotations of human suffering – hence "surgical strikes", "collateral damage", "soft targets" and all the other euphemisms for death and destruction which the media armchair generals were only too happy to parrot from the modern military vocabulary. This conception of war as something acted out by machines as opposed to sentient human beings was perfectly encapsulated by President Bush's National Security Advisor, Brent Scowcroft stating that: "our goal was not to kill people. Our goal was to destroy the Iraqi army."[1] No wonder, then, that those sections of the British press which were perfectly content to play their allotted role in this process, which John Taylor has described as "de-realisation" and Paul Virilio as "the aesthetics of disappearance", reacted with such fury when the BBC and ITN showed even highly sanitised images of the consequences of the 1991 allied bombing of the Amiriya bunker in Baghdad, which we now know killed over 1,600 people, mostly women and children. As Phillip Knightley explained:

> one reason for this almost hysterical reaction was that the
> reporting of the Amiriya bombing threatened the most important

element in the military's propaganda strategy – an attempt to change public perception of the nature of war itself, to convince everyone that new technology has removed a lot of war's horrors ... The picture that was painted was of a war almost without death.[2]

As Hugh Gusterson put it, the media coverage of the 1991 Gulf War demonstrated "the power of a system of representations which marginalises the presence of the body in war, fetishises machines, and personalises international conflicts while depersonalising the people who die in them".[3] And indeed, it might have been thought at the time that the way in which the media covered the first Gulf War would set the pattern for the coverage of future wars as well.

THE RIGHT PERSPECTIVE

However, such a prediction would have been proved wrong, at least to some extent, by media coverage of the Anglo-American invasion of Iraq. That this coverage was significantly different can be attributed to at least three factors. Firstly, the nature of the action itself, in which soldiers on the ground played a far greater role than in 1991. Secondly, the relatively easy availability of alternative media, many of which represented the invasion from a very different perspective from that of the mainstream media – in other words, one which regarded the action as illegal. Chief amongst these was Al Jazeera, but almost as important were the numerous websites which carried highly critical coverage of the invasion. And thirdly, in Britain at least, the press was far more divided than in the first Gulf War, with the *Guardian*, *Independent* and *Mirror* opposed to the Anglo-American adventure.

It was these last two factors which allowed British people to see images of death and injury from Iraq which the mainstream broadcasters (along with most of the press) refused to show – at least whilst the invasion was in progress. And so, for the first time, the hitherto undisputed hegemony of highly Anglo-centric notions of taste and decency in war coverage was thrown into sharp relief. In this respect, it's worth recalling a revealing anecdote told by John Simpson about the aftermath of a mortar bomb landing in a Sarajevo street:

a camera crew from the agency "pool", whose pictures could be used by everyone, arrived first and saw the immediate results of the massacre. It was instructive to see how the reporters from different countries, and different television traditions, dealt with the pictures. The Italians used almost all of them: the brains, the intestines, the gutter literally running with blood in the rain. The French used the gutter and the bodies. The Americans used the gutter. We used none of these things: just the covered bodies being put into the ambulances, the empty pram, the abandoned shoes.[4]

Newspapers are, of course, "free" to report and comment on matters in any way that they choose – or indeed to ignore them altogether – but broadcasters have a statutory obligation to inform their audiences impartially of the facts. But they have other obligations too, and some of these undoubtedly complicate their informational role. For example, the BBC's *Producers' Guidelines* argue that

> there is a balance to be struck between the demands of truth and the danger of desensitising people. With some news stories a sense of shock is part of a full understanding of what has happened. But the more often viewers are shocked, the more it will take to shock them.

They also state that: "the dead should be treated with respect and not be shown unless there are compelling reasons for doing so. Close-ups should generally be avoided. When such scenes are justified they must not be lingered over." Furthermore, flatly contradicting the idea that a picture is worth a thousand words, they maintain that: "editing out the bloodiest scenes need not result in a sanitised version of events. A good script is vital in conveying the reality of tragedy."[5]

The Broadcasting Standards Commission's *Codes of Guidance*, which apply to all the terrestrial channels and also to BSkyB, contain almost identical provisions, but also add that

> images shown on television can have an overwhelming impact. While broadcasters should not shy away from showing the conse-quences of violence, they must also take care in the choice of accompanying words to ensure that they put the scenes into the right perspective and ensure that those exercising editorial judgements are aware of the impact such material may have on the audience.[6]

Leaving aside thoughts about just what constitutes the "right per-spective", especially in time of war, these policies inform the general climate on propriety and the public record. But, they are not developed in a vacuum, and take into account the views of the audience, the government, pressure groups, and, of course, the press. Many of these, for varied reasons, are hostile to the showing of violent images at any time – particularly during military action. We also have to bear in mind that in an increasingly competitive broadcasting environment, in which news provision plays a key commercial role, TV executives may well be concerned that factual images of death and injury are, quite literally, a turn-off.

In explaining why the BBC was unwilling to show explicit images of death and injury during the invasion, BBC director of News Richard Sambrook stressed the views of the audience, arguing that

> the fundamental question is what people will tolerate, and that shifts over time. Shocking people is an issue. You have to take care, certainly during daytime, but you can put stronger images on *Newsnight* than the *One O'clock News*; stronger on current affairs than on news.

Noting that Al Jazeera showed far more disturbing scenes than did British broadcasters he commented that: "the Arab world is used to seeing more gory shots". However, this is simply to ignore the fact that most European public service broadcasters, too, are *far* less squeamish than British ones. It's also hard not to detect a note of cultural condescension in Sambrook's remark; after all, if Arab viewers are indeed used to more gory shots than their British counterparts, maybe it's because many of them inhabit countries torn apart by brutal conflicts – conflicts in which the west is highly complicit. Equally Anglo-centric is Sambrook's admission that

> there will be images of British and Iraqis that we wouldn't show under any circumstances, but once you get past that point you have to be more sensitive with UK casualties – it is more difficult to show dead UK soldiers than dead Iraqis. Nonetheless, that is secondary to the issue of taste.[7]

Nick Pollard of Sky News, however, was rather more forthright:

> I wouldn't say that we wouldn't ever show pictures of UK casualties either dead or wounded. We've shown pictures of dead civilians in Basra and Baghdad. And it's absolutely illogical to say that it's fine

to show dead Iraqis, civilians or soldiers, by the dozen, but not dead coalition soldiers. Although you do have to be careful with shots where you can recognise individual soldiers, we should show what's going on to the people of the countries who are waging the war ... We shouldn't show only the process, we should show the effects as well. Bodies and injuries are part of it.

In particular, he raised the all-important point that broadcasting regulations dealing with the portrayal of violence in general should not be applied to the representation of violence in wartime, stating that: "I'm not sure they are quite appropriate to the situation we're in now – we might want to show more than we would normally show under the regulations."[8]

Meanwhile, much to the fury of the government and the jingo press, Al Jazeera regularly showed uncensored pictures of the Iraqi victims of the invasion. It also showed pictures of mutilated bodies of British soldiers, and shots of US prisoners of war. The latter was condemned by Geoff Hoon as "a flagrant and sickening breach of the Geneva Convention", even though he must have known that the Convention does not apply to the media, only to states or "detaining powers". Many in the press were quick to agree with him, but, of course, this did not stop them showing pictures of Iraqi prisoners of war. Earlier they'd been quite happy to show pictures of the detainees at Guantanamo Bay – whose rights under the Geneva Convention are indeed being denied and violated on a daily basis.

THE VIEWERS' VIEWS

Given that the limits of public taste and tolerance are frequently cited as the main reason for self-censorship by the broadcasters, what *does* the public think about the reporting of military action?

The most detailed of the limited amount of evidence available, is to be found in David Morrison's *Television and the Gulf War*. Morrison's findings are quite complex, but it is undeniable that few of those interviewed for this project thought that television coverage of war should include close-ups of the dead or seriously injured. In the case of a battle involving Iraqi casualties 42 per cent thought the scene should be shown only from a distance, so that the dead were not recognisable, whilst 43 per cent thought it should be shown only after the dead and seriously injured had been removed. In the case of a battle involving British casualties the figures were 48 per cent and 34 per cent respectively. Scoring highly amongst the reasons why some of the interviewees thought that various disturbing scenes should not be shown *at all* were: "upsetting for relatives of victims/prisoners" (with British relatives coming in for rather more consideration than Iraqi ones); "upsetting for adults"; "don't need to see it/can imagine it"; and "children will get upset".

According to Morrison, his findings demonstrate that the majority of those who felt that certain images, such as those of the Amiriya bunker or the slaughter on the Basra Road, should not be shown at all:

> considered that they had enough imagination to grasp what had taken place without the need for detailed visual representation ... For the majority of his interviewees felt that the function of news was seen to be that of relaying what was happening in the war and in relaying what was happening it was not considered necessary for the news to include close-up shots of injury, but merely establish that injury had occurred.

He concludes that: "very few people really wish for the full horror of war to be shown on their screens".[9]

CYNICAL EXPLOITATION

In times of war, then, it's not altogether surprising that broadcasters feel that they have to take into account their viewers' apparent preference for visual restraint and understatement. In addition, the BBC knows that its numerous enemies in the press are simply itching for any opportunity to decry it as "unpatriotic". Chief amongst these, of course, are the papers owned by rival broadcaster Rupert Murdoch. His permanent campaign against the BBC found expression in the *Sun*'s high-profile, week-long attack on the Corporation for showing a documentary about Al Jazeera in its *Correspondent* slot on BBC2 on Sunday 1 June 2003. What the *Sun* opportunistically latched onto was the extremely brief, and heavily pixellated, footage of the dead bodies of Staff Sgt. Simon Cullingworth and Sapper Luke Allsopp, who were killed in an ambush during the war, footage which the BBC, along with the other UK broadcasters and the press, had refused to show at the time of its original release. The programme had in fact already been postponed for a month because the original screening would have coincided with the soldiers' funerals. The *Sun* referred to the footage variously as an "atrocity", "sickening" and "beyond comprehension". Thus, for example, a lengthy article on 28 May, headed "Bloated, Biased and Disloyal to Britain", rapidly forgot the unfortunate relatives and launched into the main point of the story: a furious tirade against the BBC. Amongst other things this alleged that: "senior officers aboard Britain's Gulf flagship Ark Royal banned BBC News 24 and switched to Sky News after sailors labelled the BBC the Baghdad Broadcasting Corporation" and quoted "TV arts pundit" (and sometime Murdoch employee) Jonathan Miller to the effect that: "what Britain needs is a public broadcasting system that answers to viewers, not a bloated BBC hooked on extracting money with menaces from every home in the land".

Courageously the BBC held its ground, and the programme was broadcast intact, but sadly, if all too predictably, not before Tony Blair and Geoff Hoon had given ample credence to the *Sun's* campaign, thus neatly demonstrating yet another source of pressure on the broadcasters to censor themselves.

MORAL SLEEP AND HISTORICAL AMNESIA

That the broadcasters do censor themselves in times of war (as indeed at other times) is, as we have seen, undeniable, and we have explored – although not endorsed – some of the reasons why they do so. Of course, no one would argue that the most horrific images should be shown at primetime – even with due warning. But ever since the 1991 Gulf War there has been growing criticism of the degree to which broadcasters are shielding viewers from the true horrors of wars in which their own country is involved. Thus, for example, Martin Bell has argued that

> people have to be left with some sense of what happened, if only through the inclusion of pictures sufficiently powerful at least to hint at the horror of those excluded. To do otherwise is to present war as a relatively cost-free enterprise and an acceptable way of settling differences, a one-sided game that soldiers play in which they are seen shooting but never suffering. The camera shows the outgoing ordnance, but seldom the incoming.

He concluded that

> we have retreated too far, certainly, in British television ... We should flinch less. We should sometimes be willing to shock and

to disturb. We should show the world more nearly as we find it, without the anaesthetic of a good taste censorship.[10]

The way in which such censorship operated during the 2003 invasion of Iraq was all too clearly illustrated in "The True Face of War" (5 June 2003), the third episode of the Channel 4 series *The War We Never Saw*. This showed clearly that there were significant civilian casualties during the American advance on Baghdad, and that these, exactly like those slaughtered on the Basra Road in 1991, were inadequately covered by British broadcasters. A particularly telling moment occurs when Stuart Webb of ITN describes filming a civilian vehicle in which three people had been blown apart and incinerated:

> as I panned along one body I hurried my pan because I realised I couldn't use it anyway, and I stood there for about five minutes just looking for one image to shoot that could be acceptable on British TV, and the only thing I could use was the hand of one of the victims.

This is particularly chilling, as it suggests that British television journalists are tempted to censor the raw material of historical record, because they see little point in filming images which they know cannot be shown.

In the event, Webb's pan, and much other equally horrifying footage, was indeed shown in this exemplary programme. Similarly, on 14 February 2003, the *Guardian* devoted the whole of its *G2* section to a series of appalling images from the first Gulf War all bar one of which had never before appeared in the mainstream British press. But nowhere in these assaults on what John Taylor has aptly described as "the moral sleep and historical amnesia that can exist when such imagery goes unseen or unreproduced", is it ever adequately explained why it was felt that these images could not be shown in Britain.[11] Could such admirable interventions actually be a sad confirmation of Taylor's proposition that: "terrible images and accounts belong to war's peripheral history" as opposed to its contemporaneous representation?[12]

IN OUR NAME

During the 2003 invasion itself, a *Guardian* editorial asked:

> how much should we – the passive viewers, readers and consumers of war – be shielded from or exposed to, the full horrors of what

is going on? Our parliament voted for this. To that extent, if no further, the death and pain is in our name. Many of the weapons which cause the daily carnage in Iraq are loaded in, and despatched from, the middle of the gentle Gloucestershire countryside. Can we reasonably turn our eyes away from what happens when they reach their hot and dusty destination six hours later?[13]

To which one might add: there is all the difference in the world between, on the one hand, choosing to turn one's eyes away from images that one does not want to see, and, on the other, being denied the ability to make that decision by the prior censorship of those images. As Kevin Williams has forcefully put it:

> wars prosecuted by democratic societies are done so in the name of the people. If the public supports a war then it has a responsibility for the consequences. Citizens have rights and responsibilities, and surely one of the responsibilities in wartime is to see – or at least to be provided with the opportunity to see – the price being paid to prosecute the war, whether this is the body of your neighbour's son or innocent civilians killed in the crossfire. Even if people do not want to accept their responsibilities it is difficult to argue that they have a right to be protected from seeing what happens on the battlefield. This would appear to deny a necessary democratic impulse.[14]

Of course, just as those presented with the opportunity to see disturbing images may reject it, so those who choose to look at those images may choose to read them in a variety of ways. To put it bluntly, those viewing horrific pictures do not necessarily read those images as a condemnation of that war. Thus David Morrison's interviewees, even when confronted by imagery of the Amiriya bunker and the Basra Road, were buttressed by their acceptance of the war as both just, and given the perceived intransigence of Saddam Hussein, inevitable. Basically, blame for all the suffering was placed at Saddam Hussein's door, and this fact mediated the impact of the images seen.[15]

The obvious point here is that how people react to such images will depend largely on how they understand the conflict in the first place. But how they understand it will, in turn, have been shaped, although of course not wholly formed, by the media's representation of the conflict. It is frequently suggested today that violent images from war zones may induce "de-sensitisation" or "compassion fatigue", and thus should be censored. However, there is no more evidence that watching violent images "makes" viewers indifferent than that it "makes" them violent, whereas there certainly *is* evidence that large numbers of viewers fail to understand *why* the scenes of violence which they are witnessing are happening in the first place, and are thus left completely bewildered by them.[16] The answer to this problem lies, surely, in more knowledge not less. However, whether television, particularly in the midst of a highly controversial conflict in which this country is deeply involved, can provide such explication, given its well-rehearsed difficulties in dealing with matters of political controversy in the past, remains somewhat doubtful.

IGNORANCE AND SUPERFICIALITY

Let us remind ourselves of Susan Sontag's remark that

> a photograph that brings news of some unsuspected zone of misery cannot make a dent in public opinion unless there is an appropriate context of feeling and attitude ... Photographs cannot create a moral position, but they can reinforce one – and can help build a nascent one.[17]

In other words, even if British television had shown appalling pictures of, say, the consequences of the American bombing of the two Baghdad markets, which massacred at least 76 civilians, it would probably have made little difference to many people's attitude to the event, and to the invasion as a whole, if it had been presented in the context in which the sanitised images were shown, namely one riddled with equivocation and evasion about where the true blame for the atrocity lay. As Sontag concludes: "what determines the possibility of being affected morally by photographs is the existence of a relevant political consciousness".[18] Mainstream news programmes give little succour to such consciousness.

In the end, however, it's hard to avoid the conclusion that, in their attitudes to images of death and injury in military actions undertaken by this country, both the regulators of British broadcasting and large sections of the audience on whose behalf they allegedly regulate do need – to put it bluntly – to grow up and get real. Wars involve bloodshed and slaughter, and those involved in them, even indirectly, have a moral and political responsibility to face this surely obvious fact. Audiences can, of course, choose not to do so, but the broadcast media should not help them to bury their heads in the sand. Furthermore, if people choose to join armed forces then they knowingly put themselves in a position of risk, and, in the modern media-saturated world, they and their relatives simply have to accept the fact that images which they might prefer were kept private may be beamed around the globe: after all, banning them from British television hardly banishes them from the screens of other, less squeamish and complicit, nations. And as for civilians – the reactions of those in the scenes of carnage finally shown in "The True Face of War" made it abundantly clear that they actively *wanted* the inhabitants of the aggressor nations to be made to face the human consequences of their governments' actions. For these reasons, then, it's extremely hard to disagree with Susan Sontag when she argues that:

> No one after a certain age has the right to this kind of innocence, of superficiality, to this degree of ignorance, or amnesia. There now exists a vast repository of images that make it harder to maintain this kind of moral defectiveness. Let the atrocious images haunt us. Even if they are only tokens, and cannot possibly encompass most of the reality to which they refer, they still perform a vital function. The images say: This is what human beings are capable of doing – may volunteer to do, enthusiastically, self-righteously. Don't forget.[19]

NOTES

1. Quoted in John Taylor, *Body Horror: Photojournalism, Catastrophe and War*, Manchester: Manchester University Press, 1998, p. 179.
2. Phillip Knightley, *The First Casualty*, London: Prion, 2000, pp. 494–5.
3. Hugh Gusterson, "Nuclear War, the Gulf War and the Disappearing Body", *Journal of Urban and Cultural Studies*, Vol. 2, No. 1, 1991, p. 51.
4. John Simpson, "Depicting Violence on Television", in Andrea Millwood Hargrave (ed.), *Violence in Factual Television; Annual Review 1993*, Broadcasting Standards Council/John Libbey, 1993, p. 104.
5. BBC, *Producers' Guidelines*, British Broadcasting Corporation, 1996, p. 75.
6. Broadcasting Standards Commission, *Codes of Guidance*, Broadcasting Standards Commission, 1998, p. 31.
7. "What Can You Show?", *Media Guardian*, 31 March 2003, p. 7.
8. Ibid.
9. David Morrison, *Television and the Gulf War*, John Libbey, 1992, pp. 30, 33, 38.

10. Martin Bell, "TV News: How Far Should We Go?", *British Journalism Review*, Vol. 8, No. 1, 1997, p. 15.
11. Taylor, *Body Horror*, p. 6.
12. Ibid., p. 183.
13. "Hold Our Tongues", *Guardian*, 28 March 2003.
14. Kevin Williams, "Something More Important Than Truth: Ethical Issues in War Reporting", in A. Belsey and R. Chadwick (eds), *Ethical Issues in Journalism and the Media*, London: Routledge, 1992, p. 161.
15. Morrison, *Television and the Gulf War*, p. 38.
16. See in particular Greg Philo et al., "The Israeli-Palestinian Conflict: TV News and Public Understanding", in D. Thussu and D. Freedman (eds), *War and the Media*, London: Sage, 2003, pp. 133–48.
17. Susan Sontag, *On Photography*, New York: Farrar, Straus and Giroux, 1973, p. 17.
18. Ibid., p. 19.
19. Susan Sontag, *Regarding the Pain of Others*, New York: Farrar, Straus and Giroux, 2003, p. 102.

19
Normalising Godfatherly Aggression

Edward Herman

It is fascinating to see how effectively the US propaganda system has normalised and even put a very good face on its government's straightforward aggression against – and conquest and colonial occupation of – a small, distant country. It is especially remarkable that this has happened across the board, through all major media venues, despite the fact that the media are not directly owned and controlled by the government. All of them, however, are part of a national establishment that shares an ideology and worldview, and their integration into that establishment has been increased by the steady centralisation and intensified commercialisation of the media, their control by a narrowing elite, and their heavy reliance on the government as a news source. The media have also been kept in line by the increasingly powerful right-wing contingent of media owners, editors and pundits. There is a right-wing echo chamber that pushes for imperial violence, especially when organised by a right-wing executive, and assails media deviants for lack of patriotic ardour. (It can also punish a supposed "liberal" executive, hated by the right wing, like Clinton, for the Lewinsky caper, but protect George Bush from any serious media bother for his failure to prevent 9/11 despite inside and outside warnings, for his inside trading of Harken stock, and for his and his colleagues' Enron-energy policy conflicts of interest.)

Normalisation of government policy, no matter how vicious and contrary to the public interest that policy may be, follows easily from the acceptance and internalisation of patriotic premises and the view that the media are part of a team fighting the good fight. From the 1991 Gulf War case of CNN's top reporter Christiane Amanpour marrying top State Department public relations officer James Rubin in the midst of that conflict, without any media mention of possible conflict of interest, to Judy Woodruff's and Wolf Blitzer's comradely "we" in talking with – and never asking challenging questions of – their official counterparts, the team spirit has dominated not only CNN but all the US networks. Network sourcing of the news on the

Iraq crisis has been overwhelmingly through present and former government officials (76 per cent in a FAIR study). The mainstream print media have not been quite as atrocious, but they have been loyal members of the team as well. The result has been the dominance of "press release journalism", a high media gullibility quotient and easy management by government officials, and the attrition or death of criticism and investigative reporting that challenges the official lines.

In the case of the 2003 Iraq invasion and conquest, the first aim of official propaganda was to sell it to the public. This was accomplished by the three gambits: demonisation, claims regarding the demon's possession of weapons that threaten US national security, and the failed diplomacy and inspections gambit. The media co-operated beautifully in pushing these propaganda themes. Saddam was demonised quite effectively – not a difficult task -but the media also accomplished the more difficult task of deflecting attention from the earlier alliance with and support of the demon. This was in line with Big Brother's propaganda techniques as described in Orwell's *Nineteen Eighty-Four*, where "any past or future agreement with him [the demonised enemy] was impossible. The Party said that Oceania had never been in alliance with Eurasia. He, Winston Smith, knew that Oceania had been in alliance with Eurasia so short a time as four years ago." The mainstream media have not said that an agreement between the United States and Saddam is impossible, they simply refuse to discuss and reflect on the one that existed for an extended time period. The picture of Donald Rumsfeld shaking hands with Saddam Hussein back in December 1983 as he helped cement the alliance with the demon was not shown on the TV networks.

The second propaganda gambit was to focus intently on Saddam's alleged continued possession of weapons of mass destruction (WMD) and their threat to US national security. The media pushed this theme by following the government's party line that this was a really important issue and that we were dealing with a real threat, and by providing saturation coverage of government charges on these matters. But as with the first gambit, important Orwellian complements were also applied: namely, suppressing inconvenient evidence, avoiding experts who would challenge the party line, failing to call attention to and criticise the shifting claims and stream of lies, and refusing to discuss and analyse either the supposed threat to US national security or the possible hidden agenda rationalised by the WMD-threat charge.

On Iraq's WMD, Scott Ritter, the former top weapons inspector, claimed that when he left in 1998, 90–95 per cent of Iraq's chemical and biological weapons had been destroyed and any remaining anthrax or sarin would be useless sludge. It was recently disclosed that the number one Iraqi expatriate, Hussein Kamel, whose testimony had been repeatedly cited by US officials, had told his interrogators in 1995 that Saddam Hussein had actually destroyed his chemical and biological weapons and had none left, a point not made public until March 2003.[1] The *New York Times* handled these matters by never allowing Ritter any opinion space and not reporting the *Newsweek* disclosure of Hussein Kamel's 1995 claim. It also never featured the fact that Saddam had not used his chemical and biological arsenal during the first Gulf War, but had only employed such weapons when supported by the United States during the war with Iran; or that CIA head George Tenet had told Congress that Saddam was unlikely to use them against the United States unless in defence when under attack.

Despite many thousands of lines on the Iraq controversy, the *New York Times* never provided a single article analysing the shifting Bush claims and enumerating the serial lies, whose exposure was a commonplace in the foreign media and internet sources.[2] The pattern of suppressions, plus massive conduiting of administration claims, plus refusal to analyse or allow contesting analyses, permitted a nonexistent threat to be made into a real one. An important measure of the effectiveness of fear-mongering and disinformation in making the public ready for aggression is the fact that whereas 3 per cent of Americans believed that Saddam Hussein had had something to do with 9/11 immediately after the event, 45 per cent believed this by the time of the invasion. This was the disinforming result of the coordinated efforts of the war-makers and media.

After an internal debate the Bush administration had agreed to seek UN Security Council approval of its attack on Iraq, instead of just attacking without such sanction. It then waged an intense campaign of propaganda, bribery and threats to get other members of the Security Council to approve its aggression. It argued that inspections had failed and that an attack or threat of attack was needed to get the demon to "disarm". All intelligent and honest observers understood that the inspections were a charade as far as the Bush administration was concerned, and that "disarmament" was a cover for an intent not only to displace Saddam Hussein but to occupy and control Iraq. This last was even acknowledged when the United States made clear that Saddam's exit wouldn't suffice – there must be a military occupation of Iraq.

The media collaborated fully in these various charades. They accepted that the Bush administration was engaging in "diplomacy", when it was only buying and coercing other governments to sanction its plan to commit aggression. With patriotic ardour they framed the issue as one of support for Bush versus disloyalty, helping produce a small-scale demonisation of the French for failure to go along. They portrayed this campaign to bully the UN into approving an invasion and occupation of Iraq as a test of UN "relevance", not a threat to its independence, integrity, and ability to prevent the "scourge of war" and outright aggression. They failed to discuss openly the fact that Bush intended regime change and was using inspections as a pretext, and was actively subverting the inspections by denigration, false charges, and providing information that Hans Blix called "garbage".

Other important requirements of a propaganda system trying to put a good face on aggression are to pretend that what its leadership is doing is only a legitimate response to a threat; that it has a right to engage in such intervention by violence, and that international law has no bearing on the case. This is done in large part by playing dumb and relying on the demonisation and inflated threat to transform an unprovoked attack into self-defence and a response of good to evil. You don't aggress if you are only defending yourself and serving freedom, and the media have never used the word aggression to describe the US attack on Iraq, just as they never did when the United States invaded Vietnam (by invitation of a client government that it imposed, and whose leadership it changed at pleasure).

But international law is clear and the UN Charter is explicit that war is an unacceptable means of settling international disputes, and the 1945 Nuremberg War Crimes Tribunal stated clearly that "to initiate a war of aggression is the supreme international crime". Nuremberg judge Robert Jackson also stated that this greatest of war crimes is criminal when engaged in by anybody, not just the Germans. The pathetic front man for the great powers, Kofi Annan, was quoted a few days before the US attack as saying plaintively that such an attack would be in violation of the UN Charter! But Annan did not propose any action to prevent this major violation, nor did he resign in protest at this trampling on UN Charter fundamentals, and no other country or major institution of the "international community" called for a serious response to open aggression.

The media largely steered clear of discussing international law and the UN Charter – it is inconvenient and by patriotic assumption they make it inapplicable to the good and benevolent United States, whose leaders were simply protecting US national security and bringing liberty to the Iraqis. On the rare occasions when the media allowed international law to be addressed they chose their sources carefully. The *New York Times* gave byline space to international law experts Anne-Marie Slaughter and Gary Bass to apologise for US policy and assail the dilatory UN, and just as it steered clear of Ritter, Hans von Sponeck and Denis Halliday on Iraq WMD and sanctions, so it ignored critical international law experts Francis Boyle, Richard Falk, Michael Ratner and Burt Weston. From 1 January 2002 to 24 April 2003, Slaughter, Bass and Yale Law School super-apologist Ruth Wedgwood together had 13 bylined columns in the *New York Times*, *Wall Street Journal*, *Washington Post*, *Los Angeles Times* and *Time* magazine, whereas the four dissident experts had a grand total of one column. The media clearly choose their experts on the basis of conformity to the party line.

Slaughter's contribution in the *New York Times*, entitled "Good Reasons for Going Around the UN" (18 March 2003), describes the Bush course of action as "illegal but legitimate". She cites the independent International Commission on Kosovo as saying that while the invasion is "formally illegal" it was "legitimate in the eyes of the international community". By "international community" Slaughter and her favoured commission obviously don't mean the people of the world, and they don't mean a majority of UN or Security Council members. They are referring to a mystical group that would include the International Commission on Kosovo and unknown and unspecified others who agree with the US position. Slaughter then says that the invasion would be legitimate in retrospect if "irrefutable evidence" is found that Saddam possessed WMD, or if the Iraqis "welcome their coming". She doesn't explain how "welcoming" could be measured, although I suspect that Slaughter was satisfied with the US-organised pulling down of Saddam's statue and a street full of cheering Iraqis holding US flags.

On the weapons, what if they were not found? Given that that was the issue and basis of "formal" illegality, wouldn't there be retrospective real illegality and shouldn't the perpetrators be tried for war crimes? Slaughter doesn't consider these possibilities. Even if WMD are found, if the inspections process had been continued it is possible that they could have been removed without a devastating war. Again,

Slaughter doesn't consider this. Further on in her article, she argues that UN constraints "cannot be a straitjacket, preventing nations from defending themselves or pursuing what they perceive to be their vital national security interests". The implication that this applies to the US attack on Iraq is merely taken for granted, and if applicable here would certainly apply to Nazi Germany's attack on Poland in 1939. We have here crude and silly apologetics for aggression.

With the approach to war and war itself, the media spent a great deal of effort and space describing the mobilisation process, the plans, the debates over strategies, and the course of the war as seen by Rumsfeld and company and the embedded journalists. As in all recent US military attacks on Third World countries, the media pretended that this was a "war" as opposed to a straightforward attack by a distant superpower on a virtually defenceless target state – an unlevel playing field par excellence, and a massacre of enemy forces that had been disarmed, bombed, spied upon under the guise of inspections, and starved for the prior dozen years. These pretences were essential to allowing the defeat of Iraq to be a military marvel and matter of pride, rather than a source of embarrassment and shame at beating up yet another hapless and deliberately crippled victim.

As in all recent US attacks, the media followed the government's lead in steering clear of details on civilian casualties. The official position was that our high-tech precision weapons were civilian friendly and that we were going to great pains to avoid civilian sites. This became the media mantra, and the media also proceeded to steer clear of looking at the characteristics of the weapons used or the actual effects on civilians. Al Jazeera's practice of showing pictures of civilians injured and killed was considered improper by US officials and the US media. One important reason for this is that it would deflate the claims of a civilian-friendly war by bringing home an important but carefully evaded reality. The media did an outstanding job of evading this reality. They had devoted endless news reports, commentaries, and pictures to the several thousand victims of 9/11, but the much larger number of dead and seriously injured Iraqis were almost entirely invisible in the US media and to the US public. As NBC reporter Ashleigh Banfield noted recently, it was a "bloodless war" in which "you didn't see what happened when the mortars landed. A puff of smoke is not what a mortar looks like when it explodes, believe me."[3]

With the victory and occupation, the media continued to avoid the hospitals and the general condition of a citizenry suffering from a water crisis, food shortages, a breakdown of public services, and a medical care crisis, exacerbated by belatedly exploding ordnance and land mines and the looting of hospitals as well as homes, stores and public facilities. The media focus was on signs of celebration of the "liberated" Iraqis. Most notable was the coverage of the pulling down of the statue of Saddam Hussein in Baghdad's Firdos Square, featured throughout the media. It is now well established that this was organised by the US military, whose machinery actually pulled the statue down, and that only a tiny crowd was participating, comprised mainly of recently imported Chalabi supporters. The media uniformly served as agents of disinformation in this contrived celebration, by failing to show a picture of the entire Square, which was surrounded by US tanks and empty of Iraqi celebrants, and by failing to discuss the organisers and participants.

What are the principles and gambits required to deal with a post-aggression occupation? The first principle is to take it as given that the aggressor has the right to rule. The media have done this across the board, reading from the successful victory some kind of vindication of aggression, as if the French and global majority in opposition questioned the ability of the United States to defeat a tiny, disarmed victim. The assumed right to rule is asserted regularly: "The coalition alone retains absolute authority within Iraq," according to Lt General David McKiernan, the US ground forces commander, and that is reported and not debated in the media, who find this easy given their ready acceptance of the right of aggression (by their country).

During and immediately after the 2003 invasion US mobile investigative teams visited 90 of the top 150 most-promising WMD sites identified by US intelligence, but none of these provided a smoking gun. The media have expressed no surprise and little interest that no WMD have yet been uncovered, despite the occupation and search, and despite the fact that the fearsome presence of WMD was the rationale for invasion. They have reported the Bush refusal to allow the UN inspectors to return to do the job, and insistence that only US or US-approved personnel do the search, but the media don't see a conflict of interest here or express any suspicion that this might facilitate the planting of weapons to meet the demand. You may be sure that they will not provide anything like former CIA analysts Ray McGovern's and David McMichael's detailed analysis of the numerous occasions on which US officials have forged and planted evidence in the past.[4]

Not finding any hard evidence, US officials have turned to claims of Iraqi scientists who allegedly worked on Saddam's WMD and are now prepared to tell the "truth". This is a plausible fallback position, as scientists can easily be found who will trade off saying what US officials want said for money, rights to travel and settle abroad, and exoneration from penalties for punishable actions in the past. This has been a long-standing way of getting official claims "confirmed" and publicised (the most famous case dealing with Soviet diplomat Arkady Shevchenko was written up by Edward Epstein under the title "The Spy Who Came in To Be Sold", *New Republic*, 15–22 July 1985). The media have always co-operated and today as in the past they never suggest that the witnesses – now Iraqi scientists – are extremely vulnerable to pressure, and that their "evidence" cannot to be taken seriously without independent support.

The *New York Times*, which has regularly fallen for propaganda lies in the past (see its own self-serving confession in its editorial with the revealing title "The Lie That Wasn't Shot Down", 18 January 1988), has set a new standard for gullible propaganda service with Judith Miller's front page article "Illicit Arms Kept Till Eve of War, an Iraqi Scientist Is Said to Assert" (21 April 2003). Miller didn't even talk with the scientist, but merely passed along statements he allegedly made to US government agents. And he says everything the government would like him to say: that Saddam Hussein had chemical weapons destroyed just before the war (no explanation by him or discussion by Miller of why they didn't choose to use the weapons); some had been sent off to Syria in the mid-1990s; and "more recently Iraq was cooperating with al-Qaeda". Miller doesn't discuss the credibility problem – the possible gain to some Iraqis from saying what the government wants said, or the record of fabrications by the Bush administration (and its predecessors). This is propaganda that is almost surely disinformation, but the *New York Times* gives it front page space, in its great tradition of pushing convenient lies. (It often doesn't shoot them down even with a time lag – the paper has never acknowledged that its pushing the Bulgarian-KGB link to the shooting of Pope John II in 1981 was a lie, and it even suppressed the 1991 revelation by CIA official Melvin Goodman that the CIA knew it was a lie because they had penetrated the Bulgarian secret services.)

With the WMD not found after a month-long search, and any that might appear belatedly and under pressure – and those claimed by confessing scientists – possibly not convincing to a suspicious world, the "coalition" has put ever-increasing stress on the aim of giving the Iraqis their freedom. The media have supported this new stress by featuring evidence that Saddam Hussein was a brutal ruler and by giving prominence to Bush administration claims and promises regarding a democratic Iraqi future. Equally important has been the media failure to give context and ask questions: Didn't the US and Britain support Saddam for many years; and if so, doesn't this suggest that Iraqi liberty is unlikely to be a driving motive? Why not liberty for Saudis, Kuwaitis and Palestinians? Is concern for Iraqis welfare compatible with having smashed its infrastructure, killed and wounded many thousands, and allowed its great cultural heritage to be destroyed? Does the US record in other places where it has intervened heavily, such as Guatemala, Vietnam, Indonesia, Nicaragua and Afghanistan, suggest that it will bring liberty and contribute to nation-building? Are its contracts and threats to freeze out countries like France and Germany from Iraq operations compatible with the free choice of Iraqis? Are its plans as spelled out in government documents and earlier statements of objectives and its recent suggested intention to maintain military bases in Iraq compatible with Iraqi freedom?

A focus on such questions is incompatible with the normalisation of aggression and occupation, and the propaganda system skirts past them. It postulates the right of the United States to aggress, occupy, decide who are good and bad Iraqis, organise the reconstruction – first and foremost of the oil industry – and decide at least for now on Iraq's direction, very possibly toward privatisation of the oil industry and integration into the global market as a US client state. Whether the Bush administration can get away with this is not certain, but it will try and its media will continue to do their best to put this aggression-occupation bringing "liberty" to the Iraqis in a good light.

NOTES

1. John Barry, "The Defector's Secret", *Newsweek*, 3 March 2003.
2. Raymond Whitaker, "Revealed How the Road to War Was Paved With Lies", *Independent*, 27 April 2003; Carla Binion, "Bush Lies and Manipulates Public and Congress", *Online Journal*, 25 April 2003 – Binion gives detailed references to sources on official lies.
3. Andrew Grossman, "Banfield Lashes Out at Own Network", 28 April 2003, <http://story.news.yahoo.com/news?tmpl=story&u=/nm/20030428/tv_nm/television_banfield_dc>.
4. "Ex-CIA Analysts on the Pretext for War", <http://www.counterpunch.org.vips04262003.htm>.

20
Little Ali and Other Rescued Children

Patricia Holland

INNOCENT CHILDREN

On 2 April 1995, Nick Cohen reported in the *Independent on Sunday* that seven-year-old Irma Hadzimuratovic had died in Great Ormond Street Children's Hospital, after spending two years paralysed from the neck down and fed intravenously. The brief news item was a media trace of a war that had faded from the headlines. In August 1993 Irma's name had dominated the British press when she was injured in a Serb mortar attack on a market in Sarajevo, capital of Bosnia and centre of a ferocious civil war. Her picture, showing her bruised and damaged face and broken body, had outraged the public. "Demands for action were so great that the Government was forced to fly her and 20 other injured children to Britain." In fact her doctors had failed to get her included in the UN quota for evacuation, so had turned to the media to create the public furore that saved her life. (We do not learn the fate of the other 20 children. In fact refugees from the Balkans had rapidly shifted out of one context of news reporting – children rescued from war zones – and into another with a far less sympathetic tone – immigration and asylum seekers.)

In 1993 Irma's plight had symbolised that of all innocent victims who are the horrific consequence of war. She represented every victim, but she was also an individual and her need was tangible. Ten years later, in the war on Iraq, it was Ali Ismaeel Abbas, a twelve-year-old who lost both arms in a US attack, who played this double role. He became the abstract symbol who was living out a painful reality. He was the representative of all injured children, but at the same time he was a unique child whose needs were overwhelming. Little Irma was removed from the Balkans, goodwill messages relayed by press and television echoing around her. Ali, too was taken out of his overstretched, under-resourced hospital in Baghdad after intense media coverage of his case. He was conveyed to Kuwait, by a "convoy

185

led by a US navy doctor" who "ruffled Ali's hair" and said "I'm here to help" (*Mirror*, 16 April 2003). Irma's next two years were spent in obscurity, pain and suffering; at her death the staff at Great Ormond Street paid tribute to her courage and forbearance. Ali has been made many promises, but his future is not yet known.

Amongst the emotions which the reporting of a war seeks to arouse, the sequence of outrage/pity/empathy/relief which can be called up by the story of a rescued child, is clear cut and dignified. Such humanitarian feelings are free from the ambivalence and guilt which attach to the fiercer emotions such as anger, disgust, horror, aggression, hatred, patriotism, triumphalism which are routinely marshalled by war coverage. The story of a rescued child is a powerful one. The pictures help to sell papers and they boost donations to charitable agencies.

While most critiques of war reporting rightly focus on factual accuracy, and on absences and distortion, it is also important to consider these softer aspects of news which pose a different set of questions. What about the tone, the appeal, the cultural placing of these reports which *do* make the headlines – particularly the human interest stories? How are they constructed? How does their emotional content relate to judgements about the war? What are the uses to which such stories are put?

Two aspects are important here: simplification and the appeal to emotion. In the increasingly broad spectrum of information and communication, one role of the popular press is to *simplify* news stories, cutting through the cacophony of voices and seeking to unify the response of a mass audience by highlighting, shaping and going for the gut. We can note the structuring of narrative themes in the coverage of an event and the construction of partly mythical "characters" who are selected out from the mass and given a role to play in stories that develop day by day like the plot of a drama. Characters are presented in ways which will evoke sympathy, hatred or pity, whichever is appropriate, and tension is built as the story develops. (*Will* campaigners succeed in getting Ali/Irma/another desperate child airlifted out? Buy tomorrow's paper.) Just as in a fictional drama, these narrative structures create "positions" which may be occupied by many different real life individuals.

The starkness and clarity created by such simplifying practices has a power that is difficult for the rest of the media to ignore – despite argument, research and in-depth journalism. The broadsheets and much of the coverage on radio and television – to say nothing of innumerable websites and email circulars – can be scoured for greater complexity and multiple perspectives, but the underlying drama developed in the tabloid headlines echoes back and forth across the entire news output. It carries not only the structure of a narrative, but a sense of what will be recognised as *properly directed* sympathy, *properly directed* hatred, *properly directed* support.

Stories about damaged children are of great importance to the narratives of war, and images of severely injured infants and toddlers in Iraq were used by all the media to point to humanitarian values few could dispute. "What everyone can agree on is that the children of Iraq are in no way to blame. It is not their war, yet many of them have become victims," wrote the *Mirror* (9 April 2003). At one level the story is irresistible. A child is horrifically injured, his picture catches the imagination of the world. Public outrage causes the great and powerful to intervene on his behalf, and he is rescued.

However, in postmodern wars, which involve communities as much as armies, and where civilians are more at risk than soldiers, it has become difficult to separate those who are implicated from those who are not, and the myth of the eternal innocence of childhood is less easy to sustain. Contemporary images of childhood include children armed to the teeth as soldiers in Uganda, Sierra Leone and other parts of the warring world. They include children throwing stones, children with slingshots and even a baby dressed as a suicide bomber. Children may well be potential aggressors, exploited by adults, or using their own childhood as a protection. *Guardian* correspondent Suzanne Goldenberg writes of Iraqi children who go up to American soldiers and smile while swearing at them in Arabic – highly amused that the Americans think they are being friendly (25 April 2003).

In the simplified narrative with instant appeal, it is easier to deal with childhood when children are helpless and totally unable to fend for themselves. Most of the British press worked hard to create an image of children outside the conflict and to protect them from guilt by association. Before the story of Ali broke, the pro-war *Sun* was running a fund-raising campaign, "Give a quid for an Iraqi kid" (the money was eventually passed to Save the Children) and, on the day when the captured American soldiers were "paraded" on Iraqi television, the *Mirror* used a picture of a child with horrific burns, "Still anti-war? Yes, bloody right we are" (24 March 2003). When children are visibly injured, sympathy can be unrestrained, and the simplicity of the story can be preserved. In a perverse way a picture of an injured child is a reassuring image and difficult questions can be pushed aside by the imperative to help. When children are in desperate straits the way is open for a familiar drama, the story of child rescue.

But the work of simplification is never totally straightforward. Even as the soap opera plot develops, the images that provide so much of its emotional content pose challenging questions – about politics, about childhood and about the role of the imagery itself – which provide a disturbing undertow to the simple narrative. They clearly demand that something should be done: but they open up questions of what can be done and who should do it. Their appeal is to general sympathy for the universal value of childhood: but, especially in times of war, they pose questions about specific national, cultural and ethnic difference. If children are outside politics, who is responsible for the children of the enemy? After all, for a combatant, children too are sometimes targets – perhaps not intentional, perhaps regrettable, but targets none the less.

Finally the photographs pose questions about the status of the image itself, for pictures are notoriously slippery and open to multiple interpretations. As Thomas Sutcliffe pointed out in a thoughtful article in the *Guardian*, "images that would once have been the stock in trade of enemy propagandists – dead or injured children, shattered buildings, wailing mothers – are now firmly part of the repertoire of ordinary reporting" (14 April 2003). What sort of pleasure do such pictures give in a media climate with an undeniable taste for shocking imagery? The pictures of Ali served many purposes; they were fund raisers, a way of boosting sales, an argument sometimes for the legitimacy of the war, sometimes against it – in particular a weapon in the battle between the pro-war *Sun* and the anti-war *Mirror* – as well as the centre of a humanitarian story about a real child.

ALI

Reviewing the photographs of the 2003 war, Nicci Gerrard writes of the single image as an icon which "we select from the melee of events … we recollect in pictures". And the image of the razed body, stumps for arms and "remarkably untouched face" of Ali Ismaeel Abbas – taken in Al-Kindi hospital in Baghdad by the Reuters photographer Faleh Kheiber – became such an icon. The twelve-year-old had lost both arms and suffered 60 per cent burns to his torso in a US missile attack which killed his mother, who was seven months pregnant, his father, his brother and six other relatives. He was "the bereft innocent who has captured the imagination of the world" and "the human face of the price that is paid in a 'just war'" (*Observer Review*, 13 April).

In the photograph Ali is lying against a pink patterned cushion, a crude metal hoop with peeling white paint keeps the covers away from his body which is dreadfully scarred and smeared with cream. His mouth is stretched in pain, his eyes tearful, his bandaged head supported by hands of a woman (identified as his aunt) – although all that is visible in the picture is part of a hand and a red patterned top. (Paul Vallely pointed out that his expression could be interpreted as a grimace of pain or an uncomprehending stare, depending on which caption-writer you encountered (*Independent*, 12 April).) Most shocking are the stumps swathed in bandages which are all that remain of his arms. On his right, half of an upper arm projects awkwardly away from his body, on his left there is a mere lump. "It is a miracle that his lovely face was unscathed," wrote Anton Antonowicz of the *Mirror* – the paper that made greatest use of Ali's image (11 April). The poignant visibility of his injuries together with his facial beauty, often commented on, makes Ali a good candidate for iconic status, in comparison with Zahraa, aged four, and Abdullah aged eight, whose faces are mutilated and spoiled (*Mirror*, 15 April). To a western viewer the patterns against which he rests suggest an Iraqi orientalism and we miss the clean white surfaces which we would expect to signify a medical photograph. It was "a historic image that made the world weep" (*Mirror*, 9 April); "the image that refuses to leave the retina no matter how many times you blink" (*Evening Standard*).

But, even as it lifts a moment from "the melee of events", a picture of this sort gathers a new penumbra of meanings. Although this single photograph was selected out and reproduced across the tabloid and broadsheet press, it only fully makes sense within the context of the narrative within which it is placed, in its flow, its totality, the attitudes that hover around it, and the uses to which it is put. Every single picture has shadows behind it of many other pictures. In this case we are reminded of those other images of maimed and damaged children circulated during wars and disasters, Irma Hadzimuratovic amongst them. Many commentators mentioned Nick Ut's picture of a screaming child running towards the camera, her body scarred by napalm in Vietnam 1972. Half-remembered pictures have already taught us how to interpret and how to react as new images are created within the genre.

The reports which accompanied the pictures repeated Ali's appeal "Can you help me get my arms back? Do you think the doctors can get me another pair of hands? If I don't get a pair of hands I will commit suicide" (*Reuters*, 6 April, taken up by most of the press). The structure of an appeal was established from the first. This was a classic appeal from child to adult; from the suffering world to the rich, confident, capable, technologised world, long established in the imagery of charities and aid agencies as well as in the press. And the reaction was immediate. "My wife's grief was devastating and she wept for over an hour," wrote one reader to the *Mirror* (11 April). In parliament an Early Day Motion congratulated the *Mirror* for publishing the picture and called on the government to treat Ali, his family and others like him "in a financially generous fashion" (9 April).

His cause was rapidly taken up by charities and newspapers, many of them claiming credit for bringing his plight in front of the public. A lawyer raised the case with the Dorset Orthopaedic Centre "after seeing his picture in the *Daily Telegraph*" (9 April); someone from Hamburg tried to contact him through the *Independent* (12 April). The *Mirror* told its readers it had been swamped with calls. The paper launched an appeal together with UNICEF and one reader immediately sent £250 (April). Three other newspapers started appeals; a Maharani offered to pay his medical fees; a firm which manufactures prosthetic limbs said it would provide them half price; the shadow international development secretary, Caroline Spelman, opened Ali's Fund in aid of children injured in the conflict; the Limbless Association set up a fund. The Association originally said it would to bring him to its Roehampton centre, and eventually paid for his care in Kuwait. Donations, which had been slow up till that point, began to flow in.

That first photograph was rapidly followed by others. Freelancers, news agencies, staff photographers from around the world made sure that his plight remained in the public eye. On 10 April he was moved from Al-Kindi when that hospital was devastated by looters, to Saddam General in a poor suburb of Baghdad. Journalists visited him there, talked to him, promised help and touched him, as if to make a tangible link between the real-life boy and their readers. "I tell him I'll try to help and stroke his face," wrote Anton Antonowicz of the *Mirror* (11 April).

The doctors pointed out the danger of septicaemia because of the lack of basic hygiene. One is reported as saying "it would be better if poor Ali died" (*Sunday Telegraph*, 13 April), but, the *Mirror* front-paged a letter from nurse Fatin Sharhah. "Dear Mr Prime Minister and Mr President," it said, "many journalists have visited Ali and taken his picture but he is still here ... He will die if he stays ... You have all this technology to bomb us, to make the missile that burned Ali's house. But you cannot spare one aircraft for one day to save a life?" (14 April).

The bad publicity and political pressure apparently did the trick. "Tony Blair ordered all the stops to be pulled out," reported the *Mirror*. This was to be a happy ending story – at least in the short term – and the press could claim a prominent role. "The Pentagon came under pressure from Downing Street ... and ... the breakthrough followed a day of frenzied negotiations between US military officials, Iraqi doctors, Ali's family and journalists" (15 April). The double-page spread showed Ali stretchered out of the hospital and included portraits (from the family album) of his dead mother, father and brother. In fact, as Esther Addley later revealed in the *Guardian*, despite the self-congratulatory tone, British journalists and fund raisers had played no role at all in the rescue, which had been under-written by a wealthy benefactor from Perth and negotiated and organised by an Australian journalist, Peter Wilson. In his view "the British press were just disgraceful", crowding into Ali's room, putting the sterile environment at risk and behaving as if they owned him (1 August).

Ali was installed at Ibn Sina hospital in Kuwait and the press continued to report and to photograph his remarkable progress. He gets to see new limbs; there's a setback as he "fights bug"; he is given a successful skin graft; he orders a kebab for dinner; Manchester United stars sign a T-shirt for him, he is comforted by relatives, and talks to the *Metro* reporter on a mobile phone – all against a new, high-tech background of tubes, drips, measuring equipment and doctors in gowns and masks. Finally he walks. "A gentle smile replaces the look of anguish that moved *Mirror* readers to raise an incredible £350,000 for our Ali appeal to help Iraqi children" (7 June).

"This gives me hope for my future," Ali is reported as saying, adding that if people knew his story, it might help others. "I saw how important children are to the world." "People should protect children" (*Metro*, 7 May).

THE REAL STORY?

Reviewing Ali's story, the *Sun* drew a clear analogy with the state of Iraq itself, disabled for its own good, to be built up again with high-tech prosthetics and kindly western help.

> Can war be right, we asked ourselves, if such things are happening in our name. Today Ali is on the mend. His shattered life will be slowly rebuilt. He cannot wait to be fitted with new limbs. The allied leaders, especially Tony Blair, always said Iraq could not be freed without civilian casualties. It is terrible that Ali had to suffer. But in his smile there is hope for a new beginning. (7 June)

With its powerful anti-war stance, the *Mirror* had used Ali's story for a different purpose. "Ali's suffering was the symbol of the pain of the Iraqi people, innocent victims of a cruel dictator and a cruel war" (7 June). Its correspondents, Anton Antonowicz and Stephen Martin had taken the opportunity to give deeper insights into occupied Baghdad. We learn that the reason Ali ended up in a Baghdad slum was that here he had the protection of the mosque. "The local mullah organised his own militiamen to defend the hospital ... the chaos is such that aid agencies cannot operate" (12 April). And when he was finally moved to Kuwait, "permission ... had to be given not just by US and Kuwaiti officials but by the Muslim leaders who now run the slums of Saddam City following the fall of the Iraqi regime" (16 April). Chief Surgeon Mowafak Gabrielle was not prepared to speak to the script, "there are hundreds of Ali's here", he said, "all kinds of cases, amputations, internal injuries, burns ... I've had 5 hours' sleep in the last 72 hrs ... This is what war does." The *Mirror*'s leader pointed out that British medics were at the time being ordered home from Basra. The "world, so shocked by the terrible ordeal of one young boy, must not turn their back on the thousands like him" (11 April).

For John Pilger Ali's story was an unacceptable distraction from the real story. Tony Blair pledging "to do everything to help" "must be the ultimate insult to the memory of all the children in Iraq who have died violently in Blair's war and in the embargo Blair enthusiastically endorsed". He pointed out that as Ali was flown to Kuwait, the Americans were preventing Save the Children from sending a plane with medical supplies to northern Iraq, where 40,000 are desperate" (*Independent on Sunday*, 20 April).

However, Samia Nakhoul, Bureau Head in Reuters' Baghdad office, has said that the Ali story was one of the most important she had covered, as it drew attention to the plight of Iraqi children. She had heard of Ali, and it had taken a couple of days to track him down before she and photographer, Faleh Kheiber, went to see him in Al-Kindi hospital. Things felt very different on the ground in Baghdad. There were problems finding food and water; journalists were hassled by the Iraqi authorities, who threatened to confiscate their equipment – especially their essential satellite phones; some journalists had been expelled.[1] Samia Nakhoul and Faleh Kheiber were themselves injured when a US tank shelled the Palestine Hotel in Baghdad where the foreign journalists were based, killing two of their Reuters colleagues. And certainly, in the British press, although Ali was highlighted, other children were constantly present.

EXPLOITATION?

Ali's story neatly encapsulated the relationship between the west and the nation it was attacking – either by pushing aside the fact that "we" are complicit in the attack, or enabling us to accept that, as the *Sun* had argued, this was a way of assuaging guilt and even justifying the action. The accepted relations between adults and children are easily transferred into relations between the paternal west and a childish nation. In a familiar narrative it is assumed that the west has the power and the duty to console and to offer aid. It is one small step to assume that it has the right to punish as well.

John Pilger argues convincingly that "the saving of Ali substitutes a media spectacle of charity for our right to knowledge of the extent of the crime committed against the young in our name". But that's not all there is to it. In his book *States of Denial*, sociologist Stanley Cohen explores the ways in which populations may learn about atrocities and suffering. Invariably understanding is partial, partisanship is balanced against factual information, readers need to protect themselves against too much horror, denial and a refusal to comprehend must be recognised as part of the social response.[2] The images and simplifying practices I have been discussing make a contemplation of war possible by those distant from the events themselves. The story allowed readers to feel that they had some purchase on events which are otherwise out of their control. In some ways this may be seen as negative – enabling us to tolerate the intolerable; in other ways it may enable readers to face some difficult questions. "We could not stop the war but the least we can do is to help those our country has bombed and humiliated," wrote *Mirror* reader Shakoor Ahmed of Leeds (11 April). At least, as I have argued, it has provided less obvious ways of raising questions which might otherwise not be asked.

Ali's image may have been exploited, but there is no doubt that he benefited from the media intervention, and the aid agencies got a boost, too. Save the Children, who have long struggled to keep a balance between images which are realistic and respectful, and the need to raise funds, say that donations to their fund had been low until the story of Ali broke.[3] But it was Ali himself who was able to encapsulate what was happening to him in a way that points to the limits of a view which sees children as merely passive: "I feel the whole world is feeling my feelings. I feel I am living a challenge I have to go through" (*Metro*, 7 June).

NOTES

1. Samia Nakhoul speaking at a meeting organised by *The Media Society*, 10 June 2003, with additional information from Reuters photographer, Goran Tomasevic.
2. Stanley Cohen, *States of Denial: Knowing About Atrocities and Suffering*, Cambridge: Polity, 2001.
3. Save the Children, *Focus on Images*, London, 1991/98.

21
Watchdogs or Lapdogs?
Media, Politics and Regulation:
The US Experience

Granville Williams

"If Dwight Eisenhower were alive today he'd be warning about the dangers of the military-industry-*media* complex."

Reed Hundt, Chair, Federal Communications
Commission (FCC), 1993–97

The Pentagon Papers and Watergate controversies during the Vietnam War provide revealing insights into the political pressures on the media in times of war and crisis.

The Pentagon Papers were produced by order of the Secretary of Defense, Robert McNamara, as an internal study to see how the Vietnam War developed, but the 47 volumes revealed how deceitful successive governments were about their involvement in Indochina since the Second World War, and in the conduct of the Vietnam War. Daniel Ellsberg worked on the Pentagon Papers but when he took the courageous decision to leak them to various media outlets, the TV networks would not cover them. Sanford Unger notes in his book, *The Papers and the Papers*:

> The networks' reluctance to touch the Papers was perhaps the clearest evidence of the extent to which they felt intimidated by the Nixon administration's attitude to the press. They knew how easy it was to spark a costly and threatening investigation by the FCC, which controls their broadcast licenses.[1]

The *Washington Post* was threatened by the Nixon administration twice. The first occasion was in its legal battle, in alliance with the *New York Times*, to publish the Pentagon Papers in 1971. The *New York Times* published large sections of the Pentagon Papers until the Nixon administration got a restraining order, and the paper stopped publication. Ellsberg was then contacted by Ben Bagdikian, a national editor on the *Post*, who obtained the Papers from him. The *Washington Post*, unlike the *Times*, had broadcast holdings and was more vulnerable to the FCC. The *Post*'s lawyers were worried that the courts might rule that the paper had violated the law by publishing classified documents, and make the *Post* of "bad character", giving the FCC grounds to revoke its ownership of television stations. Sam Husseini points out, "For that reason, as well as others, the *Post* only published articles about the Papers, not extended excerpts as the *Times* had done."[2]

The second occasion was the Carl Bernstein and Bob Woodward investigation into Watergate, which began in 1972. The Nixon administration used an array of weapons in an attempt to dissuade the paper's journalists, and its proprietor, Katharine Graham, from publishing its investigations. When Carl Bernstein called Nixon's Attorney General, John Mitchell, to check his involvement in the Watergate affair, he received the blunt, inelegant response: "All that crap, you're putting in the paper? It's all been denied. Katie Graham's gonna get her tit caught in a big fat ringer if that's published."

In her autobiography Katharine Graham cites memos which demonstrate the extent of the Nixon administration's desire to do damage to the paper. But she comments, "Of all the threats to the company during Watergate – the attempts to undermine our credibility, the petty slights, and the favoring of the competition – the most effective were the challenges to the licenses of our two Florida television stations." She points out that of more than 30 stations in the state of Florida, only the *Washington Post* ones were challenged.

Why was this? On Friday 27 October 1972, Chuck Colson, a White House trouble shooter assigned to oversee the networks, sent a memo: "Please check for me when any of *The Washington Post* television station licenses are up for renewal. I would like to know what the upcoming schedule is." The result was the company had to spend over $1 million on legal costs during the two and a half years up to renewal; the share price fell by over a half from $38 to $16 or $17; and it was difficult to recruit staff reluctant to join stations with an uncertain future. Interestingly, Katharine Graham adds a throwaway comment that the threats had their effect, leading to self-censorship: "It became difficult to air the kind of advocacy editorials we wanted to, knowing they would be used against us."[3]

CBS also aired the first of what was meant to be a two-parter on Watergate on the evening of Friday 27 October 1972 with the second piece planned to go out on the following Monday. Unusually, it took up 14 of the 22 minutes of that night's network news. The following day William S. Paley, the CBS chief executive, received a call from Colson about the programme, which Paley described in his memoirs as "pretty vicious". The result was a top level meeting with the Head of News, Richard Salant and other CBS executives at which Paley attacked the first programme, claiming it violated CBS standards by mingling fact and opinion. He did not mention the call he had received from Colson.

Participants in the meeting were clear about what Paley wanted.

Although Paley did not explicitly refer to the second part, Salant knew the chairman well enough to decipher his message: shorten the segment, or even better, kill it. "Bill Paley is the master of never giving an order, but he could make himself perfectly clear," said Salant.

The programme was delayed until the Tuesday, shortened to seven minutes, and the subject of a scalding memo from Paley the following day saying the piece was "unworthy of our fine traditions".[4]

Paley in his memoirs is very evasive about his interventionist role in the Watergate reports: "I am accused – and quite inaccurately – of having interfered with the content of a news broadcast." But he does point out that the networks were under considerable threat from the Nixon administration. Vice President Spiro Agnew on 13 November 1969 in a major address attacked the news organisations of all the networks as being "in the hands of a tiny, enclosed fraternity of privileged men elected by no one and enjoying a monopoly sanctioned and licensed by government". He went on: "As with other American institutions, perhaps it is time that the networks were made more responsive to the views of the nation and more responsible to the people they serve." Paley comments:

The message was clear, the threat was unmistakable. The Nixon administration was reminding all broadcasters that they were licensed by the government and regulated by one of its agencies, the FCC, which they thought had the power to make us "more responsive" to the views of the man elected to the White House.[5]

Thirty years later these events provide a useful comparison for an analysis of the extent to which regulation and ownership of the media influenced reporting of the Iraq war and the stance media organisations took towards investigating or questioning the statements by the US government over the reasons for, and conduct of, the war on Iraq.

In the US and Britain there was considerable opposition to war with Iraq, including regular large protest rallies in major cities. In both countries organisers of these events felt that they were either misreported or ignored. In December 2002 one US journalist suggested, "It's not unusual for those with dissenting opinions on controversial issues to complain that the news media don't take them seriously. But when it comes to coverage of opposition to a possible US invasion of Iraq, the critics might have a point." The author cited ombudsmen on the *Boston Globe*, National Public Radio and the *Washington Post*, and the public editor of Portland's *Oregonian* who all agreed with readers' and listeners' criticisms of the news organisations for not giving enough coverage to anti-war protests.[6]

One of the press officers for the huge 28 September 2002 march in London analysed the invisibility of the march in the overwhelming majority of the British media, and commented, "Any news is better than no news. Being marginalized is what does the worst damage. It says your views don't matter, you're not part of the legitimate debate."[7]

Media organisations in the US also intervened more actively to limit the effectiveness of the anti-war movement. Viacom is one of the top five global media groups, owner of the CBS television network and MTV as well as Viacom Outdoor, the largest outdoor-advertising entity in North America. MoveOn.org wanted to put its message "Inspections Work. War Won't" on buses, billboards and buildings in four major American markets, but in Washington, Los Angeles and Detroit Viacom controls a significant share of the outdoor-advertising space. Wally Kelly, chief executive of Viacom Outdoor, personally decided not to run the ads. Another group, TrueMajority, founded by Ben Cohen who was previously co-founder of the Ben and Jerry ice-cream company, had anti-war ads featuring celebrities refused by CNN, Fox, Comedy Central and four New York affiliates.[8] When CBS televised the Grammy awards they warned all prospective winners that if they attempted to mention the war they would be taken off air, and only Sheryl Crow subverted the ban by appearing onstage with NO WAR emblazoned on her guitar strap. In contrast to the tradition of protest songs in the Vietnam era, it has been suggested that if a major artist did record a protest song, no US radio station would play it because US radio has largely been consolidated into two national networks – Clear Channel and Infinity (owned by Viacom) – both notoriously conservative.[9]

Indeed Clear Channel Communications was in the forefront organising pro-war sentiment and rallies on the first weekend of the war. One rally, near to Richmond, Virginia, heard Glenn Beck, a conservative radio host, urging the crowd, "Don't let these peace protesters confuse you." In the previous weeks, his programme, which goes out three hours a day, five days a week on more than 100 stations, helped promote many similar demonstrations under the banner, Rally for America. Clear Channel insisted the events were simply pro-troop rallies, grass-root events undertaken independently by local stations that carried Beck's programme. But as Eric Boehlert points out, Clear Channel "played a key role in giving war supporters a voice by providing a turnkey service; staging the events, acquiring any necessary permits, taking care of security, assembling speakers, and of course relentlessly promoting the events on Clear Channel radio stations." The founder and chief executive of Clear Channel, Lowry Mays, is a staunch Republican, a generous contributor to the party, a good friend of George Bush Sr, and close to the President. Boehlert also cites a speech given by the actor and anti-war activist, Tim Robbins, at the National Press Club in April 2003, when Robbins said:

> A famous middle-aged rock-and-roller called me last week to thank me for speaking out against the war, only to go on to tell me that he could not speak out himself because he fears repercussions from Clear Channel. "They promote our concert appearances," he said. "They own most of the stations that play our music. I can't come out against this war."[10]

What is striking about US mainstream media coverage before, during and since the Iraq war has been the failure to criticise the basis for Bush's drive to war since the release of the administration's National Security Strategy in September 2002 and Bush's concoction of the "axis of evil" and the threat of Iraq to US national security. The US media, with rare exceptions, uncritically relayed government propaganda, but it was very unlikely that they would adopt adversarial or critical stances towards Bush's drive to war – they wanted political favours, and had been lobbying hard for them. If the media damaged the Bush administration politically, it in turn could damage the media commercially, and this wasn't something they were prepared to risk.

The chair of the FCC, Michael Powell, son of Defense Secretary Colin Powell, announced the results of his review of media ownership regulations, after a vote on 2 June, which went along party lines with the two Democrats, Michael Copps and Jonathan Adelstein, voting against. But behind the vote was an amazing process of corporate lobbying of politicians and the FCC, which led to the scrapping of long-standing rules to prevent the growth of media monopolies.

An analysis by the Center for Responsive Politics shows that media companies spent more than $82 million on federal lobbying efforts between 1999 and 2002, and another $26 million on political contributions. Some of the biggest media groups were the biggest spenders. AOL Time Warner spent $15.7 million on lobbying between 1999 and 2002, and another $6.2 million in political donations; Disney spent $16 million on lobbying and $2.8 million in contributions; and the Hearst Corp. (which owns newspapers and television stations and filed comments with the FCC urging repeal of the newspaper/televison cross-ownership ban) spent $394,000 on lobbying and contributed $180,000 in political contributions. The Center's analysts point out that much of the spending was connected to the FCC proceedings and that, "There is evidence that media conglomerates intensified their lobbying on Capitol Hill in the months leading up to the vote."[11]

Another independent watchdog, the Center for Public Integrity, explored the close relationship between the FCC and the interests it regulates, and its report makes disturbing reading. An examination of travel records reveals that FCC officials have taken 2,500 trips costing nearly $2.8 million over the past eight years, with most of the costs covered by the telecommunications and broadcast industries the agency regulates. This was in addition to about $2 million a year in official travel funded by taxpayers. Other findings in the report show that FCC commissioners and agency staff attended conventions, conferences and other events all over the world, with the top destinations Las Vegas, New Orleans and New York.[12]

Michael Powell has insisted that he and the other FCC commissioners were not influenced by the lobbying and the money: "We collected a thorough record, analysed our broadcast ownership rules from the ground up, and wrote the rules that match the times."

However, the Center for Public Integrity report reveals a disturbing reliance by the FCC on outside information providers:

> When the Center was constructing its database of media companies, researchers and reporters were repeatedly referred by FCC staff to private companies for basic information on ownership, audience reach and cable subscribers. Getting market share information, which is key when reviewing whether broadcasters are within existing FCC limits, was all but impossible without going outside the agency.

SOME CONCLUSIONS

Major changes have taken place in the US media since the events around the Pentagon Papers and Watergate. One clearly is the closer supportive relationship between the Bush administration, the FCC and big media. Another key change has been the relentless move to greater media concentration in fewer and fewer corporate hands.[13] For the vast majority of Americans these changes have taken place without public discussion or informed consent. The corrupt process of lobbying by the media industry of key politicians and regulators was the exact opposite of an open democratic discussion on media ownership rules and the consequences of any changes. Indeed Michael Powell reinforced the exclusion of the public role and strengthened the influence of the media industry by holding 71 off-the-record meetings with industry executives in the months leading up to the FCC vote, but only five were held with organisations representing the public interest. He also limited public input by organising only one official hearing on the rule changes.

However, the US media industry did not speak with a single voice on media ownership rules. The National Association of Broadcasters, which represents radio and television stations, lobbied aggressively to keep the FCC rules limiting media ownership intact. All four of the US television networks – ABC, CBS, NBC and Fox – have now withdrawn from NAB because its membership and finances are dominated by the smaller affiliates that would become targets for takeover if the ownership of TV networks is lifted from 35 per cent of US TV households to 45 per cent.

The anti-war movement was built on wide-ranging support including religious, trade union and community groups, and the anti-globalisation movement. Americans are now becoming aware of the scale and impact the media rule changes will have on an already deeply commercialised media system, and are beginning to build a similar broad-ranging protest movement. In a review of the range of opposition mounting against the FCC, two commentators concluded that Powell "may ultimately be remembered not for loosening the rules but for pushing so hard he woke America up, forcing public interest concerns back into the debate over media ownership".[14]

Finally, these concerns have an international resonance. A fiercely debated Communications Bill, before the UK parliament in the 2002–03 session, has three areas of direct relevance to the US experience. Firstly, the Bill gives a green light to the creation of a single ITV system, and at the same time lifts the prohibition on non-European ownership of ITV, making it a target for US-based global media groups. Secondly, the restriction on media groups with a dominant share of newspaper circulation owning terrestrial TV channels will be lifted in the case of Channel 5. Rupert Murdoch, who owns newspapers with almost 40 per cent of UK circulation, and the satellite system BSkyB, would be able to acquire the free-to-air channel and build its audience through cross-promotion and utilising programming acquired from his global media empire.

Finally, a new regulatory structure, OFCOM, is being created which is modelled on the FCC. Amongst the places FCC officials visited in the eight years covered by the Center for Public Integrity report was London (98 times). As this chapter was completed, the following item was tucked away on an industry news website:

US, UK watchdogs nuzzle
In an attempt to co-ordinate regulatory policy between the US and the USA, the chairman of the new media and communications watchdog, Lord Currie of Marylebone of Ofcom, is set to meet his counterpart at the US Federal Communications Commission when he visits Washington this week.[15]

This is not good news for those who want diverse media, regulated in a clear, accountable way, and reporting accurately and independently on events in times of crisis.

NOTES

1. S. Husseini, *The FCC, the Media, and War*, September 2001, <http://www.tompaine.com/feature2.cfm/ID/4569>.

2. Ibid.
3. K. Graham, *Personal History*, Vintage: New York, 1997, pp. 479–82.
4. S.B. Smith, *In All His Glory: The life of William S. Paley*, New York: Random House Trade Paperbacks, 1990, p. 477.
5. W.S. Paley, *As It Happened: A Memoir*, New York: Doubleday & Co., 1979, pp. 313–14.
6. K.S Wenner, "Major Rally, Minor Play", *American Journalism Review*, December 2002.
7. M. Gosling, "Dreams and Nightmares ... A Tale of Two Demos", *Free Press*, November/December 2002.
8. M. Hastings, "Billboard Ban", Newsweek/MSNBC News, <http:// www. msnbc.com/news/872684.asp>.
9. A. Petridis, "Sound of Silence", *Guardian Friday Review*, 14 March 2003.
10. E. Boehlert, "Habla usted Clear Channel?", 2003, <http://www.salon. com/tech/feature/2003/04/24/univision/print.html>.
11. C. Pope, "Media Groups Spend Millions Lobbying the FCC", *Seattle Post-Intelligencer*, 3 June 2003.
12. Center for Public Integrity, "Well Connected: FCC and Industry Maintain Cozy Relationship on Many Levels", 22 May 2003, <http://www. publicintegrity.org>.
13. B.H. Bagdikian, *The Media Monopoly*, 6th edn, Boston: Beacon Press, 2000; R.W. McChesney, *Rich Media, Poor Democracy*, New York: The New Press, 1999.
14. J. Nichols, and R.W. McChesney, "FCC: Public Be Damned", *The Nation*, 2 June 2003.
15. Advanced-television.com <http://www.advanced-television.com/2003/ News_archive/june16_23.html>.

22

The BBC: A Personal Account

Abdul Hadi Jiad

Ithaat London (London Radio), as the BBC is traditionally known in the Arab World, had been associated in my mind, since I was a teenager in Iraq, with an influx of varied and extensive reporting of events and a provision of information that no other media source was able to match. Although the signal of Radio Moscow was strong and uninterrupted, large proportions of the male population in my town would brief each other on what Ithaat London had said about local, regional, international, political, economic and other issues.

It was easily detectable that Radio Moscow was a propaganda tool for an ideology, and Ithaat London was "colourless". Certainly both of them share in one main objective, which is to persuade through a variety of means, whether direct, like Radio Moscow, or indirectly and implicitly as the BBC does.

However, the majority of Iraqi politicians and party activists, whether they were Ba'athists or communists or others, whose differences and political intolerance had notoriously ended up in bloodshed, would always agree on one thing: that Ithaat London, in effect, was fundamentally a propaganda tool for another ideology: imperialism/colonialism. Their evidence was that the BBC World Service, which was set up in 1932, was originally one of the departments of the Colonial Office, the UK ministry which controlled the overseas colonies and territories. Until the late 1950s its signal used to be beamed out of Cyprus as Ithaat ash-sharq al-Adna (Radio Near East) to serve colonial purposes.

Unaware of that history, and certainly being indifferent to politics at the time, my ears were tuned to that ugly wooden box late one night when the radio dial caught a programme, "Teaching English by Radio", in which a male Arab voice and a female English voice, were repeating English sentences and expressions with their syntax and Arabic meaning in a teaching session for listeners. There was no ideology or political propaganda in that programme, which gave a mail box address in Baghdad for correspondence. I wrote to them and asked for a transcript.

Months later my English teacher at Al-Musayab High School came to the classroom and, with no comment but with a stern look of warning that I was unable to comprehend at the time, handed me an envelope that was marked "opened by Censorship". It was sent by the BBC.

I was overjoyed that the BBC responded to me, being the only one in my town to have such a privilege and which soon became the talking point of the neighbourhood. However, I never dreamt or expected that, in about fifteen years' time, my future career would land me in the studios of Bush House in Central London.

The BBC operates on the principle of presenting fairly and equally the views of all sides in a story. It has issued a bulky *Producers' Guidelines*, which is updated regularly, that addresses most of the principles and guidelines to impartial and fair reporting with recommendation of how to report various events and controversial stories, whether related to elections or to terrorist organisations and actions. Those guidelines, which are excellent and attractive on paper, are the guardians of professional journalism.

The most critical and tormenting moment in my professional career with the BBC was on Wednesday 13 February 1991, just on the eve of Valentine's Day. At dawn, two 2,000-pound laser-guided bombs burrowed through ten feet of hardened concrete and detonated, punching a gaping hole in Baghdad's Amiriya bomb shelter – and incinerating over 400 Iraqi civilians. It is considered the single largest civilian massacre in modern air warfare.

The Pentagon claimed the attack was against an Iraqi military command and control centre, but one of the first journalists to arrive at the scene was the BBC reporter Jeremy Bowen. I was presenting the Current Affairs special war programme live on air with two of my colleagues on the fourth floor of Bush House, when a senior producer brought in the copy of Bowen's piece from Baghdad which gave a graphic description of the charred bodies of children and women.

My colleagues and I found ourselves in a dilemma, torn between professional requirements of impartiality and objectivity and human and personal considerations. Being already persuaded by the BBC and guided by its principles and guidelines, we aligned ourselves with the impassionate professional against the passionate personal. On air we read Bowen's description of the human tragedy as dispassionately as we could, through eyes filled with tears.

The professional journalistic output of the BBC World Service is rich and diverse in many areas of human activity, whether linguistic, cultural, ethnic, political or in arts and sciences. There is a daily flow of programmes in over 40 languages, reflecting the globe's varied and colourful cultural and political spectrum, with the main objective of engaging the receptors (audience) and pulling them away from other competitors.

However, the content of the programmes has always drawn the attention and criticism of professionals, politicians and, of course, the target audience, according to their own set of criteria. The BBC Arabic Service is a model example because it broadcasts in 23 Arab countries, each of which has its own political and historical background, though they may share in religious and some social traditions.

A major shake-up in BBC senior management thinking on how to professionally handle coverage seems to have taken place in the aftermath of the Iraqi invasion of Kuwait and the subsequent Gulf War in which the United Kingdom was a major partner and, as some believe, an instigator. I can reveal now that confidential "working" papers, with very limited circulation, were produced in 1992 for the BBC Arabic Service, to deal with Gulf affairs, Islam and economic development as well as a shifting global strategy from a western (read British) perspective. Those papers determined, and recommended, the way ahead for coverage.

On the staffing level the national structure of the Arabic Service was dangerously destabilised in that over 60 per cent of professional staff were recruited from Egypt and the remaining 40 per cent were drawn from ten other Arab nationalities. All the managers were of Egyptian national origin. The recruits had been drawn mostly from Egyptian media, which is notoriously government controlled, and had kept their jobs with the Egyptian government. Such a heavy Egyptian presence made the Arabic Service sound like an extension of an Egyptian local radio station that toed, on major political issues, the Egyptian official line. Non-Egyptian staff adapted a complaint from a listener and described the Arabic Service as radio Tanta (Tanta is a poor, remote locality in Egypt), in which heavy Egyptian accent and dialect are the normal linguistic rendering on air.

That fact led to a flow of professional and racial complaints as staff from other national origins found themselves less favourably treated in professional exposure, development, promotions, bonuses and other issues. Over 30 tribunal cases of racial discrimination have been issued against the head of the BBC Arabic Service, Gamon McLellan, who took up his post after the 1992 review. Still, he remained in his post and the senior management did not investigate him.

Since the Egyptian government supported the 1991 Gulf War coalition, and sent three brigades to support the military operations, Iraq stood no chance of fair or unbiased reporting. The majority of interviewees on various issues had always been of Egyptian origin, even on matters not related to Egypt. Dozens of letters and complaints from listeners had highlighted the problem.

One of the major examples was in 1998–99 when a media war erupted between Iraq and Egypt. The BBC Arab Service stringer reported the Iraqi side and the Service office in Cairo reported the Egyptian reaction. Both went out on the morning programme, which would be repeated on *World at One*, which is a flagship of the Arabic Service. So far this sounds like the BBC as its guidelines state: impartial, unbiased and objective reporting of views of parties to a story. The editor was an Egyptian and I was the producer. However, half an hour before the programme was due on air, the head of the Arabic Service, McLellan, and the Egyptian editor withdrew the Iraqi stringer tape and edited it removing the majority of quotes or attacks against the Egyptian government. In response to my enquiry they told me that the Egyptian information minister was upset and asked us not to broadcast the Iraqi attacks.

Another example was during the "Desert Fox" military attacks against Iraq in 1998. Several Arab and non-Arab TV stations reported attacks on civilian targets inside and around the Iraqi capital Baghdad. US and UK sources admitted that some missiles hit civilian targets. In a morning live interview from Baghdad, the Iraqi stringer described civilian buildings, including the Natural History Museum, that were hit by missiles and air raids. The head of the Arabic Service and the same Egyptian editor were angry with both the presenter and the stringer and did a confidential investigation after translating the full live Arabic interview into English.

The BBC Arabic Service did not have a correspondent or stringer in Baghdad from when I left in 1989 until 1998. In the Egyptian capital there had always been a full-fledged office with two staff correspondents. Several months prior to the outbreak of military hostilities against Iraq in March 2003, the BBC management started its preparations for the incidence of war which indicated to us that the decision of war had already been taken. The preparations included briefings by the management, Foreign Office and Ministry of Defence.

Other indicators included the BBC campaign, as far back as September 2002, to send reporting staff to "hostile environment", chemical and biological warfare training courses. The management had even recalled dozens of correspondents and local stringers to undergo that training. Each person cost the BBC between £2,000 and £5,000 per course. The BBC World Service also sent dozens of its staff and stringers. The Arabic Service also sent its staff and brought in its stringers from the Middle East to join the training courses. During the last two months of 2002 the BBC management issued directives and guidelines of how to cover the war and the placements of reporters and crews. Various aspects had also been discussed in senior management meetings with limited participation.

The Arabic Service played a major role in targeting the Arab audience, including Iraq, since all the analysis indicated that the main worry for the US and UK planners was the reaction of the Arab people to the war against Iraq. The BBC Arabic Service decided to set up an additional office in the Egyptian capital, an action which had raised many eyebrows because Baghdad, not Cairo, was the target area and better coverage could have been gathered in neighbouring Jordan or even friendly Kuwait. The additional Cairo office was staffed with more than ten Egyptian staff, the majority of whom were locally recruited. Soon after the outbreak of military hostilities against Iraq in March 2003 McLellan instructed his staff to stop receiving or broadcasting any of the Baghdad Iraqi stringer pieces – according to sources inside the Arabic Service.

The second major incident in the run-up to the war against Iraq was an illegal, sudden, and on the spot dismissal of two senior journalists from the Arabic Service, an Iraqi and a Palestinian. I was the Iraqi who on the day of dismissal, 19 February 2003, was the editor of the Arabic Service day programmes. It was a normal working day when I chaired the editorial meeting and distributed work. Suddenly the head of the Arabic Service, Gamon McLellan, took me to his office and pretended to discuss ideas about covering the Iraqi crisis and impending war. I was unaware that he was trapping me until Mark Byford, director of the BBC World Service, had finished dismissing my Palestinian colleague. Minutes later, Byford stormed into the office to dismiss me without a warning or investigation or disciplinary hearing or even the right of appeal.

Byford acknowledges in his profile and biography posted on the internet that he was a friend of Geoff Hoon, the Defence Secretary, since they were both at Leeds University.[1] The more telling indicator was Byford's letter to the *Guardian* (on 26 February 2003) in which he admitted that there was communication with the Foreign Office on dismissing us. He claimed that he did that as a matter of "courtesy". Surprise! How many appointments and dismissals had he discussed with the Foreign Office? Why? Was the BBC an independent public service or a government mouthpiece during the war? When dozens of trade unions protested to the Foreign Secretary, Jack Straw, demanding an independent enquiry, the Foreign Office dismissed that outright. It said, in a formal letter (14 April 2003), "we have no reason to believe that the BBC World Service or the BBC have acted improperly and therefore do not feel the need for an independent enquiry". The Foreign Office was aware of the reasons and was not told only as a matter of "courtesy".

The BBC is an excellent organisation with excellent professional and employment guidelines and policies. The problem arises when a few managers, or the policy maker, breaches those policies either to discriminate or to hijack the Corporation to serve the politician.

NOTE

1. See <http://www.leeds.ac.uk/alumni/html/news/review/issue6/markbyf.htm>.

23
Mass Deception: How the Media Helped the Government Deceive the People

David Edwards and David Cromwell

AMONG THE KNOWLEDGEABLE

In June 2003 the media erupted with outrage at the allegation that Tony Blair "duped" the public and parliament into fighting a war that had been secretly agreed with George Bush in September 2002. Equally outrageous, however, was the stubborn refusal of the media to discuss these issues before senior politicians blew the whistle.

Martin Woollacott summarised the standard pre-war media view in the *Guardian* on 24 January: "Among those knowledgeable about Iraq there are few, if any, who believe he [Saddam] is not hiding such weapons. It is a given."[1] This was nonsense but because it was rarely challenged Blair's "passionate sincerity" about the supposed Iraqi threat also became a "given". The *Observer*'s Andrew Rawnsley described how Blair was "genuinely disturbed – it would not be going too far to say petrified – about Saddam Hussein's potential ability to use weapons of mass destruction".[2] The BBC's Laura Trevelyan declared that Tony Blair "passionately believes" that Saddam had to be confronted if future generations were not to be haunted by our inaction (BBC *News at One*, 14 January 2003).

The editors of the anti-war *Mirror* wrote the day after Blair's crucial 18 March speech to parliament: "Even though the *Mirror* disagrees strongly with Tony Blair over his determination to wage war on Iraq, we do not question his belief in the rightness of what he is doing." The *Daily Telegraph*'s editors wrote: "Any fair-minded person who listened to [the] debate ... must surely have concluded that Mr Blair was right, and his opponents were wrong.'

The *Independent*'s editors wrote:

Tony Blair's capacities as a performer and an advocate have never been in doubt. But this was something much more ... this was the most persuasive case yet made by the man who has emerged as the most formidable persuader for war on either side of the Atlantic. The case against President Saddam's 12-year history of obstructing the United Nation's attempts at disarmament has never been better made.

Remarkably, this praise across the media spectrum was heaped on a speech packed full of lies and deceptions that could easily have been exposed by journalists.

Cambridge academic Glen Rangwala has analysed the first reference in Blair's speech to an UNMOVIC working document of 6 March 2003, entitled "Unresolved Disarmament Issues". Blair noted that Iraq "had had far reaching plans to weaponise VX". The quotation used by Blair was from a "background" section of the UNMOVIC report on Iraq's policy before 1991. In the key *new* section on VX nerve gas in the same report, UNMOVIC reported that the method used by Iraq to produce 1.5 tonnes of VX before 1990 – a "threat" repeatedly mentioned by US and UK politicians – did *not* lead to stable results. According to the weapons inspectors: "VX produced [by the Iraqi method] must be used relatively quickly after production (about 1 to 8 weeks)."

Rangwala explains the sheer audacity of Blair's deception: "In other words, Blair's first piece of 'evidence' was about a substance that the weapons inspectors consider to have been no threat since early 1991. Tony Blair didn't tell the MPs that."[3]

This could be mistaken for ignorance, except that it fits a consistent pattern of careful distortion. The government's September 2002 dossier on Iraqi weapons of mass destruction (WMD) contained four mentions of the claim that Iraq was able to deploy WMD within 45 minutes of the order being given. Senior intelligence officials – outraged at the abuse of their work – told the BBC's *Newsnight* programme (4 June 2003) that the original mention of a 45-minutes response time referred to the length of time it might have taken the Iraqis to fuel and fire a Scud missile, or to load and fire a multiple rocket launcher. The original intelligence said nothing about whether Iraq possessed the chemical or biological weapons to use in these weapons. The government had turned a purely hypothetical threat into an immediate and deadly threat to make war possible.

Other lies include repeated claims that inspectors were thrown out of Iraq in 1998 (they were withdrawn), and that inspectors were forced to leave because the Iraqi regime had completely failed to co-operate (co-operation had resulted in near-total disarmament). Blair has also blamed the Saddam regime for the mass death of Iraqi children under sanctions (the UN and aid agencies have blamed 1991 Gulf War damage to infrastructure and the effects of sanctions).

To create the proper black and white contrast between our noble leader – forced to confront his children with the prospect that his principled stand might cost him his job – and theirs the public was told that Saddam was surrounded by "a rogue's gallery of the world's most wanted men", in the words of ITN's Nicholas Owen (ITN *Lunchtime News*, 3 April 2003). Skulking in the shadows was "Chemical Ali", described by ITN's Tom Bradby as "a diabetic with a high-pitched whine" (ITN *Lunchtime News*, 3 April 2003). Another senior Iraqi figure was described as "an unstable psychopath who suffers from hyper-tension".

Even when our leaders were clearly responsible for major loss of civilian life, the media managed to sanitise the horror. Standing beside a deep crater that had once been a restaurant and residential area in the heart of Baghdad – destroyed in a US attempt to kill Saddam Hussein – ITN reporter John Irvine said merely: "It's the Americans who are setting the agenda" (ITN *Evening News*, 7 April 2003). As though auditioning for a part in a Hollywood action movie, Irvine concluded: "After this, Saddam Hussein is a dead man walking."

SILENCING DISSENT – THE WAR WE COULD HAVE STOPPED

It was only possible to be persuaded of Blair's sincerity by ignoring highly credible experts who argued that Iraq had no significant WMD capability, and that the US–UK case for war was therefore an audacious fraud. Former chief UNSCOM weapons inspector, Scott Ritter, has long insisted that Iraq was "fundamentally disarmed" between 1991 and 1998, with 90–95 per cent of its WMD eliminated by December 1998. Of the remaining capability, Ritter wrote last year: "It doesn't even constitute a weapons programme. It constitutes bits and pieces of a weapons programme which in its totality doesn't amount to much, but which is still prohibited."[4]

Responding to Colin Powell's infamous 5 February speech to the United Nations, Ritter said:

He just hits you, hits you, hits you with circumstantial evidence, and he confuses people – and he lied, he lied to people, he misled people ... The Powell presentation is not evidence ... It's a very confusing presentation. What does it mean? What does it represent? How does it all link up? It doesn't link up.[5]

UNSCOM's executive chairman Rolf Ekeus reported to the Security Council in April 1997 that "not much is unknown about Iraq's retained proscribed weapons capabilities".[6] In May 2000, Ekeus added, "I would say that we felt that in all areas we have eliminated Iraq's [WMD] capabilities fundamentally."[7] Ritter, the CIA, the International Institute for Strategic Studies, and others, also pointed out that with extremely limited shelf lives any remaining WMD would long since have become "harmless sludge".

Time and again UK government spokespeople like Blair, Jack Straw, John Reid and Mike O'Brien made damning references to thousands of litres of missing anthrax. They asked, ironically, if we were supposed to believe that Saddam had simply mislaid them. Not once did an interviewer respond with the basic facts: that Iraq is only known to have produced liquid bulk anthrax, which has a shelf life of just three years. The last known batch of liquid anthrax was produced in 1991 at a state-owned factory blown up in 1996.

Crucially, Ritter pointed out that any attempts to reconstitute the WMD programmes would have been immediately detected by the most intense and sophisticated surveillance operation in history – it just couldn't have been done without western awareness.

If these arguments had been granted the exposure they merited, public support for the war would surely have collapsed. What is so remarkable, and so damning, is that these elementary but obviously crucial points were almost literally never raised in our media before the attack on Iraq.

According to the *Guardian/Observer* website, Iraq has been mentioned in 7,118 articles between 1 January and 6 June 2003, with 961 articles mentioning "Iraq and weapons of mass destruction". Out of these, Scott Ritter has received twelve mentions and Rolf Ekeus two. The *Independent*'s website records 5,872 articles mentioning Iraq, with 931 mentions of "Iraq and weapons of mass destruction". Ritter records 24 mentions, Ekeus four. There have been no mentions of Ritter or Ekeus in either paper in May or June – the period covering the media furore on WMD.

Ritter, the most outspoken whistleblower, was not interviewed by BBC TV News, *Newsnight*, or ITN in the months heading up to the war. He was last interviewed on a terrestrial BBC channel by David Frost on 29 September 2002. When asked why *Newsnight* had failed to interview such an important source, editor George Entwistle answered: "I don't particularly have an answer for that; we just haven't" (interview with David Edwards, 31 March 2003). By contrast, *Newsnight* "just has" interviewed war supporters like Ken Adelman, Richard Perle and James Rubin endlessly over the last six months.

We are living in a time when the propaganda function of even our most respected media is clear for all to see. In October 2001, as Britain helped the US pound Afghanistan – one of the poorest countries on earth – into rubble, the *Guardian*'s editors commented on a speech by Blair:

> The core of the speech – intellectual as well as moral – came when he contrasted the west's commitment to do everything possible to avoid civilian casualties and the terrorists' proven wish to cause as many civilian casualties as possible, a point which Jack Straw followed up powerfully in the Commons yesterday. Let them do their worst, we shall do our best, as Churchill put it. That is still a key difference.[8]

With tens of thousands dead, injured and sick in Iraq, with the country's health and social systems looted and wrecked, and with clear proof of "the west's commitment to do everything possible" to wage war, regardless of the cost in human life, this is surely one conceit "the country's leading liberal newspaper" will not be repeating any time soon.

NOTES

1. Martin Woollacott, "This drive to war is one of the mysteries of our time – We know Saddam is hiding weapons. That isn't the argument", *Guardian*, 24 January 2003.
2. Andrew Rawnsley, "How to Deal with the American Goliath", *Observer*, 24 February 2002.
3. Glen Rangwala, "Evidence and Deceit: How the Case for War Became Unstuck", *Dissident Voice*, 2 June 2003, <http://www.zmag.org>.
4. Scott Ritter and William Rivers Pitt, *War On Iraq*, London: Profile Books, 2002, p. 24.
5. "Ritter Dismisses Powell Report", *Kyodo News*, 7 February 2003.
6. Quoted, Glen Rangwala, "A Threat to the World?: The facts about Iraq's weapons of mass destruction", 4 April 2002, <http://middleeastreference. org.uk/latw020404.html>.
7. <http://www.casi.org.uk/discuss/2000/msg00701.html>.
8. "Blair Plays it Cooler – A new tone, but few new answers", Leader, *Guardian*, 31 October 2001.

24
Covering the Middle East

An interview with Robert Fisk

23 May 2003

Pacifica Radio: Over the course of a quarter century covering the Middle East can you describe the kinds of press restrictions you have been operating under at different times?

Fisk: You know I think we mischaracterise it with the word "restrictions". In most cases journalists turn up on assignments on major stories, certainly in the case of the American media, with a clear idea of what limits there are and what constraints there are. This of course particularly applies in the Arab/Israeli dispute. Where the concern that a criticism of Israel, however soft and remote will elicit an over-emotional response and the reporter will be accused of being an anti-Semite or a racist, has produced a situation in which journalists, American journalists covering the Middle East question, particularly new arrivals, are so sensitive and so careful of the way they report things, always putting the word "alleged" or "reported" around anything which might impugn the integrity of an Israeli army officer or Ariel Sharon the prime minister, their reporting is almost unintelligible. I want to know what the reporter thinks, not what Israelis or Palestinians say. I know that. So in a sense, once a major story breaks in the region, the restrictions are very much, the front line runs very much through the mind of a reporter I am afraid to say.

If you take the case of the 1991 Gulf War, any journalist who remotely tried to question, I mean American, I questioned it, the British press questioned it, but anyone who questioned the motives of that war was immediately accused of being a Saddam lover, a man who was obviously for terrorism, who hated America, etc. Even worse was the reaction of 11 September. I was actually crossing the Atlantic on 9/11. Of course the plane turned around when the US closed its airspace. And from the satellite phone on my seat in the plane, I was on deadline, I realised this was a Middle East story, it must be Arabs, we didn't even know that then. And I wrote an 800-word story that said "so it has come to this. The lies of the Balfour declaration, the promises that we made, the lies, British to the Arabs, all the deceit of the decades, all the one-sided peace process, all the suffering of the children of Iraq", I thought, and I said "seems to have produced this international crime against humanity", which is what it was. And the most extraordinary response to this, emails saying I was in league with the devil that I had a pact with bin Laden. A Harvard professor went on Irish radio saying I was an evil dangerous liar, that to be anti-American, and whatever that is, I suppose I was being accused of it was the same as being anti-Semitic. In other words to be opposed to Mr Bush you become a Jew hater, a Nazi, a racist. An extraordinary attempt, even if you were British to stop you from asking why.

An American journalist for example could ask who and how they did it. That was acceptable. It was alright to say they were Saudi Arabians, they were Arabs. Those were the countries they came from. But to then ask what was wrong with the countries they came from was absolutely forbidden, it was a no no, it was a taboo question. Not for us, we kept pushing it through the British press. But in America it was unpatriotic to ask that question because it meant you were giving credit to terrorists.

And so, by and large journalists don't need restrictions they restrict themselves, in this country I am sorry to say.

Pacifica: Do you recognise a goal of objectivity; do you see a distinction between writing commentary and what a reporter thinks, and reporting facts?

Fisk: I think we are dealing here with a problem in American journalism school, which thank god we Brits don't go through. We do politics and history and other subjects at university. I think that the foreign correspondent is the nerve ending of a newspaper. My paper sends a correspondent to live abroad to tell us what happens there, not to tell us what two sides are saying, I can read that on the wire.

Over and over again for example, when I am in Jerusalem or Damascus, or Cairo, I talk to my American colleagues – who are just like me, same jobs much better salaries of course, but the same role. And what they tell me is fascinating. They really have a deep insight many of them, into what's happening in the region, but when I read their reports it's not there. Everything they have to tell me of interest has been erased. When they want to put forth a point of view, they ring up some guy in America who has very little knowledge usually in one of the places I call the think-thanks, the think-tanks, the Brookings Institute, the Rand Corporation, and this guy blathers on for two paragraphs of bland prose, and this is put in as opinion. But I want to know what the reporter thinks, if you send a reporter to a region, you send him there because you think he is intelligent, fair, decent reporter; you don't have to ask him to give 50 per cent of every paragraph to each side. I mean if you follow the rules that a journalist seems to have to follow in the Middle East, what do you do say if you cover the slave ship and the slavery campaign? Do you give the same amount of time to the slaves and the slave ship captain? Or what if you are covering the Second World War, do you give the same amount of time to prisoners and an SS guard? No. You have to have some sense of morality, and passion and anger. You know when I am at the scene for example of the slaughter of Hamer in 1982, where the Syrian army crushed the people of Hamer, up to 20,000 dead, destroyed their mosques in the old city. I managed to get in there, and my piece if you read it now, drips with anger at the way in which this massive armed force run by the then president's brother was erasing a city and its history and its people. If you read my account of the Sabra and Shatila massacre carried out by the Israelis' allies in 1982 as Israeli soldiers watched, the same thing happens. We should not be employed to be automatons to effectively just be a voice for spokesmen. We should be out there telling it how it is, how journalism used to be.

Pacifica: But if a sense of passion, morality, anger leads to a journalist like yourself being considered pro-Palestinian —

Fisk: I'm not considered pro-Palestinian.

Pacifica: But do you ever hear that characterisation and does it undermine your credibility?

Fisk: Absolutely not. Of course Israelis who don't like to see their misbehaviour narrated into the paper will say you're pro-Palestinian, pro-terrorist. Of course they do. And I have many times written about Arab misbehaviour and immorality and immediately I am accused of being a Mossad agent. Indeed I appeared at a conference in Boston called the Right of Return conference, in which I criticised the corruption of Arab American groups, in which I criticised their total disassociation from the actual, the dirt and filth of the refugee camps, and emails soon began to go around from various Arab students around the United States saying I had been Judaised, this apparently based on the idea that I give a lecture once a year in Madison Wisconsin organised by a Jewish family, and that I was a member of Mossad. And you get it from both sides, and you have to take it. But if you see, you want to be an uncontroversial journalist, and I am not a controversial journalist, I am a correspondent for a mainstream newspaper and I do my job. But if you are going to be frightened by people who are going to use this cheap language, if you are going to write so carefully not to offend anyone, then you are going to produce the path that appears in the American media now.

Pacifica: Governments tell us that they are protecting journalists by creating closed military areas, by restricting journalist access to battle zones, do you accept that?

Fisk: Well that is what the Soviets said when they labelled cities closed military areas in the Soviet Union. Look: during the Israeli occupation of Lebanon I learned very quickly that whenever the Israeli army declared an area a closed military area it meant they were doing something which was meant to be hidden, and every time they did that I got into the town to see what they had been doing and invariably there had been extra-judicial executions, torture, or prisoners taken away and not being seen again, like what has happened here. Exactly the same happens in the West Bank. The moment they declared Bethlehem a closed military area, I am talking about the first of the reoccupations of the West Bank by Sharon's soldiers, I went straight into Bethlehem, and I did the same in Ramallah. Our job as journalists when we hear the words closed military areas is to go straight in because that is where the story is. It has nothing to do with our protection. Indeed in the case of the Israelis they have shot so many journalists and wounded so many journalists the last thing I think they are interested in is the protection of journalists.

Pacifica: Have you ever written a story and looked back, and felt you jeopardised civilians or soldiers or anyone by reason of your story?

Fisk: No. I will give you a very practical example. And that is geography. It is very easy to do a colour piece. "As we walked up the hill I saw a tank on my right." I always go through my copy saying have I identified that hill? Because if I have I am giving a Palestinian, or an Israeli, or a Hezbollah a chance to get that tank. Of course they knew about it anyway, they know more about the military location than we do. But I am going to make sure we are not even open to the accusation. If, by reporting for example the massacre of Sabra and Shatila we are accused of being anti-Semitic because we make people dislike Israel, well I am sorry that is an argument I want to be involved in. Because my job is to report what I have seen. And of course when a country, Syria at Hamer, for example, Israel at the time of Sabra and Shatila, Iraq at Halabja, when a nation uses its armed forces and behaves in a despicable way that amounts to a war crime, well, it may be that our reporting makes people angry at the country, well tough luck, that country shouldn't have committed those war crimes.

Pacifica: There was great controversy in America when the entire tape of an Osama bin Laden broadcast was edited for the American availability but was broadcast in full on Al Jazeera. What is the role of the internet, of access to Al Jazeera and other news sources on Americans and people around the world getting a complete picture of what is going on?

Fisk: Well, we haven't fully understood yet the implications of the internet. Once the internet allowed Americans to tap into English-language newspapers abroad, not just the *Independent* but the *Guardian*, the *Financial Times*, the French press if they read French, or *El Pais* which is very good or is very good in Spain, suddenly a new depth was given to them. They were not reading in the English press what they were reading in the *New York Times*. I could tell immediately. At the moment at almost a thousand letters a week I am getting almost 50 per cent from America. Now that is an indictment of the American media for a start. I should be getting 20 per cent from America and 80 per cent from the United Kingdom, but in fact more than half is coming from America, and many of them complain about what they refer to, as one did, of the lobotomised coverage in the American press. Now what is the effect of this? I think that more and more Americans are saying, "hold on, why can't we read this in our newspapers, why can't we watch this on our television?" Yet again and again, even despite the fact, I don't think the American media realise the extent to which ordinary American citizens are looking at foreign publications, in itself an appalling reflection on the worth or lack of it in the American media. Continually, still, American reporters hedge their bets. I was reading an article which was referring to Sabra and Shatila which the Kahan Commission of Israel said that Ariel Sharon was personally responsible, page 93 I think it was. And the article in the Associated Press referred to him "allegedly facilitating the militias that went into the camp". A total cop out. He was personally responsible. He sent the militias into the camp, where 1,700 Palestinians were murdered. So I think what's happening with the internet, there is a profound change coming among Americans interested in the region, or who have an intellectual interest in the Middle East. As for all the other Americans who are not interested in the Middle East, I don't know. But certainly the internet is profoundly changing, not fast enough, but profoundly changing the way Americans look at regions that are not properly covered by their newspapers and television.

Pacifica: We call our programme Clear and Present Danger. What from your perspective is the clear and present danger to free press in the United States?

Fisk: I will sum it up very briefly. The relationship of the press and television to government is incestuous. The State Department correspondents, the White House correspondents, the Pentagon correspondents, have set a narrative where instead of telling us what they think is happening or what they know is happening, they tell us what they are told by the spokesman. They have become sub-spokesmen. Spokesmen for the great institutions of state. When an American correspondent visits the Middle East they turn up in Beirut, Damascus or Cairo and where do they go? The first visit is to the American Embassy for a briefing with the ambassador, the economic adviser, the defence attaché and no doubt the CIA spook. Then they go and see an Arab Minister of Information who almost never knows any information about anything ever. Then they write a story. Now it's not always that bad, but that is the main theme which is followed.

So what you have I think is a general consensus in America, which I hope is breaking up, that to challenge American foreign policy is in some way, not just insensitive, but unpatriotic. Especially foreign policy in the Middle East which is still a taboo subject. You know in America you can talk about lesbians, gays, and blacks but not about the relationship with Israel and the US administration or Congress. So I think it is this cosy, incestuous, dangerous relationship between press and administration, between sources and access which causes many of these problems.

25
Why the BBC Ducks the Palestinian Story

Tim Llewellyn

Watching a peculiarly crass, inaccurate and condescending programme about the endangered historical sites of "Israel" – that is to say, the Israeli-occupied Palestinian Territories – on BBC2 in early June 2003,[1] I determined to try to work out, as a former BBC Middle East correspondent, why the Corporation has in the past two and a half years been failing to report fairly the most central and lasting reason for the troubles of the region: the Palestinians' struggle for freedom.

The approach of the programme – made by Arts rather than News and Current Affairs – reflected the general run of BBC domestic coverage of the issue: the strained effort at "balance"; the failure to question the circumstances of the beleaguered historical sites (why *are* they beleaguered?); the acceptance of the "equivalence" of the two peoples fighting over this territory, the indigenous population and an occupying army; the assumption on which the whole programme was built: that in the then looming Anglo-American invasion of Iraq these historical and holy places might be damaged by missiles fired from Iraq. Perhaps BBC Arts was not aware before their team arrived that many ancient Arab monuments had already been besieged, shelled, violated, ransacked, bulldozed, and in many cases closed to their worshippers and their inheritors by Israel's occupying army.

A week earlier, in a BBC News documentary about the wall that Israel is building between the Israelis and the Palestinians[2] – much of it encroaching on occupied Palestinian land, destroying houses and olive groves and dividing families – it was again felt necessary to leaven the images of Arab suffering with the "balance" of how awkward the wall would be for a handful of illegal Jewish settlers. To explain this, a sympathetic Irish woman settler told that side of the story in the vivid English of her people.

It was not that the BBC did not tell the Palestinian story graphically and shockingly – but that "the other side" of the story had to be told as well, diluting the central and violent issue of The Wall and all it symbolises of Israel's fears, greed and brutal dismissal of its Arab neighbours.

Since the beginning of the Aqsa Uprising, or Second Intifada, in September 2000 there have been countless examples throughout the BBC's news broadcasts, discussion programmes, features, documentaries and even online of this muddying of the clear waters of the Israel–Palestine crisis. Elsewhere in this book academics and analysts such as Greg Philo give a scientific, *actuarial* account of this carelessness with the public broadcaster's duty. Without the room to print my long litany of the BBC's sins of omission and commission, I can best highlight my findings this way: Channel 4 News at 7pm is the only mainstream television news/current affairs bulletin that has tried consistently to do justice to this story, which sits at the centre of world affairs and the west's political engagement overseas.

Where Carlton TV has shown John Pilger's graphic *Palestine is Still the Issue*[3] and Channel 4 Sandra Jordan's death-defying story of the International Solidarity Movement[4] the BBC has made no effort to tell us truly – as did these two documentaries – how this occupation demeans and degrades people: not just the killing and the destruction, but the humiliation, the attempt to crush the human spirit and remove the identity; not just the bullet in the brain and the tank through the door, but the faeces Israel's soldiers rub on the plundered ministry walls, the trashed kindergarten; the barriers to a people's work, prayers and hopes.

In the news reporting of the domestic BBC TV bulletins, "balance", the BBC's crudely applied device for avoiding trouble, means that Israel's lethal modern army is one force, the Palestinians, with their rifles and home-made bombs, the other "force": two sides equally strong and culpable in a difficult dispute, it is implied, that could easily be sorted out if extremists on both sides would see reason and the leaders do as instructed by Washington.

In London, respectful BBC presenters talk calmly to articulate Israeli politicians, spokesmen and apologists in suits in studios; from Palestine comes the bad-quality, broken voice on a dusty wire from some wreckage of a town. It is true that BBC teams risk their lives in the midst of the violence, but soon they are back in their Jewish Jerusalem studios, finding the balance for their pieces, so that the rolling tragedy of occupation can somehow be ameliorated by the difficulties inside Israel.

When suicide bombers attack inside Israel the shock is palpable. The BBC rarely reports the context, however. Many of these acts of killing and martyrdom are reprisals for assassinations by Israel's death squads, soldiers and agents who risk nothing as they shoot from heli-copters or send death down a telephone line. I rarely see or hear any analysis of how many times the Israelis have deliberately shattered a period of Palestinian calm with an egregious attack or murder. "Quiet" periods mean no Israelis died ... it is rarely shown that during these "quiet" times Palestinians continued to be killed by the score.

In South Africa, the BBC made it clear that the platform from which it was reporting was one of abhorrence of the state crime of apartheid. No Afrikaaner was ritually rushed into a studio to explain a storming of a township. There is no such platform of the BBC's in Israel/Palestine, where the situation is as bad – apartheid, discrimi-nation, racism, ethnic cleansing as rife as ever it was in the Cape or the Orange Free State.

We are not reminded, continually and emphatically, that this strife comes about because of occupation. Occupation. Occupation. This should be a word never far from a reporter's lips, stated firmly and repeatedly as the permanent backdrop to and living reason for every act of violence on either side.

Much of the explanation of events the BBC offers from the scene reminds me of the "on-the-one-side-on-the-other-side" reporting that bedevilled so many years of BBC reporting from Northern Ireland. The performance in the London studios is little better. Presenters and reporters are, on the whole, not well briefed on the Middle East. They are repeatedly bamboozled by Israel's performers. Time and again, presented with an Israeli or some inadequately flagged American or other apologist for Israel, the presenter will accept the pro-Israel version of the truth at face value, respectful of an American accent, a well-dressed politician or an ex-diplomat (who is often nothing like as disinterested as it would appear),[5] while pressing hard on the recalcitrant Arab.[6]

The Arab view is not properly heard. This is partly an Arab problem, in that there are not enough articulate and willing Arabs readily available to go to studios or answer the telephone. But this is only part of the problem: the BBC has been plied with lists of suitable people by organisations such as the Council for the Advancement of Arab–British Understanding, the Arab League, individual embassies and private people, only for these lists to be ignored. Whether this is through inefficiency or deliberation, it is hard to say. I do know, for example, that the ambassador for the Arab League had, between January 2003 and the end of the Iraq war in early April, appeared once on BBC TV; a colleague of mine who is one of Britain's most articulate and intelligent Palestinian spokespersons is missing almost completely from mainstream BBC television and rarely heard on domestic radio.[7]

Why is the BBC so poor at covering Israel/Palestine (for the purposes of this chapter I am concentrating on the BBC's domestic output – BBC World Service and to some extent BBC World TV could easily be the product of a different organisation)?

In the past dozen years or so, the BBC has become a vast, impersonal, extremely successful organisation – a corporation in a very modern sense, rich, powerful, crushing the opposition, riding high and expanding in many directions. It is on the verge of being a commercial organisation, with its diversity of interests. Certainly the spirit of its Charter has been bent nearly to breaking point. It certainly behaves like a commercial company in its ruthless pursuit of ratings and the descent of its terrestrial TV channels down-market, proper current affairs programming being a significant victim of this process.

The difference between the BBC and other private concerns, however, is that in the BBC's case its only shareholder is the British government: it prospers or fails by its licence fee, which is fixed by the government. The more generous the government is to the BBC the more unwilling is the BBC to cross that government in any significant way. Why rock a comfortable boat? It is also true that the more one owns the more one loathes to lose it. This was not true of the BBC of the 1960s, 1970s and 1980s. Since the advent as director general of John Birt,[8] the Blair government has smiled on the BBC. We thus have what might be termed a Blairite tendency at the BBC, an unwillingness to cross New Labour on matters close to its heart; and the Middle East has been at the very centre – outside Europe – of Tony Blair's foreign policy concern.

The Blair vision of the Middle East – that the Americans have all the answers, but need a little gentle coaxing from Whitehall, that the Israelis are victims of terror, and "terror" is our main universal enemy, that the Palestinians are their own worst enemies and must do what they are told – will have been sensed at the BBC and passed on down the line.

It is no secret that Blair is very close to Israel. His old crony and party financier, Lord Levy, has been rewarded with the post of special adviser on Middle East matters. Lord Levy is a peer who has close contacts with Israel and a multi-million pound villa near Tel Aviv – his son Daniel Levy worked in the office of Israel's former Justice Minister, Yossi Beilin. The first stress in any New Labour comment on the Palestine–Israel crisis is always on Israeli security or on "terror", that easy *bête noir* of the modern politician (the BBC has uncritically accepted "The War on Terror" as a phrase with meaning).

Thus there is much for the BBC to be aware of as it peers out over the carnage in the Occupied Territories. The process of getting the boys in the front-line *into* line does not work by diktat from above but by hint and nudge and whispered word, almost, in such a very *English* way, by extra-sensory perception – rather as until the mid-1960s a Tory Party leader would *emerge* rather than be chosen.

Eager to help in this insidious process, squatting there in the gardens of Kensington, is the Israeli embassy, emanating influence and full of tricks, with many powerful friends and supporters. The first bloody month of the Second Intifada took the Israelis by storm. Their responses were crude and ill-thought-out. They received a highly critical international press after Ariel Sharon stormed on to the Haram al-Sharif, the Palestinians erupted and the Israelis started their killing spree. The Israeli machine recovered quickly, and immediately turned its attention to the BBC. One experienced reporter in the field told me how producers from *The Today Programme* would ring the office in Jerusalem with story ideas launched by the Israeli embassy; how the Israeli version of events was so often received as the prevailing wisdom in London; how Israel successfully amended the very language of reporting the crisis.

For a short while on BBC news, "occupied" territories became "disputed". We heard much of Palestinian "claims" of occupation rather than of the 33-year-long fact of it. Illegal Jewish settlements near Jerusalem became "neighbourhoods". Palestinians *are* killed (it happens); but *Palestinians kill* Israelis (that is deliberate); dead Israelis have a name and identity, dead Arabs are – just, well, dead Arabs. When Palestinians die their bereaved vent "rage" at apparently riotous funerals; Israeli survivors express shock. The list goes on. The news-speak of the crisis was adjusted to favour the Israeli side.[9]

Then, unfortunately, the BBC's experienced team in Jerusalem was removed at the beginning of this new upheaval in Israeli–Palestinian affairs – not through any Zionist-inspired plot but because correspondents' and producers' contracts or tours of duty were expiring. I do not wish to malign the new reporters' professional expertise, as reporters, but it was a bad moment for an across-the-board reshuffle. The BBC should have staggered the changeovers and deployed people more experienced in Middle East or even in similar crises – the Balkans, for example.

London and its attendant Israeli pressure teams were thus writing on blank sheets for a while. The worst excesses of that early period have ended and the use of language is more accurate – though phrases like "ceasefire", implying the existence of two armies, and "terrorist", too often used as a synonym for "resistance", underscore the already false projection of the conflict. Through it all, the policies of artificially striving for balance and equivalence remain, and the people on the ground have neither the skills nor strength to resist this policy or circumvent it with subtlety. To be fair to them, perhaps they would quickly be removed if they tried.

The matter is further complicated by the cornucopia of BBC news outlets that now exists. This phenomenon harms news coverage in many ways. As the head of BBC Newsgathering, Adrian Van Klaveren, told a media conference in London in February: "We [the viewers and listeners] are victims of the broadcasting culture where there is so much broadcasting that none of us, even an interested audience can hear any more than a fraction of what [the BBC] do."[10] This cuts many ways. Mainly, it means that the BBC can banish the awkward squads who might raise (or answer) real questions about the Middle East to the watches that end the night. Critics who say the Palestinian or Arab view has not been aired can be referred to the World Service at 3.00am, or News 24 at 6.00am, and so on.

Anyone who listens to *The World Tonight*, on Radio 4 at 10.00pm, will know that the level of programming and presenting is far more searching and alert to the twists and nuances of foreign affairs than *Today*. A few hundred thousand may listen to radio at 10.00pm (in competition with the BBC's main TV news and its oversimplifications and star "brand" reporters), while millions tune in to *Today*, which throws its heaviest weight into domestic matters and is inconsistent and often badly briefed on foreign affairs, particularly those in the Israeli-occupied Territories.[11]

The profile of the listening and viewing world is changing. Many people, especially the young, now listen to and watch all kinds of channels at all times of night and day. Stations like BBC Asia Network and Radio Five Live are boisterous and irreverent, with well-informed callers, many of them from Muslim, Arab, Asian and other ethnic groups. Britain's political leaders and Israel's supporters, however, do not apply themselves to these people's forums. What they care about are the mainstream outlets, *Today*, *The World at One*, *PM*, *Breakfast News*, the one o'clock, six o'clock and ten o'clock television bulletins. The BBC, alert to this, shapes the tone of its correspondents' and reporters' coverage, and its presenters' and producers' attitudes accordingly: very cautiously, in lockstep as close as can be with the government and the policy-makers at No.10 Downing Street.

In fact, the coverage of the Blair government and its personalities is often more critical than coverage of Israel.

One reason for this may be the phrase that terrifies the managers of the Corporation, though it is widely misused, abused and manipulated: this is anti-Semitism. Anything critical of Israel is liable to raise that spurious charge; spurious or not, BBC bosses do not want to hear it let alone try to answer it or argue against it intelligently. At a recent writers' festival in Sydney, the Palestinian author Ghada Karmi, who has good reason to know about this phenomenon – *Woman's Hour* apparently refused to consider her book *In Search of Fatima: A Palestinian Story* for serialisation or author-interview unless an item of "Jewish balance" could be found – strongly criticised the BBC's nervousness about anti-Semitism, which, she told a large and appreciative Australian and international audience of writers and journalists, was seriously undermining the BBC's fairness in dealing with the complexities of the Middle East. The novelist and broadcaster Sarah Dunant publicly confirmed this view to the conference, saying that all European journalists were constrained in their reporting by this consciousness of avoiding anti-Semitism.[12]

For example, lurid Israeli stories of anti-Semitism in the Arab press are taken at face value, while similar abuse of Arabs by Israelis is rarely reported. Both phenomena exist but only one is belaboured.

As I write this chapter, in mid-June 2003, the BBC has consigned a profile of the Palestinian intellectual, author and activist Edward Said, a giant mind of his time by any measure, to a late-night showing on BBC4, a minority channel.[13] It was not advertised; its time was changed from 8.30pm (a prime slot right after the BBC4 news bulletin) to 10.00pm at the last minute, again without publicity. Much of this kind of programming is shunted to the late hours or minority channels.

The only decent documentary the BBC has made about Israel, a searching examination of the Vanunu affair, was also postponed a day, from a prime time, and dismissed to a late-night showing.[14] (To be fair to the BBC, Carlton also put John Pilger's Palestine programme out late at night. After it was shown, the chairman, Michael Green, excoriated the programme, saying it should never have gone out.[15] Many other friends of Israel joined Green in complaining to the ITC about bias, but the Commission resoundingly endorsed and vindicated the programme.[16] At least the chairman of the BBC Board of Governors does not publicly revile his organisation's programmes hours after they have been transmitted.)

There are less easily avoidable reasons for the BBC's mishandling of the Palestine–Israel issue. Much of the seeming bias in the coverage – and not just at the BBC – is endemically and accidentally cultural. To a westerner sitting at a screen in London a dead or suffering Arab in the rubble of a bazaar is more remote than a dead or suffering Israeli in a shopping mall with a Wal-Mart in-shot; studios favour good English-speakers rather than men with heavy accents; producers like quality sound and vision. It is a presenter's inclination, in many cases, to take more seriously a representative of a state and an authority, a uniform or a dark suit, than a denizen of what is, after all, not quite a state but still a national revolutionary and resistance movement, a man perhaps in a *keffiyeh* or a militia uniform, speaking poor English or being translated or subtitled.

All this is true, but it is no excuse. The BBC has to work hard to counter this cultural drift. It has to strive for *proper* balance between the state and the stateless. Conscious effort and caution has to be applied at all times, and it is not easy in busy, overworked, high-turnover newsrooms.

The BBC has to be courageous. It has to do more to understand and have presented properly the Arab–Palestinian case. It has to find those many Palestinians and Arabs, and their interlocutors and experts on the region, here and in the Middle East, who can put and explain the Palestinian case. It is, after all, not so different from the plight of the Africans, Indians, Coloureds and liberal-minded Whites who struggled for so long in South Africa, and about whom the BBC reported with fairness and integrity.

The news chiefs should move more people out of West Jerusalem. It should base a news team in the West Bank – not just some luckless stringer but a senior, known correspondent who can force his or her way onto the main bulletins (what the BBC likes to call a "brand" reporter). Here the reporters will feel what daily life under occupation is like, live it and empathise with the people crushed under it, as news crews lived the invasion of Baghdad or as we experienced the Israeli invasions and occupation of Lebanon – from the inside, not just down there on a visit.

It seems, however, that the policy-makers at the BBC are not as brave as the reporters, producers and cameramen they send into the field. It is more troubling for a boss to field an angry phone call from the Board of Deputies of British Jews or receive an abusive letter from Golders Green or to read a bilious article in the *Daily Telegraph* than it is for a camera crew and correspondent to venture down the road to Nablus, past those trigger-happy roadblocks and into those dangerous alleyways, and still find their cut story watered down with the countervailing view from a balcony in West Jerusalem.

Despite all this, the sheer imagery of the crisis – tank against stone, soldier against civilian – is making its weight felt. The British public are becoming more and more uneasily aware that the words do not quite match the pictures. The euphoria that greets each new peace plan – the "road map" is the latest – and is picked up so eagerly by a flag-waving, cheer-leading broadcast media no longer takes with it, I think, the average viewer.

The Corporation's timidity about telling the truth from Palestine is not about informing the viewer, however, but about keeping protectively in step with government and projecting its future into the twenty-first century.

NOTES

1. *The Road to Armageddon*, BBC2, 8pm, 7 June 2003.
2. "Behind the Fence", *Correspondent*, BBC2, 7.15pm, 25 May 2003.
3. *Palestine is Still the Issue*, Carlton TV, 11.00pm, 16 September 2002.
4. "The Killing Zone", *Dispatches*, Channel 4, 8pm, 19 May 2003.
5. Two good examples of misrepresentation are those of Martin Indyk and, more especially Dennis Ross, both former US diplomats whom the BBC regularly trundles out to pontificate from apparently Olympian, though expert, detached heights about the Israel–Palestine crisis. It is never pointed out that both men are Zionists and former members of the powerful American Jewish lobby organisation, AIPAC.
6. One outstanding example of this was the *Newsnight* of 30 November 2001, BBC2, when Jeremy Paxman gave the former Israel Prime Minister, Binyamin Netanyahu, an astonishingly easy ride then bullied the British Palestinian barrister – Michel Massih – an inexperienced TV broadcaster – with repeated rapid-fire accusations about suicide bombs and terrorism. The BBC bosses reprimanded Paxman. Paxman is not alone in this

tendency to let Israelis get away with it but treat Arabs as if they are prisoners at the bar.

7. If three London Palestinians – Dr Ghada Karmi, Afif Safieh, the Palestinian ambassador-equivalent in London, and Abdel Bari Atwan, editor of the Arabic language daily *Al Quds Al Arabi* – were to fall under buses tomorrow, the Palestinian case would almost cease to exist as far as the BBC is concerned. It has to be said that they are all used far more sparingly than the importance of crisis demands.

8. When John Birt came into the BBC in the late 1980s, first as deputy Director-General than as full DG, his main task was to bring into line a BBC the Thatcher government saw as a rival centre of power. He did his job well. His successor, Greg Dyke, while not bucking government has developed the commercial nature of the Corporation.

9. Martin Woollacott, the eminent *Guardian* foreign affairs columnist, described this well at a media conference in Dubai in April 2002, saying "the Israelis have captured the language".

10. "Reporting the World", a media conference at the *Guardian/Observer* building on 20 February 2003.

11. One excepts from this *Today*'s brilliant post-Iraq War coverage – but this is essentially a domestic political story.

12. Sarah Dunant is a regular presenter of BBC Radio 3's *Night Waves* and has broadcast intelligently on, *inter alia*, Palestinian cultural affairs. It must also be pointed out that no decent journalist would have any dealings with real anti-Semitism – it is the false, blanket charge of anti-Semitism and the obsessive fear of incurring it that actually devalues the currency of language and paradoxically assists real anti-Semitism.

13. *A Profile of Edward Said*, by Charles Glass, BBC4, 10pm, 9 June 2003.

14. "Israeli Nuclear Power Exposed", by Olenka Frenkiel, *Correspondent*, BBC2, 11.20pm, 17 March 2003.

15. *Guardian*, letters, 20 September 2002.

16. ITC ruling handed down on 17 January 2003.

26
Black Holes of History:
Public Understanding and
the Shaping of Our Past[1]

Greg Philo and Maureen Gilmour

In March 1999, President Clinton made a public apology in Guatemala. It was an extraordinary event and we asked a group of 280 young people why he might have done this. We were engaged in a study of what people knew about the history of their world and this was one of a series of questions which we put to groups of students.[2] Very few of them knew why Clinton had apologised. Three per cent wrote correctly that it was because of US involvement in "dirty wars" in support of right-wing regimes. Ten per cent believed he was apologising for the Monica Lewinsky affair – a subject which people knew much more about. The majority simply did not know. Yet Clinton's apology was remarkable. It followed the publication of a report by an independent commission which concluded that the US was responsible for most of the human rights abuses during a 36-year civil war, in which 200,000 people died. Clinton was reported as saying: "It is important that I state clearly that support for military forces or intelligence Units which engaged in violent and widespread repression of the kind described in the report was wrong" (*Guardian*, 12 March 1999).

At the same time the American government de-classified documents which showed the US had "initiated and sustained a murderous war conducted by Guatemalan security forces against civilians suspected of aiding left-wing guerrilla movements" (*Guardian*, 12 March 1999). The documents revealed that the US set up a safe house in the presidential palace in Guatemala City which became the headquarters for the "dirty war". A State Department cable from October 1967 revealed that security operations included "kidnapping, torture and summary execution". Twenty-five years later, a CIA cable confirmed that civilian villages were targeted because of the army's belief that the Maya Indian inhabitants were aiding guerrillas. As the *Guardian* also reported:

> A report released this month by the Guatemala Truth Commission confirmed that entire communities were massacred. It said children were killed, abducted, forcibly recruited as soldiers, illegally adopted and sexually abused. Foetuses were cut from their mothers' wombs and young children were smashed against walls or thrown alive into pits. (*Guardian*, 12 March 1999)

Such events are intensely controversial and their history is often contested. Yet in this case the source was the US president and the documentary proof came from the US government itself. We put the same question – of Clinton's apology – to a group of 49 American journalism and media students and to another group of 114 high school students from Germany. In these samples 8 per cent of those from the US knew the correct answer and 4 per cent of the Germans, but the great majority did not know or thought it was related to Monica Lewinsky.

The United States has been involved in many "dirty wars" in Latin America and there have been extensive accusations of human rights abuses. Right-wing military regimes were supported in countries such as Brazil while some elected regimes were attacked or displaced as in Nicaragua and Chile. In another question, we asked: "Who were the 'Contras' in Nicaragua?" These were the private army financed by the US in the 1980s to attack the left-wing Sandinista government. The great majority of the students had not heard of them. We also found that the abuses of the Soviet communist system had apparently vanished into a similar black hole. We asked: "What were the Gulags in the Soviet Union?" These were the slave labour camps which were established under Stalin's regime and which Solzhenitsyn wrote of in his books *The First Circle* and *The Gulag Archipelago*. Five per cent of the British students and 8 per cent of the Americans knew what they were. The German students were better informed and 30 per cent gave the correct answer.

Popular history is likely to be shaped by the priorities and interests of those who produce it. In controversial areas it may serve to legitimise past actions or to celebrate them. This is expressed in the phrase "history is written by the victors". When beliefs about historical events do exist they are likely to have been coloured by the cultural struggles which characterise the writing of history and its popular construction. Beliefs about a major conflict such as the Second World War can vary between different societies. This is partly because history is told from the side and perspectives of those involved. We are taught about the famous battles which involved "our" soldiers and watch popular films and TV programmes about them. But such memories are coloured by a second level of cultural struggle which developed after that war. This was the Cold War between east and west, which provided another filter for our perception. In the Second World War, the Soviet Union was allied with the United States and Britain in a common struggle against fascism. But after the war, the west and east were divided as ideological enemies. This meant that the contribution of the Soviet Union to the winning of the Second World War was not only neglected but was actually obliterated in some popular accounts. We can look for example in the manner in which anniversaries of the war were conducted. The 40th anniversary of D-Day was on 6 June 1984. The early 1980s was a period in which the American Right had become dominant under President Reagan. This signalled an intensification of the Cold War, an intention to increase defence expenditure and extensive rhetoric on the "evil empire" of the Soviet Union. When President Reagan attended the D-Day ceremonies in Europe, the commemoration of what was actually a joint struggle against the Nazis was turned into a straightforward attack on the Soviet Union. This is an extract from President Reagan's speech which was shown on British television news: "The Soviet troops that came to the centre of this continent did not leave when peace came. They are still there, uninvited, unwanted, unyielding almost forty years after the war" (President Reagan, ITN/Channel 4 News, 6 June 1984).

The effect was to remove consideration of the role of the Soviet armies in the actual war. This was discussed at the time by an "alternative" weekly news programme made by Channel 4, under the title *Diverse Reports*. Its role was to highlight stories that were missing from other news programmes. It produced a feature on the D-Day story and began by pointing to gaps in national news coverage. ITN/Channel 4 News had reported for example that: "The Union Jack rose under the Queen's proud and watchful eye, to join the flags of all the nations who fought and defeated Hitler" (7.00pm, 6 June 1984). This news extract was shown on *Diverse Reports* and the programme commented on it that: "not quite all, the Soviet flag was missing" (27 June 1984). The programme then went on to describe the decisive role of the Soviet Union in the combat. It noted that the

Battle of Stalingrad in 1943 was a key defeat for the Nazis in which they lost an elite army of a quarter of a million men. This was followed by the Battle of Kursk Bulge which was reported to be the biggest tank battle of all time. The German army was again routed and a significant proportion of its ground armour destroyed. D-Day was still a year away. By 1945 the western allies had defeated 170 German divisions; the Soviets had defeated 607. The Soviet losses were enormous with an estimated 20 million dead (compared to around 1 million for the western forces).

Ten years after Reagan's speech, President Clinton came to Europe for the 50th anniversary of the D-Day celebrations. By then the Soviet bloc had collapsed but the US president's speech still highlighted the role of the Allies and spoke of them as "beginning to end" the war: "Here the miracle of liberation began ... the forces of democracy landed ... on beaches such as these an army landed from the sea to begin to end a war" (BBC1, 5.45pm, 6 June 1994).

We asked the students the question: "In the Second World War, which Allied country defeated the most German divisions?" Just 18 per cent of the US students and 29 per cent of the British gave the answer as the Soviet Union (65 per cent of the US students and 48 per cent of the British put Britain or the US). Interestingly, the German students were better informed and 73 per cent named the Soviet Union.

We also asked about the war in Vietnam, which the Americans eventually withdrew from in 1975. It is believed that the US dropped 3 million tons of explosives in this war, which would have been more than the total tonnage dropped by the US and Britain in the Second World War (including the atomic bombs). In Vietnam, just under 60,000 Americans were killed. Vietnamese deaths were estimated at over 2 million. The question which we put to the students was: "In the Vietnam War, how many casualties were there on each side, how many US personnel, how many Vietnamese?" To this, 37 per cent of the US students replied that it was more Americans or that the numbers were about equal. The same percentage replied that it was "a lot more Vietnamese". The remainder thought it was "a few more Vietnamese" or did not know. For the British, 34 per cent thought it was "a lot more Vietnamese" and for the German students it was 36 per cent. In our popular culture, US films have portrayed their forces as involved in heroic and bloody action against a deadly enemy. They do not typically discuss the millions of mostly civilians who were killed or injured. When the British students were told of the actual casualties, an audible gasp came from them. What is clear is that many of these young people including the Americans, had no idea of the scale of death which had been imposed on Vietnam.

Our understanding of contemporary events can be shaped by our knowledge of history. To investigate this further we undertook an additional study of public understanding of the Israeli–Palestinian conflict. We used the same sample groups as above, but also interviewed a further 100 people in focus groups.[3] For most people, the main source of information about world events is television news. A recent study by the Independent Television Commission found that in 2002, 79 per cent of the population regarded the television as their main source of world news.[4] For our own study, we analysed the content of television news and found that there was very little information given on the history and origins of the Israeli–Palestinian conflict. We examined 91 bulletins from BBC1 and ITV1 in the first weeks of the Intifada, between 8 September and 16 October 2000. The news was transcribed and the lines of text which were devoted to different themes were counted (e.g. how many described fighting/violence or peace negotiations or explanations of the conflict). In over 3,500 lines of text, just 17 explained the history of the conflict. It is perhaps not surprising then that many of the people in our audience groups knew very little about its origins. We asked our large samples of students the question: "Where did the Palestinian refugees come from and how did they become refugees?"

For the British students only 8 per cent replied that the Palestinians had been displaced or lost their homes and land when Israel was created (19 per cent of Americans and 26 per cent of Germans). This history has in fact been contested. Israel for many years claimed that the refugees had left voluntarily or because they were ordered to by their leaders. More recently historians have disputed this and have given documented accounts of the events. The Israeli historian Avi Shlaim for example has shown in his very detailed history, *The Iron Wall*, how the military forces of what became Israel embarked on an offensive strategy which involved destroying Arab villages and the forced removal of civilians:

> Palestinian society disintegrated under the impact of the Jewish military offensive that got underway in April (1948), and the exodus of the Palestinians was set in motion ... by ordering the capture of Arab cities and the destruction of villages, it both permitted and justified the forcible expulsion of Arab civilians.[5]

The intention, as Shlaim comments, was to clear the interior of the future Israeli state of what was seen as potentially hostile "Arab elements". Shortly after in May 1948 a major war broke out between Israel and its Arab neighbours which occasioned more people to flee. Many of the refugees moved to Gaza (which came under the control of Egypt) and to the West Bank of the Jordan River (under Jordanian control). In 1967 Israel fought a further war with its Arab neighbours and in the process of this, occupied Gaza and the West Bank, thus bringing the Palestinian refugees under its military control. East Jerusalem, which has great religious and cultural significance for both Israelis and Palestinians, was also occupied (taken from Jordan). These military occupations were bitterly resisted by the Palestinians, not least because Israel built "settlements" all across the militarily occupied territories. This was much more than simply building houses and farms. As Avi Shlaim suggests, they were part of a policy of exerting strategic and military control by, for example, "surrounding the huge greater Jerusalem area with two concentric circles of settlements with access roads and military positions".[6]

In the focus groups for our study, we were sometimes asked by the group members about the origins of the conflict. In response they were given a very brief account based on the work of Avi Shlaim quoted above. Although the account given was extremely brief, it could have a very dramatic effect on their understanding. This exchange occurred in a group of males, interviewed in London:

Moderator	Would it help you when you are watching the news, if you knew that history?
First Speaker	Yes.
Second Speaker	A lot more.
Third Speaker	Absolutely.
Second Speaker	If they did refer more to the history, the whole thing would mean a hell of a lot more for a lot of people.
First Speaker	That's right, we need to know more.
Third Speaker	It's so fragmented and vague, I mean to try and explain it to my children, I found it difficult – I'm

> not the sharpest tool in the box anyway, but
> having said that, on what I was given by the
> media, a great deal of it was blank, and you just
> filled in the blanks that I didn't have a clue about
> – 1948? Was there a war in 1948? Well now I know
> there was. (Low income male group, London)

There were some reservations about how much historical detail could be included in news. But overall there was a strong feeling in the groups that it was difficult to understand the present without some knowledge of the past. As a student from Glasgow put it:

> I've not heard any historical context from the news at all. They
> don't tell us that – they don't say. They leave it on the short scale.
> "This fighting was due to yesterday's fighting, which was due to
> the day before." But they don't go back to all that, I don't know
> anything about that [history]. The reporter will say: "The Israelis
> fired into a Palestinian refugee camp today in response to a
> Palestinian suicide bomber yesterday" but they won't say why the
> Palestinians are fighting or why the Israelis are fighting – it doesn't
> go back any length of time. (Male student, Glasgow)

The lack of historical knowledge made it very difficult for people to understand key elements of the conflict. For example, some had written that "land" was an issue but there was a great deal of confusion over what this meant. Another participant described how his understanding included no sense of the Palestinian case that land had been taken from them:

> The impression I got was that the Palestinians had lived around
> that area and now they were trying to come back and get some
> more land for themselves – I didn't realise they had been actually
> driven out, I just thought they didn't want to live as part of Israel
> and that the places they were living in, they decided they wanted
> to make self-governed – I didn't realise they had been driven out
> of places in wars previously. (Male student, Glasgow)

Some people saw the conflict as a dispute between two countries or peoples, who had a strip of land between them that they both wanted, as in this exchange:

Moderator   How did this land conflict come about?

Male Speaker   They are right next to each other and they are trying
                  to get a bit more off each other.

Moderator   Do you see it as two countries, two groups and two
                  countries and they are both fighting over this bit of
                  contested land?

Male Speaker   That is it, yes.

Moderator   So something in the middle of it all?

Male Speaker   It is like the border and they are trying to take a bit
                  off each other. (Low income mixed gender group,
                  Glasgow)

The same point is made in another group: "I didn't realise – I didn't
know all the geography of Palestine being occupied. I thought there
was Palestine, then there was Israel and then there was the border in
between that they were fighting over" (Female office workers,
Glasgow). Another sees the conflict as a "nice piece of land" that
they are both fighting over, without any sense that land has been
taken:

Female Speaker   I just thought it was disputed land, I wasn't under
                  the impression that the Israeli borders had changed
                  or that they had taken land from other people. I
                  just had the impression that it was a nice piece of
                  land that both, to put it simplistically, that they
                  were fighting over and I thought, it was more a
                  Palestinian aggression than it was Israeli aggression.

Moderator   Did anyone else see it this way? (Five out of ten
                  people in this group assented.) (Student group,
                  Glasgow)

There were similar problems in understanding terms such as
"occupied territories". Because many in the groups did not
understand that Palestinians had been subject to military occupation
after 1967, there was some confusion over what the word "occupied"

meant. It was sometimes understood simply to mean that people were on the land, as in a bathroom being occupied, rather than as signifying a military occupation. There was similar confusion over who were the settlers. In a large group of 300 students who answered a questionnaire for us in 2001, there were actually more people who believed that it was the Palestinians who were occupying the land and were the settlers than who believed that it was the Israelis and that the settlers were Israeli.

In conclusion it is clear that a limited knowledge of history can produce great confusion about the nature of contemporary conflicts and the reasons why they are so intractable. The gaps in our history also have an ideological function. Those who seek to present the current actions of the west as merely benign and defensive would prefer that the violent consequences of past interventions remain undiscussed and unknown. But if we are to understand our present, we must not let our past disappear into the black holes of a partial history.

NOTES

1. The funding for the research on which this chapter is based was provided by the Economic and Social Research Council whose support we would like to acknowledge.
2. For a fuller account of this study see G. Philo/Glasgow University Media Group, *Bad News from Israel*, London: Pluto Press, 2004.
3. These included three groups of people who were students plus one group of elderly/retired people and another ten groups of 25–50 year olds selected on the basis of gender and income.
4. Independent Television Commission, *The Public's View*, London: ITC, 2003.
5. Avi Shlaim, *The Iron Wall: Israel and the Arab World*, London: Penguin, 2000, p. 30.
6. Ibid., p. 582.

Part 4
Alternatives

Part
Literature

27
Al Jazeera's War

Faisal Bodi

Just as the overthrow of Saddam Hussein failed to end the US-led war on Iraq so too has it proved incapable of settling the information war that began with the build-up to the invasion. No sooner had the Ba'athist iron-man been hauled down in the centre of Baghdad than President George W. Bush and UK Prime Minister Tony Blair found themselves weathering a political storm at the eye of which lay the charge that they had cooked up a *casus belli*.

With newspapers and politicians on both sides of the Atlantic berating "dodgy dossiers" and "sexed-up intelligence" it seemed that the chickens of misinformation had come home to roost. A *Newsweek* poll in July 2003 found 38 per cent of Americans saying they believed that their government had deliberately misled them on the war. A *Guardian* ICM poll in the same month recorded a 2 per cent rise in the already high number of Britons who believe the invasion was unjustified. Limited Congressional and parliamentary investigations got underway to probe the stated reasons for the attack. The fog of war was clearing over a battlefield on which it increasingly appears it had not so much descended as been imposed to conceal the real motives for the invasion.

From their million-pound, state-of-the-art media complex at US Central Command in the Gulf emirate of Qatar, US and British forces ran an operation of military sophistication designed to prop up their comrades in arms through the war. Just how far they depended on massaging the truth was revealed with the landing of the first missiles in Baghdad's suburbs in the morning of 20 March. A volley of around 40 "precision-guided missiles" rained down on what the Pentagon described as "targets of opportunity" in a "decapitation attack" on Saddam Hussein.

Since winning the battle for hearts and minds was a political priority, it mattered less that the invasion forces were making headway in the theatre than they were seen to be doing so. Even if it failed in its stated objective, the attack had the propaganda value of topping the news agenda for the outset of the war, a clear war aim.

For days afterwards, it allowed news presenters and pundits to speculate over whether the "pinprick strikes" had succeeded in severing the snake's head. Even when Saddam showed up on Iraqi TV the following day to prove he was alive and well, the terms of western media discourse continued to follow the contours of US–British policy with speculation widening to talk of Saddam "doubles" and nobody bothering to question the ethics of assassinating the leader of a sovereign nation.

The "decapitation strike" pre-empted a widely touted blitzkrieg curtain-raiser to the war proper dubbed "shock and awe". Presented by the US as a decisive display of technological military superiority the concept was in fact a euphemism for hammering the enemy into swift submission. One of the tactic's original promoters, Harlan Ullman, explained in the 7 April 2003 issue of *USA Today* how it was informed by the US's defeat of Japan in the Second World War:

> Shock and awe's overarching goal is to render an adversary defense-less and force it to surrender … Hiroshima and Nagasaki are historical examples of this goal. In August 1945, Japan was prepared to fight to the death. The home islands were blockaded, and people were starving. B-29 firebomb raids were routinely immolating tens of thousands of Japanese. US casualties from an invasion of Japan were estimated at a million soldiers … After the second atomic bomb … Japan surrendered unconditionally abandoning its suicidal resistance. The reason was shock and awe. Tokyo could understand a thousand plane raids killing hundreds of thousands of Japanese citizens. But one plane, one bomb and one city gone? That was incomprehensible, both shocking and awesome.

Although the author goes on to say that the same degree of force was inconceivable in Iraq, the passage does indicate that "shock and awe" did not preclude the loss of civilian casualties. Yet again serious discussion of the concept and its implications failed to find its way onto the newsreels, despite the fact that Iraqi society was still reeling from the impact on health of the hundreds of tonnes of toxic depleted uranium deployed by US-led forces during the 1991 war.

One major exception was the Arab media which was possibly alone in depicting the war as an act devoid of international legal sanction. Al Jazeera's tag for the conflict was "War on Iraq", in contrast to the BBC's neutral "War in Iraq" and Fox News' jingoistic

"Operation Iraqi Freedom" which merely parroted the Pentagon's name for the campaign.

Lively debate on the vernacular animated Al Jazeera's English-language newsroom. How should we refer to the attacking forces? "Coalition" sounded too inclusive for the three armies going to war, and too benign for a force against all international legal norms. "Axis" was an option, or "invading forces". In the end, in the interests of striking a measured tone, the Al Jazeera website opted for "US-led forces". Was it appropriate to use "regime" to refer to the Iraqi government in a situation where it was clear the term was being used to demonise the enemy? We decided not. How about calling Saddam Hussein by his first name or without his presidential title? Hadn't Saddam become a loaded term?

From an early stage the decision was made to fill the website with stories and features based on themes that reflected the concerns on the Arab street rather than of western politicians. The humanitarian fallout of the invasion raised all kinds of issues: civilian casualties, toxic waste from depleted uranium, refugees, ethnic and sectarian civil strife, and the further marginalisation of the Palestinians.

Politically what would be the repercussions for the region, and were other US bogeys like Syria and Iran next on Washington's hit-list? Was this not a US attempt to reshape the Middle East in the image the pro-Israeli lobby in Washington wanted? On an economic level what would be the war's impact on the region's oil producers? How would they absorb the impact of a country with the second largest reserves coming back on stream? Was the capture of Iraq and the probable installation of a client regime a ploy to undermine the potential bloc power of OPEC?

Needless to say, with a network of journalists spanning the length and breadth of Iraq we did not need the briefings of Centcom to answer these questions. As the station would show in Basra and Umm Qasr, it could check US claims that were dutifully being reported by western news channels in addition to generating first-hand reports of its own.

From the outset of the war, reporting followed two tracks, the "embed" line laid by Centcom, and the independent line by news providers like Al Jazeera who had the courage to locate hacks in the war zone. Enjoying a greater degree of access to Iraqi towns and cities allowed Arabic media outlets to report more independently than those journalists dependent on the armed forces for their personal safety and communication equipment. Al Jazeera had a single embedded reporter, stationed with US troops in Kuwait, and representation at Centcom. But the vast majority of its correspondents were dotted around the main population centres. From these vantage points the channel offered a perspective that was almost always at variance with the Centcom-generated line that the war was proceeding as smoothly as planned.

Take the fall of Umm Qasr. According to western news networks, the south-eastern Iraqi port, first in the line of the invading troops' advance, was "captured" five times in as many days starting from the beginning of the invasion. But Al Jazeera's correspondents in the strategic town reported fighting for at least six days after Donald Rumsfeld announced on 22 March that US forces had taken the town. Ditto the Basra uprising that never was. On 26 March British military officials, followed by government figures including the Prime Minister, reported that "massive resentment amongst the population" had led to an uprising in Iraq's second city the day before. "We have no doubt that yesterday evening they [Iraqi forces] were exchanging fire with their own people," said British defence minister Lewis Moonie in a calculated attempt to demonise the enemy. Yet a phone call to Al Jazeera's correspondent in the city returned the report that the streets were quiet and there was no sign of a rebellion.

The most poignant corrective to the White House/Centcom "victory march" came on day four of the invasion with footage of several captured US soldiers being beamed around the world by Al Jazeera. The images of bruised and frightened GI's triggered uproar in London and Washington but it was difficult to believe how much of this reaction was genuine and how much related to the desire to regain the PR advantage. In the end enough of a moral outcry was whipped up to convince the major US news networks to either limit their relaying of the images to a few seconds or to still shots. That all the networks had previously shown footage of Iraqi POWs, some of them being brutally handled, seemed to have escaped the memory of those such as Tony Blair and Donald Rumsfeld now waving copies of the Geneva Convention.

The censorship of US networks was not confined to their compatriot POWs. In the *Guardian* conference previously referred to, Michael Wolff accused the US media of supine compliance "with the flag-waving agenda of the Bush administration in order to persuade the Federal Communications Commission to change its regulations" (*Guardian*, 26 June 2003). "Ass-kissing has gone to a profound degree," he said. "It's pervasive throughout these news organisations."

The relationship between news corporations and politicians imposed another barrier on accurate reporting. According to Dr Michael Niman, lecturer in journalism and media studies at Buffalo State College, America's biggest owner of radio stations Clear Channel Communications Corporation emerged from the Reagan era as the prime beneficiary of media deregulation that removed restrictions on corporations owning multiple stations. For the company which now owns 1,200 stations nationwide "supporting the Bush family's war is payback for past Republican support of airwave deregulation, and a deposit on pending deregulation plans that would allow the company to move into television".[1]

Combined with a climate of suffocating jingoism, the political debts of media owners ensured that alternative views remained on the margins of the mass media or excluded altogether. Unwelcome news such as civilian casualties was massaged.

One of the most diabolical incidents of misinformation surrounded the bombing of a Baghdad marketplace. In the early evening of 29 March an explosion rocked the shopping area in the working-class district of Shoala, killing 62 civilians and injuring around 50 more. The celebrated *Independent* journalist Robert Fisk visited the scene of the slaughter and reported seeing a foot-long shrapnel shard of the missile at the scene of the blast. He wrote that the serial number on the shard identified the weapon as an American-made Harm device, or a Paveway laser-guided bomb – both manufactured by Arizona-based Raytheon. Although US officials confirmed that one Harm missile had been released over Baghdad on the same day they refused to acknowledge responsibility for the massacre. Rather both US and British officials tried to turn the heat on Saddam Hussein, suggesting that the carnage could have been caused by errant Iraqi anti-aircraft missiles. "A large number of surface-to-air missiles have been malfunctioning and many have failed to hit their targets and have fallen back on to Baghdad," said a spokesman for British Prime Minister Tony Blair, ignoring Robert Fisk's find. That was only slightly less cynical than a source in Washington who suggested the shrapnel was planted by the Iraqi government.

Right up until the present time western news agencies are being accused of being remiss in reporting civilian casualties. Iraqbodycount.net, a project dedicated to recording the human cost of the Iraq invasion and occupation, highlights a report by the Spanish Brigades Against the War's Arab Cause Solidarity Campaign into attacks against the civilian population of Baghdad between 20 March and 5 April 2003. The report concludes:

> the damage caused to the civilian population during the three weeks in which Baghdad was attacked was in no way due to mistakes, nor did it represent the "collateral damage" of a tactical surgical war, whose sole objective had been the destruction of the city's governmental and military infrastructure. Our opinion ... is that the attacks were premeditated, designed to cause the greatest possible number of civilian victims, many being repeatedly carried out against densely populated and poor areas of the Iraqi capital. The logic of this conduct can only be explained by the deliberate will of the American and British political and military leaders to provoke terror and undermine the resistance of the Baghdad population.

The website also laments the fact that "this study has not been reported by a single English-language news or media agency, to our knowledge".

Ironically it is the Middle Eastern media that has traditionally been associated with state ownership and censorship but the political straitjacketing of western agencies during the invasion of Iraq provided a welcome foil for their news channels. Even Al Jazeera, which is owned indirectly by the Qatari government allowed its editors a degree of freedom that did not appear possible in the west. Al Jazeera's star shone, as it had in Afghanistan two years earlier, with the channel claiming to have picked up 4 million news subscribers in Europe during the first few days of the invasion. Following the capture of the US POWs visitors poured in to its temporary English website and three-year-old Arabic website at a rate that made it the most searched item on the web in the week ending 31 August.

But as it became clear who was winning the media battle Al Jazeera found itself fighting off a hacking campaign. Both its websites were knocked out for several days with the English version only returning intermittently for the duration of the war. Technical experts at Al Jazeera told me that the most serious attack was caused by a type of hacking known as flooding – the generation of a huge volume of bogus traffic to jam the site's servers – at a level only possible for large companies and governments. In the US Al Jazeera's hosting firm, under pressure from unnamed sources, cancelled its contract forcing the company to move to Europe. Another popular Arabic website Arabia.com, based in the United Arab Emirates, was also temporarily blocked by hackers.

It was probably not a coincidence that the attempt to muzzle non-compliant voices occurred at precisely the time when Americans were flocking to non-US websites for their information. A study by the Pew Internet & American Life Project on 1 April showed that in the conflict's first six days, 10 per cent of American internet users visited foreign news websites.

The war against independent reporters was to get dirtier. In the early hours of 8 April a US warplane launched a raid against Al Jazeera's Baghdad bureau and the neighbouring Abu Dhabi TV. The strike killed the former's correspondent Tariq Ayyoub and wounded cameraman Zouhair al-Iraqi. The journalists' association, the Committee to Protect Journalists, wrote to the US Defense Secretary the same day in protest:

> The strike against these facilities is particularly troubling because both Al Jazeera and Abu Dhabi TV have been openly operating from these locations in Baghdad for weeks. In addition, prior to the commencement of hostilities in Iraq both stations told CPJ that they provided the specific coordinates of their Baghdad offices to the Pentagon. CPJ has seen a copy of Al Jazeera's February letter to Pentagon spokeswoman Victoria Clarke outlining these coordinates.

It wasn't the first attempt to hit Al Jazeera in Iraq. On 2 April the Sheraton hotel in Basra being used as a base by its correspondents was shelled receiving four direct hits during a heavy artillery bombardment. Luckily the crew all escaped injury.

Two years earlier US jets had bombed the Al Jazeera's offices in Kabul hours before Northern Alliance forces entered the Afghan capital. Reporters Without Borders asked Donald Rumsfeld at the time for an explanation of the attack. It is still awaiting a reply from the US Defense Secretary but a statement in late July 2003 by his deputy Paul Wolfowitz may give some indication of why US governments consider TV stations – in Belgrade as well as Baghdad – to be legitimate targets. Al Jazeera, according to Wolfowitz, was practising "very biased reporting that has the effect of inciting violence against our troops". It is not a big leap from here to the suggestion that

American soldiers are only acting in pre-emptive self-defence, when in the words of Al Jazeera's indignant reply they routinely subject Al Jazeera's offices and staff in Iraq "to strafing by gunfire, death threats, confiscation of news material, and multiple detentions and arrests, all carried out by US soldiers who have never actually watched Al Jazeera but only heard about it".

NOTE

1. Michael Niman, "Spinning the War – Lessons in Propaganda", *ArtVoice* (Buffalo's Alternative Newsweekly), 3 April 2003.

28
Target the Media

Tim Gopsill

What's the difference, goes the journalists' joke, between the Iraqi army and the American army? Answer: the Americans shoot at you.

In the three weeks that followed the American/British coalition's invasion of Iraq 17 journalists and other media workers were killed, seven of them directly by coalition fire (both figures include two missing since a US marine attack on their vehicle on 22 March). This is the highest known death toll of journalists in such a short period.

There were several factors at work: far more people were engaged in covering this war than any before – more than 3,000 according to most estimates – and many of them were closer to heavy fighting; around 300 were in Baghdad, a city under daily bombardment; and the invasion was rapid and chaotic, with jittery troops psyched up to believe that anyone not with them was against them. But in the aftermath a lot of journalists have come to suspect that some attacks were deliberate, that the media have become a target.

On 8 March, twelve days before the invasion, the veteran BBC correspondent Kate Adie made a sensational allegation in an interview on RTE Radio in Ireland. She said she had been told by a senior officer in the Pentagon that "If uplinks were detected by any planes ... they'd be fired down on," she said, "even if they were journalists. They would be 'targeted down'."

In the frenzy of desperate opposition to the war everyone knew was imminent, the story of the RTE interview whizzed around the internet. I must have received it from half a dozen sources – and to be honest, I was sceptical. It was not that I distrusted Kate Adie, a serious if limited reporter with no particular campaigning reputation. I was prepared to believe that the Americans were capable of pointing their missiles at more or less anything. But I was mystified that they should let such a policy become known, and in such an oblique manner.

There would be nothing new in the US or Britain attacking media establishments, but thus far they had always been "enemy" targets. In the bombing of Serbia in 1996 there was a deliberate hit on the RTS state broadcasting centre in Belgrade; 13 people were killed. And in the Afghan war in 2001 a missile had hit the Kabul studio of the Qatar-based Al Jazeera station – certainly seen as an enemy by the US; this time no one was killed. The journalistic community reacted with outrage to these attacks. But to hit journalists in the field, and those on "our" side – now that would be different. The US army might have an unfortunate record of wasting its own (and coalition) troops with "friendly fire", but no one has suggested they are targeted.

I had no easy way of contacting Kate Adie (not an NUJ member) to confirm the quotes. Someone will follow this up and make a fuss about it, I thought, and filed it away. In fact there was no more about it. The story was never taken up by the commercial media.

After the war her allegation seemed much more credible. The insouciance of military leaders in the face of the death toll confirms that at the least they are not unhappy about it, and there could indeed be a sinister logic to a strategy of targeting reporters: to discourage them from independent reporting.

One US policy that was formally announced before the war was the introduction of "embedded" correspondents in military units. At a Pentagon briefing in October 2002 Defense Secretary Donald Rumsfeld described it as his "core principle". The Pentagon sold the plan to media chiefs on the basis of access to stories and the speed and ease of transmitting them. The military had another, obvious motive, which most editors were cautious about: the shaping and control of these reports. But there was another consideration too on editors' minds, and that was the safety of their staff. The "embeds" would be protected by the army units. Their free-wheeling colleagues, the "unilaterals", would not. As Brigadier General Andrew Davis, the US Marine Corps chief of public affairs, told the same Pentagon briefing: "If [unilaterals] happen on a combatant unit and they're not equipped … that endangers them, it endangers the unit, it endangers the mission. So having independent journalists wandering the battlefield really is fraught with lots of problems."

There were other straws in the wind. On the same day in November 2001 that the Americans had bombed Al Jazeera's Kabul studio, they had also hit the BBC's new studio just a few blocks away, and correspondent William Reeve, on air at the time, had a narrow escape. The target had been selected, it must be assumed, by tracking the satellite signal to earth. (The justification the Americans had given for the Al Jazeera attack was that they had detected communications with the Taliban; well, of course, the journalists had been interviewing them!) The BBC was alarmed by this and commissioned an experienced correspondent to investigate. It was even more alarmed to find that the US was making no effort to distinguish between legitimate satellite uplinks and enemy communications.

Far from dissembling about the dangers of reporting from "enemy" areas, the Americans accentuated them and successfully pressured the four main TV networks – CBS, NBC, ABC and Fox – to pull out of Baghdad before the invasion. The Cable News Network (CNN), which had built its reputation on Peter Arnett's dramatic reports from Baghdad in 1991, stayed on but was soon kicked out by the Iraqis.

In London there was government pressure to do the same. Home Secretary David Blunkett said that journalists reporting behind "enemy lines" and giving "blow-by-blow" accounts of events there were treating the US-led coalition forces and the Iraqi regime as "moral equivalents". But only *The Times* and the *Daily Telegraph* withdrew from Baghdad.

The US exodus was pleasing to the Pentagon: as Channel 4's correspondent in Baghdad Lindsey Hilsum has pointed out, the American people were the worst informed in the world on what was to happen. With the sudden expansion of Arabic TV news sources syndicating their uncensored images everywhere – there are half a dozen now, in addition to Al Jazeera – only the Americans (and to some extent the British) were ignorant of what their forces were doing to the city.

Once the ground fighting started, it took just two days for the doom-mongers to be proved right. The American armoured divisions set off for Baghdad and the British for Basra, with between them 830 correspondents embedded in their ranks. Among the handful of unilaterals was ITN's Terry Lloyd, travelling with Belgian camera operators Daniel Demoustier and Fred Nerac and Lebanese interpreter Hussein Osman in two Mitsubishi Pajeros, both plastered with tape spelling "TV" in huge letters. It took them two days to get clearance to cross the border from Kuwait. Aiming for Basra they ran into Iraqi military traffic coming in the other direction, and turned round to head back. American marines in positions by the road opened fire on the vehicles.

Demoustier, with Lloyd in the first vehicle, was able to throw himself out as the first shell hit. After an hour he was picked up by other unilateral journalists but there was no sign of his colleagues. In fact, Lloyd's body had been left in the wreck to be picked up by the Iraqi Red Crescent and taken to hospital in Basra. There he was seen, filmed and identified by the Al Jazeera crew in the city. No word has been heard of the other two crew members since.

It was to be 36 hours before ITN confirmed Lloyd's death, and at the same time it had another ominous announcement to make. Chief executive Stewart Purvis said he was calling a halt to all independent reporting in southern Iraq: "certainly for the time being we have suspended all independent reporting in the southern region. There is one satellite dish which is in operation outside the military system. We have put that on hold while we take stock." Just what Doctor Rumsfeld ordered. Unilaterals would continue to roam the north of Iraq, Purvis said – but there were no coalition units to be embedded in there anyway. There were, however, great dangers in the complex scenario in the north, and three media workers were to die in the area, including another ITN reporter, Gaby Rado of Channel 4 News. He fell from the roof of a hotel in unexplained circumstances; suicide was suspected. By 22 March there had already been a media death in the north, the first of the war: Australian camera operator Paul Moran was blown up by a suicide bomber from the pro-al-Qaeda group Ansar al-Islam which was waging a guerrilla campaign against the Iraqi Kurdish authorities.

By mid-June ITN had still got no satisfactory explanation for the death of Lloyd, despite editor David Mannion, a close friend, setting in train a thorough investigation. A team was sent to Iraq, led by a news editor, working full-time, with ITN staff and former SAS personnel from the security firm AKE. They were also of course searching for traces of the missing crew members. They found a few possible – and contradictory – leads, but most interestingly, tracked down, in Baghdad, the American marine unit that had done the shooting.

When Lloyd was killed US Secretary of State Colin Powell promised an investigation. But it is understood from ITN that when they found the unit, the marines admitted they had fired at the vehicles but added that none of them had ever been questioned, and it's hard to believe that commanders did not know who was there. ITN executives say they "got nowhere" with their attempts to get information from the British or American military.

At the time, however, the Americans did have something else to say. In Washington Victoria Clarke pronounced at a press briefing that journalists not embedded with the army were "putting themselves at extreme risk". With no apparent irony she appealed to the media to "exercise restraint, especially with journalists who are reporting freely".

NUJ general secretary Jeremy Dear commented:

> The Americans might try exercising restraint themselves when journalists are in their sights. They are saying that if independent journalists get shot they have only themselves to blame. They want all journalists to be embedded with the troops and report only what they are told. But it is especially important in wars, when there is extremely tight control of information, that brave journalists like Terry Lloyd should work independently.

Once again the British government followed the American line. Britain did not complain when its troops came under attack in "friendly fire" incidents so it was no surprise when Geoff Hoon, the Defence Secretary, said on BBC's *Question Time* that Terry Lloyd had been killed

> essentially because he was not part of a military organisation. Because he was trying to get a story. And in those circumstances we can't look after all those journalists on this kind of fast moving battlefield. So having journalists have the protection, in fact, of our armed forces is both good for journalism, and it's also very good for people watching.

After two months of pressing every button they could find, ITN chiefs did persuade the US and UK military establishments to set up inquiries. The two are running in parallel, since neither can question each other's forces. It will be quite an achievement if ITN manages to prise the truth from them.

In the north of Iraq it was the BBC that had two media workers killed. Iran-born camera operator Kaveh Golestan stepped onto an Iraqi mine, and a Kurdish translator, Kamaran Abdurazaq Muhamed, was killed in a coalition bombing raid vividly recorded, with blood spattering the camera lens, in footage featuring the BBC's venerable foreign affairs editor John Simpson. There is no argument that the convoy they were in was bombed by two USAF F-15s. Simpson reported that they had been called in by a ground commander to attack an Iraqi tank a mile away:

I had a bad feeling about it, because they seemed to be closer to us than they were to the tank. As I was looking at them – this must sound extraordinary but I assure you it is true – I saw the bomb coming out of one of the planes, and I saw it as it came down beside me. It was painted white and red. It crashed into the ground about 10 or 12 metres from where I was standing.

The bomb severed Kamaran's legs and he died from loss of blood. Sixteen others died in the attack.

Since the incident Simpson has been outspoken about US attacks on the media. "The independent journalists are upholding a great journalistic tradition," he said, "but my goodness they're taking a hammering. The system that allows this to happen, even encourages this to happen, is stupid and despicable."

The trigger-happiness of US troops has been remarked upon by just about every returning journalist. "They just didn't wait that extra second to see that the car had TV markings," said an embedded ITN reporter about the killing of Terry Lloyd. "They're scared stiff and they just shoot at everything that moves." But the Palestine Hotel wasn't moving when it took the hit that killed two journalists, and neither were the studios of Al Jazeera and Abu Dhabi TV that were bombed on the same day, 8 April.

It defies belief that these three assaults, on the day after American tanks rolled into the centre of Baghdad, could have been coincidental. The three sites were well known to commanders as media centres; nearly all the foreign correspondents in the capital were staying at the Palestine, and executives of both Al Jazeera and Abu Dhabi TV, fearful of strikes in the bombing campaign, had given the precise co-ordinates of their locations to US forces. During those three weeks they had never been hit, though, true to American form, the Ministry of Information and the headquarters of Iraqi TV were bombed. The attack on the TV station on 25 March was confirmed by the Pentagon as deliberate; an official said it was a "key regime command and control asset". The International Federation of Journalists (IFJ), based in Brussels, said the attack was "an attempt at censorship that breached the Geneva Conventions". IFJ general secretary Aidan White added: "Once again we see military and political commanders from the democratic world targeting a television network simply because they don't like what it puts out."

With hundreds of media staff in the Palestine Hotel, there are numerous accounts of the shelling, which came from a tank on the other side of the Tigris. Perhaps amazingly, all the accounts agree. Not one has given any credence to the various justifications offered by the Americans: that there was rocket or sniper fire at the tank from the hotel or surrounding area, or that there was an Iraqi soldier on the roof with binoculars, lining up sightings for snipers. For one thing, the tank would have been way out of range for any such fire. For another, what there is on the roof is a big sign reading "Palestine Hotel" (in English).

Back in Qatar, General Vince Brooks, number two spokesperson at Central Command, kept up the "it's their own fault" line by proclaiming at a briefing that journalists should not have been in the hotel.

The two killed were camera operators Taras Protsyuk, a Ukrainian working for Reuters, and Jose Couso of the Spanish channel Telecinco. At least three other journalists were badly wounded. The two slain camera operators were on the 15th floor of the Palestine, where cameras had been set up on the balconies throughout the war to film the bombing. One, from French TV, had been running throughout, with sound, and the tape shows no firing.

At the Al Jazeera office camera operator/journalist Tariq Ayyoub was seriously wounded when the network's office on the bank of the Tigris was struck by a missile. He later died. Abu Dhabi TV, whose office – again with a prominent sign on the roof – is next door on the river bank, was also hit by missiles. Staff of the two stations took refuge there and were trapped overnight, apparently held as "human shields" by Iraqi troops. Journalists' organisations around the world appealed to the US to halt the bombardment to let them out.

Reuters bureau chief Samia Nakhoul was one of the seriously injured in the Palestine. Shrapnel from the blast lodged in her brain, within a millimetre of killing her, according to doctors. She said: "I was looking through the camera lens and saw the tank on the bridge. I saw an orange flash and was calling the photographer to tell him when it hit. We were all thrown to the floor."

According to the *Independent*'s Robert Fisk, scourge of the coalition throughout the war, the American response was "a straightforward lie". He wrote:

I was driving on a road between the tanks and the hotel at the moment the shell was fired and heard no shooting. The French videotape of the attack runs for more than four minutes and records absolute silence before the tank's armament is fired. And there were no snipers in the building. Indeed, the dozens of journalists and crews living there, myself included, have watched like hawks to make sure that no armed men should ever use the hotel as an assault point.

Sky News' David Chater and the BBC's Rageh Omaar reported in the same vein.

Whatever their anger, the journalists kept at their work and next day filmed US forces using an armoured personnel carrier to pull down a statue of Saddam Hussein at a road junction just outside the hotel, reporting the scene as the coalition's great moment of triumph. Those reports have been criticised as hype, but such magnanimity on the part of people who had just been shot at is remarkable.

During the invasion two journalists were killed by Iraqi forces: Julio Anguita Parrado of *El Mundo* (Spain) and Christian Liebig of the German magazine *Focus*, were killed by an Iraqi missile south of Baghdad. Both were embedded with US 3rd Infantry, their deaths giving the lie, incidentally, to a claim by the unfortunate General Brooks that no embeds were killed. In addition, three journalists died in vehicle accidents and one from natural causes.

There was also considerable harassment of correspondents by both sides. According to the IFJ's tally of the campaign, at least 19 journalists were detained, some of them also beaten, by the Iraqi authorities and seven expelled. At least ten were shot at or otherwise attacked by Iraqi forces or irregulars, and several were beaten and robbed in Baghdad and other cities. As for the coalition, British officers three times banned Al Jazeera from reporting from Basra, and US forces detained and badly mistreated two journalists – one Portuguese and one Israeli – accusing them of spying.

All journalists accept of course that war is dangerous and anyone can get killed, but with the loss of nearly 300 media lives in wars over the last twelve years every precaution that can be is taken. War zone safety has become a hot issue, and no self-respecting employer would now let a reporter or camera operator anywhere near a war without special training. Unions also insist on watertight insurance cover – increasingly costly and difficult to find – protective gear, and proper logistical support for all correspondents in the field.

There is quite a cottage industry in media war zone training, with three companies in the UK alone laying on courses of usually from three to five days; one of them is AKE, mentioned earlier, hired by ITN to investigate the attack on its crew. They involve instruction in weaponry, first aid and self-protection, with simulated emergencies such as kidnappings that are so brutal that participants sometimes say are scarier than the real thing. Even very experienced journalists say they learn from such courses, and from other measures of protection. John Simpson, showered with shrapnel in the airborne attack he endured, said: "I would have got a chunk of shrapnel in my spine had I not been wearing a flak jacket, and it was buried deep in the Kevlar when I checked it." Yet no protection is total. It is a terrible irony that many of the war reporters who get killed are the most experienced in the field – including Terry Lloyd, who was following the advised procedure, turning round in the road when he sensed imminent danger, when his team was attacked.

The drive for training and protection has come from the IFJ, which succeeded in bringing together the World Association of Newspapers, representing newspaper owners, the International Press Institute, the employers' press freedom front, and a couple of dozen press freedom NGOs, to establish the International Institute of News Safety, launched in May 2003. The IFJ, which represents 500,000 journalists in more than 100 countries, publishes safety handbooks and has this year brought out *Live News*, a survival guide for journalists in all hostile environments.

There is an extra danger that some journalists are bringing on themselves. Apprehensive at the lawless territory they were likely to be working in, some TV crews in Iraq took to hiring local security, and these characters come with weapons – as Lindsey Hilsum says, "they feel naked without them". Worries that they could end up in firefights are not idle. This happened in Tikrit in April when a CNN crew – a seven-vehicle convoy, no less – with armed bodyguards came under machine gun fire, which the bodyguards returned, to the horror of the journalistic community when the incident was reported. One person was wounded, and the attack stopped, but what would have happened, people asked, if it hadn't? Lindsey Hilsum says: "This is one thing we can do something about and we must."

Journalists do not need to add to the perils already in store from the further imperial adventures by too conspicuously taking sides. The Australian cameraman Paul Moran, the first western journalist to die in the war – killed by an Islamist suicide bomber in the north east of Iraq on 22 March – turned out to have been working for ten years for US-inspired propaganda campaigns against the regime. When killed Paul Moran was freelancing for the publicly owned Australian Broadcasting Corporation, which, understandably perhaps, declined to comment on his work. Throughout the 1990s, according to reports that surfaced in Australia after his death, he had supplied footage to a Washington-based PR company, the Rendon Group, which was contracted by the CIA to run propaganda campaigns against the dictatorship. The reports also said Paul Moran had trained Iraqi dissidents in the use of hidden cameras to covertly film military activities and had been involved in the defection of an Iraqi scientist.

Many conflicts attract such operators. You do not have to make a moral judgement about the causes concerned to recognise that the perception that journalists are working against some armed or powerful interest must raise the stakes for all.

There is no justice in the selection of victims here. The young British cameraman Richard Wild, shot dead in the street in Baghdad on 6 July, was guilty of being among the wrong people at the wrong time, innocent of involvement with any particular enemy of the Iraqis, yet apparently seen as one.

There was quite a debate on embedding among journalists in the weeks after the US declared the fighting over, and a consensus has emerged, that it's OK to embed as long as there's plenty of unilateral material to balance it. But there is a disquieting degree of support for the process at executive level. The BBC's director of News, Richard Sambrook, said in a BBC documentary: "I think embeds undoubtedly are the future. There's no question, from the military point of view, that they provided them with, you know, kind of, a level and quantity of picture that was overall advantageous to them." Only when asked whether he was "worried" about this did he say:

> I think if we got to a position where embeds were the only form of conflict coverage that was possible then it would be one-sided and you wouldn't get the full picture of what was happening and that obviously worries me journalistically, yes.

It seemed to take a bit of getting out of him, and yes, it worries a lot of people a lot more. The combination of control on the ground and terror from the air threatens the balance of coverage, as well as the lives of correspondents. Journalists can be very brave when they're in danger, and sometimes they wish their editors and managers would be as brave in their decision-making.

It may not make that much difference as far as the military are concerned whether the fatal attacks were intentional or accidental.

They can come up with all kinds of explanations about misunderstandings and interruptions in chains of command. But if such a seasoned reporter as John Simpson, who measures words carefully, can call their conduct in Iraq "stupid and despicable", then it seems to me that the onus should not be on us to prove that the killings were deliberate, but on them to prove that they weren't.

JOURNALISTS WHO MET THEIR DEATHS IN THE 2003 IRAQ WAR

Paul Moran, 22 March, near Halabja. Freelance cameraman, Australian Broadcasting Corporation

Terry Lloyd, 22 March, near Basra. ITN correspondent

Gaby Rado, 30 March, Sulaimaniya. Channel 4 correspondent

Kaveh Golestan, 2 April, Kifri. Freelance cameraman, BBC

Michael Kelly, 4 April, Baghdad Airport. *Atlantic Monthly* (embedded)

Kamaran Abdurazaq Muhamed, 6 April, Mosul. BBC translator

David Bloom, 6 April, Baghdad. NBC correspondent (embedded)

Christian Liebig, 7 April, Baghdad. *Focus* magazine (German) reporter

Julio Anguita Parrado, 7 April, Baghdad. *El Mundo* correspondent (Spain)

Tariq Ayyoub, 8 April, Baghdad. Al Jazeera camera operator

Taras Protsyuk, 8 April, Palestine Hotel, Baghdad. Reuters camera operator

Jose Cuoso, 8 April, Palestine Hotel, Baghdad. Telecinco (Spain) camera operator

Iraqi Interpreter (name as yet unknown), 12 April, Baghdad. Malaysian media

Mario Podesta, 14 April, Baghdad. America TV (Argentina) reporter

Veronica Cabrera, 14 April, Baghdad. America TV camera operator.

Missing since 22 March: Fred Nerac, ITN cameraman, and Hussein Othmann, ITN translator.

There may also have been Iraqi journalists killed but no information is yet available.

29
Turning My Back
on the Mainstream

Yvonne Ridley

News operations for the military invasion of Iraq required quite a different approach than in Afghanistan where the ruling Taliban was oblivious to the propaganda war – a parallel battle for hearts and minds.

By kicking out all western journalists, the naïve regime ensured that the indiscriminate use of cluster bombs, civilian targeting and other horrors employed by America, Britain and the brutal Northern Alliance foot soldiers went largely unreported.

Frustrated war correspondents either covered the Afghanistan war from the rooftops of hotels in Islamabad or miles behind the Northern Alliance front lines if they couldn't bribe their way closer to the action. Print journalists were able to write round the fact they could see nothing more than plumes of distant smoke but the task proved more challenging for television reporters. Some paid the Afghan soldiers $5 a round to fire their machine guns randomly as they did their pieces to camera, giving the folks back home the impression that they were in the thick of the fighting. Who says the camera doesn't lie? A stray bullet killed an Afghan child in a nearby field, but hey, it's OK. These things happen in the fog of war!

The so-called liberation of Kabul, when it happened, turned out to be two tales of one city. According to most of the western media, garlands of flowers were thrown at the Northern Alliance while jubilant women burned their burqas and men began shaving their beards. The images were dramatic and uplifting – and very, very misleading. Many of the images were captured in exchange for much-needed dollars waved around enticingly by newshounds. Only a few papers, the *Daily Mirror* in particular, had the guts to report the sickening reality by featuring a graphic picture of a group of victorious soldiers about to blow out the brains of a Taliban soldier pleading for mercy. The headline sarcastically welcomed "our new friends" making it crystal clear the US and Britain had entered into a deal with another cut-throat regime. Enterprising Afghanis began to realise that if they could make a quick buck simply by removing their beards, there were other rich pickings to be had from some gullible journalists.

Intelligence documents began emerging revealing "the truth" behind Osama bin Laden's nuclear plans. I was told one Fleet Street hack parted with $500 for some of the al-Qaeda chief's top secret papers which later turned out to be the ripped-out contents of a university student's physics book! A trend to be repeated in the next war. The military outcome in Afghanistan was never in any doubt, but had the Taliban allowed western journalists in to their country during the build-up to this one-sided war, perhaps more civilian lives would have been saved.

As it is, civilian deaths continue to rise in Afghanistan. During my latest visit in April 2003, I went to a village near Shkin in Pakitika where there were rumours of a massacre. When I got there I was taken to a wrecked house which had been hit by a US laser-guided missile. American forces physically beat back would-be rescuers, saying the building was a Taliban stronghold. By daybreak the tiny, broken bodies of eleven children lay in a neat row in the rubble. Several days later the military returned and around $10,000 were handed over to the survivors, including one woman who had lost all her nine children. So we now know what an Afghan life is worth – less than $1,000 per child.

The Americans have outstayed their welcome in Afghanistan. The goodwill extended by the warlords has all but evaporated and the fighting and bombing continues. The country is lawless and many Afghans outside of Kabul are beginning to crave the security they had under the Taliban. However, Saddam Hussein would not make the same mistake as the Taliban. As a master of the black art of propaganda he knew the value of having the world's media report the war from Baghdad. Most were given government minders and confined to the Palestine Hotel and the Ministry of Information Centre nearby, although no less than eight Al Jazeera news crews from the trusted Arab satellite station appeared to be given a freer rein. They were filming in Mosul and Basra, as well as the capital. The Iraqi dictator knew that shocking reports and pictures of Iraqi civilian casualties would send strong messages out to the world.

But the Pentagon's spin doctors also went on the offensive to make sure the war of words went their way. They embedded more than 700 journalists with coalition troops. America needed a tame news source it could control; a lesson learned from Vietnam where independent journalists were able to report more of the truth. As well as the embedded journalists, the Pentagon also planned to spoon-feed the world's media – 700 of them – from US Central Command's base in Qatar. However, the daily diet of propaganda, weak denials, downright lies and outright hostility to anyone who dared to ask a probing question did not go down well.

One American journalist questioned the value of the briefing and was "asked to leave" and others chose to pack their bags out of sheer frustration. Fellow-journalist Tim Shipman told me later, the Americans weren't interested in journalistic integrity and ethics, and they certainly had no time for those journalists not embedded. Shipman, deputy political editor of the *Sunday Express*, who also covered the war for the daily sister paper from Qatar, said:

> As far as the British spin-doctors were concerned Qatar was the clearing house for the main strategic briefings. As far as the Americans were concerned it was yet another opportunity to conceal and distort information. The British acknowledged that we were not getting the full story but at least they recognised the legitimacy of other journalists who wanted to seek out information at the front.

For the Americans, people like Terry Lloyd were the provisional wing of the press corps and were branded "unilaterals" – turning against the media the very phrase that had been used to attack President Bush's foreign policy.

> They made it very clear that they had no sympathy for people who did not bend to their rules. Day after day they were asked who was responsible for Terry's death and day after day they feigned total ignorance about the matter, while British officials expressed amazement and despair that they did not have the guts to own up to their mistakes. American generals on the so-called podium of truth in Qatar repeatedly stressed that "no embedded journalists have been injured" as if that made attacks on the Palestine Hotel and the offices of Al Jazeera acceptable ... Either they were breathtakingly incompetent or they have crossed the line in a way that will make frontline reporting in the future a job only for people with the kind of suicidal tendencies they are supposed to be trying to defeat.

From Shipman's frank analysis it is clear the Pentagon hated journalists who chose to move around independently; they regarded them as unpatriotic and with a certain amount of distrust. Embedding reporters with the invading coalition was regarded a PR masterstroke by the White House and Downing Street, but the novelty was short-lived. Their initial reports brought a raw edge of excitement for armchair supporters who had been disappointed by the endless views of stationary tanks and desert during the 1991 Gulf War. Colourful features of living conditions made great reading, but a week is a long time in war and even the most ardent supporter became weary and fatigued ... a bit like watching the reality TV show *Big Brother* after the first eviction. A controlled media made for a boring war, which was reflected in declining newspaper sales seven days after the bombing began.

The coalition, not to mention Bush and Blair, must have breathed a sigh of relief when it was all over – except it is not. There was no great victory in Iraq – the west has won nothing and it has certainly lost the propaganda war. This was reinforced by the amount of spurious documents which began to emerge from the embers of the looted government buildings, seized upon by eager journalists looking for a scoop. Only history will tell if all the documents were planted by bungling western intelligence agencies or Iraqis following the lead of the enterprising Afghanis who duped dollar-rich journalists. The American newspaper, *The Christian Science Monitor*, has already apologised to Glasgow Labour MP George Galloway after alleging that he accepted millions of pounds from Saddam Hussein. Paul Van Slambrouck, *Monitor* editor, admitted in June 2003 that a set of documents upon which it based its story were "almost certainly" fake. He said: "It is important to set the record straight. We are convinced the documents are bogus. We apologise to Mr Galloway and to our readers." Galloway responded:

This newspaper published on its front page in every country in the world that I had taken $10m from Saddam Hussein. That was a grave and serious libel. Of course the documents were a forgery and a newspaper of that importance ought to have made the effort, both morally and legally, to establish the authenticity of those documents before they published them.

Truth is often the first casualty of this war, but thanks to fearless and honest journalists like the *Independent*'s Robert Fisk, the

Guardian's Rory McCarthy and *The Sunday Times'* Marie Colvin there is still some hope for its recovery as they continue to bring heart-rending, uncensored stories to our breakfast table.

I have to say that my experience at the hands of the Taliban in Afghanistan totally transformed my outlook on life and my role as a journalist. Before my capture I was able to cover traumatic events, conflicts and human injustices professionally but without collecting any of the emotional baggage. That all changed after my release. I remember my Pakistan guide Pasha calling me to say that American and British bombs had hit the village and district around Jalalabad I had visited prior to my arrest by the Taliban. I told Pasha that it sounded like a terrible accident; the sort of accident that happens in the so-called fog of war. He then replied: "But Madam, how can you accidentally bomb a village the size of Kama three nights running?" My blood ran cold when the harsh reality kicked in. Deliberate, indiscriminate bombing could be the only answer. Distraught, I called Labour MP Alan Simpson, a prominent anti-war campaigner, and told him and urged him to raise the issue. He said I had to tell my story at the next Stop the War Coalition rally in London because, as an eyewitness, it was important that I shared my knowledge and views. The Yvonne Ridley I knew prior to 11 September wouldn't have cared or dared to stand up in front of anyone and express an opinion. Apart from columnists, I always felt journalists should simply record events without trying to influence them. However, I turned up in Trafalgar Square and made a three-minute speech in front of nearly 100,000 people. It was a transforming moment. Since that day in October 2001, I have travelled the UK, Europe, North America and the Middle East addressing anti-war meetings, rallies and conferences.

I have also continued working as a journalist concentrating on humanitarian issues and have travelled several times to both Iraq and Afghanistan as well as Palestine. And I will continue to promote peace and justice for all, as well as question those governments, including the US and our own, which continue to carpet bomb our very freedoms and liberties while invading and occupying other countries as part of America's imperialistic plans for full spectrum dominance. There are many more like me out there. Saturday 15 February 2003 proved that, when another superpower emerged on the world stage – the global peace movement. Nearly 15 million people from around the world marched in their towns and cities to protest against the proposed war in Iraq – their views could not be so easily dismissed, nor could they be silenced.

The triumphalists aren't as vocal as they once were but as a journalist and peace campaigner, I take no satisfaction from the failure of this war. Yes, it's great that the tortures and executions under Saddam are history, but now there are sporadic beatings and killings of more innocents – at the hands of coalition soldiers. But it is not just me and you who have been lied to – consider the trigger-happy American soldiers who Bob Graham interviewed for the *London Evening Standard*. Graham wrote how the soldiers were "furious" that promises of an early return home made to them by their senior commanders turned out to be untrue. His feature would make uncomfortable reading for US and British politicians desperate to prevent the "liberation" of Iraq turning into a "quagmire of Vietnam proportions" as he put it. The soldiers from Bravo Company of the 3/15th US Infantry lost 40 of their comrades to sniper fire and bomb attacks in the 50 days after George W. Bush declared the end of the war on 1 May. In return some admitted they had killed hundreds of innocent Iraqis because they couldn't tell fighters and suicide bombers apart from ordinary people. One Corporal Richardson told Graham: "We weren't trained for this stuff now. It makes you resentful they're holding us on here. It pisses everyone off – we were told once the war was over we'd leave when our replacements get here. Well our replacements got here and we're still here."

During my first week in July 2003 as a senior editor at Aljazeera.net we carried a shocking story about how demoralised American soldiers who had lost two comrades, picked off by Iraqi resistance fighters, took their own revenge on the suspects. Acting as judge, jury and executioner, the soldiers shot dead two men and displayed their bodies in public.

Both were handcuffed as they were executed in public. The Iraqi victims were left near a crossing next to the main gate of the city for four hours. Al Jazeera's correspondent in Ramadi, Abd ul-Azim Muhammad, interviewed several eyewitnesses who all confirmed the murders. However, it is doubtful if anyone will investigate Muhammad's shocking exclusive. War crimes committed by US occupation forces in Iraq will not be investigated by the International Criminal Court (ICC) because the Bush administration refused to sign up to it. George W. Bush was following the same line as his arch enemy Saddam Hussein, who also chose to snub the court which is mandated to try genocide, war-crimes and crimes against humanity.

The tribunal's prosecutor Luis Moreno Ocampohas said on 16 July 2003 that the court does not have the mandate to prosecute such cases like the execution of the two men in Ramadi. "We have received communications about acts allegedly perpetrated by US troops in Iraq but we are not mandated to prosecute such acts since neither Iraq or the United States are states party to the court." The court, which became a legal reality in July 2002, can only act in cases involving nationals of states that have ratified the ICC statute, or events that occurred on their territories. Ocampohas said the court has also received complaints concerning nationals who are part of the US-led occupation force in Iraq, like Britain. Washington, a strong opponent of the ICC, has suspended more than $47 million in military aid to 35 countries for their failure or refusal to give US citizens immunity from the tribunal. Maybe that's one consolation for the demoralised American soldiers in Bravo Company of the 3/15th US Infantry who spoke to Bob Graham. At least they can shoot who the hell they want, when they want and know they will be immune from prosecution – just like the US soldiers who executed the two handcuffed Iraqis in Ramadi. A heated debate erupted in our newsroom as we discussed if we should use the graphic pictures of the dead Iraqis on the English website. I argued that I would not want my ten-year-old daughter clicking on to the website to be exposed to such a brutal sight. Journalist Lawrence Smallman shouted back: "What about the Iraqi children who were exposed to the execution and had to walk by the bodies? We should not disguise what is happening. The world needs to know the truth, Yvonne."

The truth is, there is no truth. The military build-up, the "shock and awe" assault and the liberation of Iraq had been constructed on a tissue of lies from politicians on both sides of the Atlantic. The British media is usually very intolerant of lies and liars. Disgraced politicians Jonathan Aitken and Jeffrey Archer were both sent to prison because they lied in court. What are we going to do with those who lie to their parliament, their country and the world? It now falls on the media to demand the truth, the whole truth and nothing but the truth because political pressure, from an ineffectual government opposition, is not working. Meanwhile armed opposition to the occupation of Iraq will continue until the US and Britain withdraw. In the words of the *Guardian*'s Seumas Milne: "It would have been hard to predict in advance that the US and the British occupation of Iraq could go so spectacularly wrong so quickly."

30
Inside the System:
Anti-war Activism in the Media

David Crouch

Do you work in the media? If so, this chapter is for you. Let me re-phrase that. Do you work? If so, this chapter is for you. It is about how the anti-war movement refused to stay on the streets and filtered into the workplaces. It is about political activism at work, but focusing on the media and specifically on the campaign Media Workers Against the War (MWAW). I am certain there are plenty of media workers out there who did excellent anti-war work and who never heard of MWAW. If you are one of those people, please, let's get in touch.

I'm going to talk about four things:

- getting active where you work;
- the media trade unions;
- how your media skills can benefit the movement;
- influencing what the media says.

Being political in the workplace is a long-term goal for some, myself included, while for others it just happened that way. Rachel (not her real name) works at a lifestyle publishing company in North London, and is a member of MWAW. She says:

> I'm not a company person, I just ended up in this job by chance. At the time of the proposed war on Iraq it was good for me to have a group of people that I can get together with and discuss things I feel passionate about. I became political after 11 September. Talking to my family I began questioning what they were reading. The reports in the papers were so biased, even down to the numbers attending national demonstrations. I bought a pamphlet for real news about the war. The company is very capitalist. There are no unions. They even had a go at us for getting people together on the email. You aren't supposed to use the email for personal

reasons, but of course everyone does. All the same, personnel told us not to use the office email to organise demonstrations.

So is the email off limits? Actually it depends – one of the activists at the *Guardian* sent out global emails to the entire company about Stop the War demos and only got a mild reprimand. Whether you can get away with blitzing the company email depends on how scared the company is of you, which will probably depend on how strong your trade union is. For people who sit in front of a computer screen – which is how most of us in the media spend our glamorous days – the email is handy, but it's still no substitute for talking face to face.

I digress. In brazen defiance of their personnel department, the North London MWAW group got organised and got active. In the early autumn of 2002 it held a lunchtime meeting in a nearby pub with a speaker from the Stop the War Coalition leadership. Night after night it got people out leafleting the nearest tube station after work for the big demo on 28 September. It leafleted the local mosque. It combined with activists from other workplaces to hold a local rally on 31 October, a national day of action. Film-maker Ken Loach and Jeremy Corbyn MP came along to speak.

"I got to know people on different floors of the building, and that gave me faith," Rachel says. "They work in mainstream companies like this but they have their own philosophies. Not all people in the media are blinkered." Media Workers Against the War was launched by Paul Foot and John Pilger in 1991 to oppose the first Gulf War. It was relaunched in 1999 over NATO's bombing of Serbia. A month after 11 September, Foot, Pilger, Rosie Boycott and NUJ (National Union of Journalists) leader John Foster addressed a MWAW meeting of 800 people in Camden Town Hall. Two outstanding American writers, Jonathan Neale and Mike Marqusee, set up a string of big meetings for media workers in late 2001 as we went flat out to stop the invasion of Afghanistan.

At the time, Helen Foot was on a short-term contract at the BBC as an assistant producer. Her experience reflects how many found themselves getting active.

I was shocked by the attacks on 11 September and frightened about what the US response would be. I remember seeing Paul Wolfowitz on *Newsnight* talking about "rogue states" and "taking out our enemies". I felt part of a dangerous world that was going to get more dangerous. I went to a big meeting at Euston. Jonathan Neale was standing in the foyer shouting: "Does anyone work for the media?" and handing out leaflets for an MWAW meeting. There were loads of people at the meeting ... and three of us decided to launch a BBC MWAW group.

They organised a meeting at Shepherds Bush by handing out leaflets outside the tube station. About 50 people came to hear Tariq Ali speak. Another meeting followed with *Express* reporter Yvonne Ridley, who turned against the war despite being captured by the Taliban. "What was good was the range of people in MWAW – print, film, photography, and not all of one political flavour," Helen says. "There was a lot of debate in the BBC at that time about what constitutes representative media debate, and MWAW campaigned for pluralism."

The invasion of Afghanistan was followed by a natural lull in anti-war activity. We took stock and tried to believe they weren't going to do the same to Iraq. The next burst of BBC activism built on what had gone before, fuelled by general discontent with management. Kathy (not her real name) picks up the story.

The group took off again in early 2003. We came up with the idea of making badges. They said: "Make it Happen: Stop the War". It was a piss-take of Greg Dyke's "make it happen" campaign – yet another efficiency drive. People fell over themselves to get a badge. They kept coming up and saying: "Psst, I hear you have badges." It was like an undercover thing. We sold hundreds. We went round in the weeks before the monster 15 February demonstration, putting together an email list of people. We got a good response, particularly in strongly unionised departments. Management sent out an email telling people not to go on anti-war demos, but it had the opposite effect. When the two journalists were sacked from the Arab service, we linked it with the war. On demos I kept bumping into people from the BBC. People were up for challenging what was being broadcast. Arguments broke out when the BBC started saying there was an uprising in Basra. The newsroom was split over the pulling down of the statue of Saddam.

The anti-war movement won the support of several big trade unions, and at its national conference in 2002 the NUJ backed the Stop the War Coalition and MWAW. The war deepened the rift between union members and New Labour; the national conference of media union BECTU (the Broadcasting, Entertainment, Cinema and Theatre Union) voted in May 2003 to ballot members on disaffiliation from Labour; the NUJ is to ballot on establishing a political fund. Meanwhile the media unions are clawing back some of the ground we lost in the 1980s. The NUJ has seen 6,000 editorial staff win union rights in the last two years; recently the *Daily Telegraph* voted 91 per cent for the union.

But union leaders' continuing loyalty to Labour means the movement here has yet to see the general strikes against war that lifted opposition in Italy, Spain and Greece to greater heights. In the main, British workers still lack the confidence to take action without their leaders' support. In the media unions there is still an argument that we have to remain "impartial" and shouldn't get involved in politics. In this situation, MWAW helped union activists to raise political questions; in turn, anti-war activity fed back into the unions and helped to radicalise their members. The "Make it Happen" badges at the BBC are a good example, but the point is a more general one.

"BECTU was slow to move on the war," says Tim Malone, a web administrator and BECTU rep at the BBC.

> The lay officials are understaffed and under-resourced. BECTU also sent out an email saying they wouldn't support people if they walked out of work on the day war started. Ironically, MWAW enabled me to be more active in the union. It meant I was able to be more vociferous. I stuck up posters on the wall by my desk. I also sent out stuff supporting the firefighters. Before I'd felt more isolated, but now there was a wider number of interested people. MWAW also meant we could reach the non-union people who were against the war. I wanted BECTU nationally to adopt an anti-war position, so I wrote to them repeatedly. Obviously I wasn't the only one. In the end the BECTU banner was on the 15 February demo, but there was still no official policy. I would have been more confident if BECTU had a policy against the war: then I could have acted at work in my capacity as a rep.

Did all this activity have any impact on the way the war was covered? Did MWAW influence editorial content? It works like this. The media are rigidly hierarchical, agendas are centrally established and a chasm of income, outlook and class separates the people at the top from the rest of us. On the rare occasions when activists find themselves in a situation where editorial content is being decided or discussed, it takes a deal of confidence to stick your neck out. That confidence can only come from feeling part of a movement and from having people in the office who will back you up.

I spoke to journalists at the BBC who tried to criticise its coverage of Afghanistan and Iraq. They described a rigid, bullying culture at the Corporation, making it hard to speak out. They all want to remain anonymous. "The idea of unbiased news coverage is wrong – news always comes from a particular angle," says one.

Some well-known presenters were disgusted with what was going on. They said how ironic it was we could hear Laura Bush and Cherie Blair talking about the plight of Afghan women, but we couldn't hear Afghan women themselves. We had fancy graphics of "daisycutter" bombs, but no concept of what was actually happening on the ground.

Another says:

Everything I said in meetings was ignored, I felt powerless. It got to me, I felt it was pointless to object. But I started working on people in other ways, by talking to individuals. I got involved in MWAW, we were having meetings and taking action. I had a group of friends who were very supportive. They said the miners had been victimised before, and so had the Irish. So it wasn't just Muslims. The BBC is so far removed from the real world. [Its star reporters are] very middle class. I'm working class and I worked my own way into journalism. People like me will never get anywhere.

Two weeks after the war began, MWAW organised a debate between Mark Damazer, deputy head of News at the BBC and Andrew Murray of the Stop the War Coalition. Thirty or so BBC staff took part. A BBC journalist recounts:

After the debate with Damazer, I noticed people in the newsroom started spending more time with me, and editors started listening, The *News at Ten* showed film of Iraqi POWs and people said it was disgraceful, it was against the Geneva Convention. Even senior news editors were shocked, they blamed it on a junior producer. Now I hear language at the BBC such as the "invasion" of Iraq, when they would never say that earlier.

Another journalist says:

> People were so angry, the BBC disseminated loads and loads of lies about the war. If there aren't angry people around them, editors will get away with it. If the war had gone on longer, the constant questions and criticism would have had a massive effect.

Most media workers are a million miles from the structures that determine national newspaper or broadcasting coverage. In the local media, however, the barriers between journalists and their audience are not so high. Sympathetic newspaper or radio staff have made a big difference to coverage of local protests, helping the Stop the War Coalition sink deep roots.

Media workers also bring to campaigns a set of useful communication skills. In the first phases of the movement, when most of the press ignored us entirely, media workers felt they had a role in getting our message out to a big audience. In September 2001 Donna Baillie, whose films of Palestine *Women in Black* and *Secret Hebron: The School Run* are now making her name as a director, was a sound recordist and freelance print journalist in London. She says:

> I joined the MWAW video group because it was the place where I thought I could be most useful. We were aware there were lots of interesting political speeches being made, but people only got to hear them if they were based in London ... So we decided to put together a video of some of the speeches and additional interviews so that people in the rest of the country could hear them as well. Members of the group interviewed George Monbiot, Tariq Ali, Tony Benn, Louise Christian and many others. The resulting video, called simply "Stop the War" proved very popular ... We also went around London covering demonstrations and interviewing the general public to get a feel for the mood on the street. These interviews proved very interesting, but we were having trouble getting them into a format where people could see them. Finding editing time at this point was practically impossible, and attempts to link up with IndyMedia to provide videostreaming of short reports on the internet came to nothing. This was a real shame. Staff on major newspapers feel they have to keep their mouths shut and "be objective"; that has to be addressed by the movement. People like me who earn shit and are freelance find it easier.

There was a definite difference between the Afghan and Iraq wars. On Iraq, the BBC was covering the protests – however patchily – and we didn't have so much pressure on us to do it ourselves.

The other way in which journalists, sub-editors and web workers contributed their skills was in establishing the MWAW website as a useful resource for the movement. Many people spent long hours sifting the wheat from the internet chaff and posting it at <http://www.mwaw.org>. Susan Casey is one of them. "I was a sub-editor full time at the Economist Intelligence Unit, but I'd come home and spend all night on the web," she says.

MWAW had a list of reliable sites, and I followed the links I found there – the whole of the web just opened up for me. I would try to post a counterpoint to whatever was on the front pages of the newspapers or TV. If there was a big statement on reconstructing Iraq, I'd go for stuff on what was happening with reconstruction in Afghanistan. It is a very well-designed site. It looks professional and is easy to access. It also has a fantastic search facility, so it has built up into a fabulous archive. People go to it because they know it will save them five hours' surfing. It is useful to collect the best stuff on one site. We got some great feedback, people said they were so happy to have found it. The BBC carried a link to the site, as did the *Guardian*. In the week the war started we were getting 7,000 hits a day – the most we ever had. We all learned a huge amount. For me personally it was a task of political education.

Other things that worked for MWAW included a rock concert, a film showing with Ken Loach, and linking up with local Stop the War groups so we could build each others' events. MWAW member Paola Desiderio photographed parliament with the slogan "NO WAR ON IRAQ" projected onto it – her photo went all round the world. Things we could do better: there aren't enough black people and Muslims at meetings; we needed stronger links with the coalition; we needed to integrate the website better into our work; and (with some honourable exceptions) we were weak on the hard grind that keeps campaigns ticking over. Oh, and please could someone hurry up and clone Tariq Ali – he was always our biggest draw.

The potential is massive. The task is immense. Iraq is not the end of it. Rather than sitting at your screen and worrying, it's better to get out and do something. And when it works, it's great. John-Henry Barac is a designer on the *Guardian*, where the MWAW group has been very successful. "We held our first meeting in a local art gallery," he recalls.

> We asked a local ballet school for chairs. We could be totally inventive and get good results. The group was a real mix – advertising staff, marketing, admin and editorial. The canteen staff helped by allowing us to put leaflets out in the canteen. We invited top speakers to our meetings to try to cut through the snobbery on the newspaper towards activism. We had four lunchtime meetings in the gallery, with Tony Benn, Paul Foot, Phillip Knightley, Jeremy Dear, Jeremy Corbyn and Stop the War Coalition leaders. At the last one 90 people turned up. The group gave people a forum to discuss alternatives. The ability of journalists to challenge the editorial line depends on their confidence, which in turn comes from the broader debate. MWAW contributed to that. We expanded to become Clerkenwell MWAW, with other local media workplaces, including Amnesty International, joining in. The Clerkenwell Firefighters Support Group wouldn't have been so strong if we hadn't had MWAW. On the day war broke out we met at 1pm outside the building; 50 people turned up. We had a brief rally and marched to Farringdon Road, carrying Clerkenwell MWAW placards. Some of us sat down in the road. By then the numbers had swelled to 80 people. So we decided to march down Farringdon Road. The public joined in and there was about 120 of us. We felt we had a very successful day. We have created something I feel confident we can re-invigorate in future. Also it's about rebuilding the sense that it is possible and important to have political meetings based around the workplace. We haven't had that for many years.

As the US and UK cast around for the next candidate for invasion, media workers will continue to organise to oppose war and the misinformation and lies that go with it.

31
Disruptive Technology: Iraq and the Internet

Alistair Alexander

As a news medium, the web came of age on 11 September 2001. While TV networks endlessly looped footage of the planes crashing into the twin towers and news anchors grasped for over-used superlatives, the internet pulsated with news, commentary and in-depth analysis that far exceeded the coverage that any newspaper or TV channel could ever muster. Much of this electronic discourse gave voice to dissent that would have previously gone unheard. And for increasing numbers of people the diversity of information on the internet highlighted the narrow priorities of the mainstream news agenda.

As the aftermath of September evolved into the war on terror, the attack on Afghanistan and a war on Iraq, the internet, through weblogs, message boards and mailing lists, provided an alternative narrative of world events and a tool for mobilising a global protest movement of an unprecedented scale. So, while the invasion of Iraq seemed precision-made to suit the voracious demands of global TV news networks – Hollywood media centres, embedded reporters and night-vision footage of POW rescues – the war also saw millions of people go online to see a very different war unfold.

No one now would question the significance of the internet as a global information resource. But, at first glance, it is striking not how much has changed, but how little. In the dot.com hysteria of the late 1990s, the mainstream media was supposed to have been swept aside by the technological tidal wave of the information revolution. Yet even in the US, the world's most connected nation, 89 per cent of people were getting most of the news from TV during the 2003 war on Iraq. Only 17 per cent of those on the internet were using the internet as their primary news source (respondents could select two media). And even on the web, it is the established offline news providers that dominate. According to Nielsen//NetRatings,[1] the number one site in the US during the war on Iraq was CNN.com with 26 million unique users in March 2003. CNN was joined in the top five by MSNBC, Yahoo!News, the *New York Times* and Fox News respectively. In the UK the picture is similar. After years of massive investment, the BBC dominates the ratings with 3 million users, according to Nielsen//NetRatings.[2] It was followed by *Guardian Unlimited*, with 1.3 million users, then Sky, CNN and the *Telegraph*.

Clearly, then, much of the content that people access online from the major news sites differs little from that which they receive from the mass media. "We're here to fill in the gap between radio in the morning and TV in the evening," ventures BBC News Online's World editor, Tim Herrmann. *Guardian Unlimited*'s news editor Sheila Pulham concurs: "What the internet can do is provide a handy mid-point between a newspaper and the demands of 24 hour TV." While a mainstream media audience passively consumes, on the web, users actively control the information they access. The content might be the same, but online it is used very differently. "There's even more immediacy to it than rolling TV news," Herrmann says, "because on the web you can find the latest thing precisely when you log on and you can also go back and unpick events at your leisure."

Both the BBC and the *Guardian* saw a huge rise in US visitors to their sites during the war. According to Nielsen//NetRatings 49 per cent of *Guardian* visitors in March 2003 were from the US. And the BBC was actually the sixth most popular news website in the US. For many Americans the web provides an escape route from the increasingly partisan news coverage of the major US news networks. "There is a constituency who wanted an alternative, less US-centric coverage of events," Herrmann argues. And, according to *Guardian Unlimited*'s chief producer, Lloyd Shepherd, they are looking for particular information: "Anything that suggests a different agenda to that of the US media – anything with Wolfowitz or Rumsfeld in the headline always does well." This surge in American traffic to UK sites reflects an emerging global pattern of people using the web to find alternative news sources to their traditional media channels; a trend that was dramatically accelerated by the war on Iraq. Europeans are also visiting US news sites in unprecedented numbers and Al Jazeera's recently launched English-language website attracted a massive global audience – before it was hacked, that is.

This pattern marks a subtle, but decisive shift in the relationship between the established news providers and their audience; web users can now compare their local news agenda to virtually anywhere on the planet.

The web is also having a profound effect on the news-gathering process. "The biggest change is that you have at your fingertips the most phenomenal range of sources of information and contacts and to a lesser or greater degree all journalists now are facing up to that and making use of it. As a resource it has revolutionised journalism," reflects Herrmann. The web might have enabled the news-gathering process to be far more effective. But it has also made the process far more transparent. If journalists are using the web to source their articles, then so can anyone.

When the US government published its National Security Strategy in June 2002, the public could download it from the White House website and read for themselves the Bush administration's rationale for pre-emptive action. A document that would have previously been circulated to a handful of journalists was read by millions across the world. Also readily available online was Dick Cheney's infamous Defense Planning Guidance that championed the "Pax Americana" over ten years earlier. And web users could visit the website of the Project for a New American Century – a neo-conservative think-tank with uncannily similar yearnings for global domination.

When the UK government published its first dossier on Iraq in September 2002, demand for the document crashed both the Downing Street and BBC websites. Herrmann points to Clare Short who, when still International Development Secretary in March 2003, first read Britain's doomed draft resolution for the UN Security Council on the BBC website. The internet has decisively levelled the information playing field.

As sociologist Manual Castells points out, "the culture of the producers of the internet shaped the medium".[3] And the open-source culture of the internet's creators – where freedom of information is paramount – is beginning to transform the content of the internet as much as it has the technology that powers it. In the open-source software revolution, freedom of information translates to a program's source code – its DNA – being freely available on the internet; a radical departure from commercial software, where the source code is a tightly guarded secret. As no one owns the intellectual property, open-source software is a public resource. Projects are collectively developed by groups of hackers, programming for nothing more than their own enjoyment and exchanging their work on the internet. In his seminal essay on the open-source movement, "The Cathedral and the Bazaar", Eric S. Raymond likens commercial software to the cathedral that is "crafted by individual wizards or small bands of mages working in splendid isolation", whereas the open-source community is "a great babbling bazaar of differing agendas and approaches".[4] And, on the internet, the mass media cathedrals have to jostle for attention in a burgeoning information bazaar. While control of the mass media might be increasingly concentrated in a handful of corporations, on the internet, a diverse and vibrant alternative news media is developing with bewildering speed; a trend that the build-up to war on Iraq dramatically accelerated. The web makes it possible for other news sources to establish themselves on little or no resources.

The war in Iraq has seen a profusion of progressive news sites, such as Alternet, Znet, Counterpunch and CommonDreams, reach beyond their core supporters to a vast global audience. With access to much the same sources as the mainstream media, they can provide an instant counterpoint to received media wisdom, focusing on the issues the press and TV networks choose to avoid. "They [Alternet users] act inversely to what we are supposed to know about people who read newspapers," says *LA Times* columnist Robert Scheer. "They want the most serious stories. They want the most analytical stories."

If the mass media is dumbing down, then the internet is where people are wising up. With an audience clamouring for in-depth insight into the war agenda, the progressive online media consistently highlighted key issues in the war on Iraq months before they flickered on the mass media radar. For example, in December 2001 Jim Lobe wrote about the neo-conservatives for *Progressive Report*, the monthly bulletin for progressive think-tank Foreign Policy in Focus:

> This circle of hawks is backed outside the administration by a network of veteran Washington hands whose political savvy, talent for polemics, media contacts, and lust for ideological combat have made them a formidable force on foreign policy since the Vietnam War.

Lobe's article triggered a surge of debate and analysis on the neo-conservatives throughout the progressive online media in the first few weeks of 2002, quickly becoming a hot topic on online discussion board and mailing lists. But it was only months later that the mainstream media registered the neocons' existence, let alone their influence. The *Washington Post* first referred to neo-conservatives on

21 August 2002, the *New York Times* on 6 October. The *Guardian* first mentioned neo-conservatives in an article on 19 August 2002.

The progressive news media was also using information from the mainstream media as well as the wealth of information on the web to present a coherent and compelling challenge to the war on Iraq – a challenge that clearly chimed with mass opinion. In March 2003 *Newsweek* first revealed that Hussein Kamel – a defector who provided the basis for US and British government claims that Iraq still had stocks of undeclared chemical and biological weapons – had said in his same testimony that Iraq had destroyed those same stocks. The article sparked a frenzy of interest on the web, but it barely registered on the mass media news agenda; the *Guardian* ran a small article but the BBC, the *New York Times* and the *Washington Post* all failed to cover this hugely significant revelation. The web has also enabled new formats of news provision to radically alter the way growing numbers of people follow global events, as traffic patterns on mainstream news sites reveal. "Before the American traffic started coming in our main entry points tended to be frontpages," says *Guardian Unlimited*'s Shepherd. "Since Americans started taking notice of us, we find that, actually, individual stories are quite often in the top five entry points."

This new US audience – like millions of other web users around the world – is using the web to define their own news agenda from an infinite range of global sources. In the last couple of years the web has seen an explosion of personal weblogs transform the way news is being consumed online. There are now estimated to be between 750,000 and a million weblogs, or "blogs", online and the number is growing fast. When global attention shifted to Iraq a new strand of the genre – the warblog – appeared. Warblogs cover every conceivable point on the political spectrum, providing a filter of the news available from the mainstream media outlets. Typically, a warblogger will post a link to a news article of interest, adding a short paragraph or comment or drawing attention to particular elements in the original article.

Bloggers scour the internet for articles and during military action, even pro-war blogs scrutinised government claims with forensic scepticism. With a solemn undertaking to "fact-check your ass", warbloggers were dissecting government claims and counterclaims to provide a raw new dimension to the media war. One leading warblog was The Agonist, created by Sean-Paul Kelley. The Agonist was started to provide a counterpoint to the ever-rightward march of the mainstream media. "We have the time and the resources to cover one story that the media ignores for a long time until it becomes fashionable again," he says. During the war, Kelley's site combined global insight and pithy comment with near constant updates as the war developed and established itself as a trusted information source with traffic rising from 3,000 to 120,000 visitors a day.

Weblogs provide an open-source platform for engaged individuals to challenge professional journalism on their own terms. The blogs are where the worlds of news hacks and news hackers collide, creating predictable friction. "It's like all stuff on the web," Mike Smartt, editor of BBC News Online, told dotJournalism, a website covering online news media. "Dissemination of information is great, but how much of it is trustworthy?" But bloggers argue that, unlike professional journalists, they have no hidden agendas. And trustworthiness, they add, is hardly a virtue most associate with the mass media anyway.

While many professional journalists remain sceptical, others are publishing blogs of their own, further blurring the line between traditional news culture and the "blogosphere". During the conflict in Iraq CNN stopped their correspondent Kevin Sites from posting to his blog. But, increasingly, mainstream news providers are acknowledging the value of the weblog format, often enlisting their own journalists to produce them. During the war, the BBC ran several weblogs from their own correspondents in Iraq. The *Guardian* went one step further, reprinting entries from Where's Raed? a weblog written by an Iraqi in Baghdad calling himself Salam Pax. His weblog was an eloquent and personal account of life in Iraq during the conflict. After one night of bombing in Baghdad, he wrote: "The images we saw on TV last night (not Iraqi, Jazeera-BBC-Arabiya) were terrible. The whole city looked as if it were on fire. The only thing I could think of was 'Why does this have to happen to Baghdad?'" As one of the only uncensored voices heard from inside Iraq, Salam Pax made an extraordinary impact on the web. In the week ending 23 March, Blogspot.com – one of the largest weblog hosts – saw 86 per cent of its traffic going to his weblog. After being cut off by the lack of electricity in Baghdad, Salam Pax resurfaced as a regular columnist for the *Guardian*; a move that might be the first of many as forward-thinking mainstream editors embrace the unmatched diversity of coverage weblogs can provide.

The web has also given rise to online activism. The anti-war demonstration on 15 February 2003 was to a great extent organised online and was almost certainly the largest co-ordinated political protest the world has ever seen. Events began in Melbourne, Australia, and then erupted in hundreds of cities across the world like a global Mexican wave before ending in San Francisco 48 hours later. With estimates ranging from 6 million to 12 million people taking part, 15 February provided the most pronounced example yet of the fusion between traditional political activism and network information technology. The alternative discussion that the internet has fuelled provided form and focus for the anti-war movement, as it has for environmental and anti-corporate campaigns in the last few years. But the web has also enabled an anti-war movement to grow exponentially with little or no resources.

In Britain, the Stop the War Coalition was formed from a series of meetings immediately after 11 September 2001, when an attack on Afghanistan was widely anticipated. Initially, however, the Coalition comprised of little more than a website and a declaration condemning an attack on Afghanistan. "We had no money and we only had a corner of an office," says Andrew Burgin, one of the Coalition's founders. "But what we managed to establish then was the website, so we had a continuity in the campaign even though we didn't have any physical resources." Out of necessity, the Coalition used mailing lists and its website to communicate with a rapidly growing network of local groups that take on much of the movement's organisation. The local groups communicate with their members and the wider movement through their own mailing lists, group text messages and websites.

Mike Healey has researched the social effects of the internet as a lecturer at Westminster University and now runs a local Stop the War group in Dulwich, South London. Dulwich is hardly a hot bed of revolutionary fervour, but meetings fill out the local hall and draw in people from every ethnic background, class, age and political persuasion. "We've used the internet to build the group," he says. "There's a lot of talk of virtual communities and what's happened here is an example of one. But the community only exists to mobilise – not to just chat online." This distributed structure has proven to be infinitely extensible, with more and more local groups continuing to be formed and the central office remaining minimal.

"A major part of campaigns in the past was always stuffing envelopes. That used to take literally days," says Burgin. "So campaigns in the past always required a much bigger labour force and more people involved." Now information is disseminated instantly at the click of a mouse at virtually no cost.

And in the US, the anti-war movement used the internet to reach middle America with equally startling results. Despite a virtual media blackout, the US anti-war movement generated a huge following with demonstrations in dozens of cities attracting hundreds of thousands. For the anti-war movement the "internet was critical" says Lynne Erskine from Win Without War, one of the main anti-war groups in the US. "Win Without War's network of 40 national organisations – including church, environmental and humanitarian groups – alerted their members to our actions mainly through email listservs and postings on their websites," she says.

MoveOn.org was created two years ago as "an online advocacy organisation" that campaigns through email on a wide range of issues. Over the last year, MoveOn concentrated on building the anti-war movement. "Over the eight months preceding the war," says MoveOn's Eli Parizer, "we tripled in size from around 400,000 to 1.4 million members." As a result MoveOn could mobilise huge numbers of people with breathtaking speed. In four days, MoveOn organised a vigil that ended up taking place in 6,700 locations in 141 countries.

The internet has obvious benefits as a campaigning tool; no-cost communication, no geographical constraints and the capacity for limitless information, chief among them. But the internet, argues Erskine, is also a "a risk-free, stay-at-home opportunity for people to learn about like-minded people". In the increasingly oppressive political atmosphere of middle America, she believes this is critical. But activists also caution that the internet is a means to an end, not an end in itself. "In Dulwich there is a virtual community online," says Healey, "but the only purpose of that is for us to hold meetings and go to protests. People are using the technology to build real-time physical opposition." Erskine agrees: "Websites alone cannot stir people who are not already poised to take action. The internet just gives people a convenient and free method of making their voices heard."

The impact of the internet on the mediascape is hardly the one predicted five years ago. Then, the information revolution was measured in soaring stock prices, corporate mega-mergers and multimedia convergence strategies. But, as the dust settles on the dot.com implosion, a different revolution is taking place online; where the information balance of power has decisively shifted from governments and "big media" to a global mass of common purpose.

NOTES

1. Nielsen//NetRatings news release: "American Web Surfers Boost Traffic to Foreign News Sites in March", 24 April 2003.
2. Nielsen//NetRatings news release: "Britons Turn to the Web for War Coverage Online", 15 April 2003.
3. Manual Castells, *The Internet Galaxy*, Oxford: Oxford University Press, 2001.
4. Eric S. Raymond, *The Cathedral and the Bazaar*, O'Reilly and Associates, 1999.

32
The Anti-war Movement

An interview with Noam Chomsky[1]

4 February 2003

Noam Chomsky: The [peace] demonstrations were another indication of a quite remarkable phenomenon. There is, around the world and in the United States, opposition to the coming war that is at a level that is completely unprecedented in US or European history, both in scope and the parts of the population it draws on.

There's never been a time, that I can think of, when there's been such massive opposition to a war before it was even started. And the closer you get to the region, the higher the opposition appears to be. In Turkey, polls indicated close to 90 per cent opposition, in Europe it's quite substantial, and in the United States.[2] The figures you see in polls, however, are quite misleading because there's another factor that isn't considered that differentiates the United States from the rest of the world. This is the only country where Saddam Hussein is not only reviled and despised but also feared. So, since September [2002], polls have shown that something like about 60 per cent of the population literally think that Saddam Hussein is an imminent threat to their survival.

Now there's no objective reason why the US should be more frightened of Saddam than say the Kuwaitis, but there is a reason. Namely that since September there's been a drumbeat of propaganda trying to bludgeon people into the belief that not only is Saddam a terrible person, but in fact he's going to come after us tomorrow unless we stop him today. And that reaches people. So if you want to understand the actual opposition to the war in the US you have to extract that factor. The factor of completely irrational fear created by massive propaganda, and if you did I think you'd find it's much like everywhere else.

What is not pointed out in the press coverage is that there is simply no precedent, or anything like a precedent, for this kind of public opposition to a war. And it extends itself far more broadly, it's not just opposition to war it's a lack of faith in the leaderships. You may have seen a study released by the World Economic Forum a couple of days ago which estimated trust in leaders, and the lowest was in leaders of the United States – trusted by little over quarter of the population. I think that reflects concerns over the adventurism and violence, and the threats that are perceived in the actions and plans of the current administration.[3]

These are things that ought to be central. Even in the United States there is overwhelming opposition to the war and that corresponding decline in trust in the leadership that is driving the war. This has been developing for some time but it is now reaching an unusual state, and, just to get back to the demonstrations over the weekend, that's never happened before. If you compare it with the Vietnam War, the current stage of the war with Iraq is approximately like that of 1961. That is, before the war actually was launched, as it was in 1962 with the US bombing of South Vietnam and driving millions of people into virtual concentration camps and chemical warfare and so on. But there was no protest. In fact, so little protest that few people even remember [it happened].

The protests didn't begin to develop until several years later when large parts of South Vietnam were being subjected to saturation bombing by B-52s. Hundreds of thousands of troops were there, hundreds of thousands had been killed, and then even after that, when the protests finally did develop in the US and Europe, it was mostly focused on a side-issue – the bombing of North Vietnam which was undoubtedly a crime. [But], it was far more intense in the south which was always the US target, and that's continued.

It's also, incidentally, recognised by the government. So when any administration comes into office the first thing it does is have a worldwide intelligence assessment – "What's the state of the world?" – provided by the intelligence services. These are secret and you learn about them 30 or 40 years later when they're declassified. When the first Bush administration came in 1989 parts of their intelligence assessment were leaked, and they're very revealing about what happened in the subsequent ten years about precisely these questions.

The parts that were leaked said that it was about military confrontations with "much weaker enemies", recognising they were the only kind we were going to be willing to face. So in confrontations with much weaker enemies the United States must win "decisively and rapidly" because otherwise popular support will erode, because it's understood to be very thin.[4] Not like the 1960s when the government could fight a long, brutal war for years and years practically destroying a country without any protest. Not now. Now they have to win and win quickly.

They have to terrify the population to feel there's some enormous threat to their existence and carry out a miraculous, decisive and rapid victory over this enormous foe and march on to the next one.

Remember the people now running the show in Washington are mostly recycled Reaganites, essentially reliving the script of the 1980s – that's an apt analogy. And in the 1980s they were imposing domestic programmes which were quite harmful to the general population and which were unpopular. People opposed most of their domestic programmes. And the way they succeeded in ramming it through was by repeatedly keeping the population in a state of panic.

So one year it was an airbase in Grenada which the Russians were going to use to bomb the United States. It sounds ludicrous but that was the propaganda lie and it worked.

Nicaragua was "two days' marching time from Texas" – a dagger pointed at the heart of Texas, to borrow Hitler's phrase. Again, you'd think the people would collapse with laughter. But they didn't. That was continually brought up to frighten us – Nicaragua might conquer us on its way to conquer the hemisphere. A national emergency was called because of the threat posed to national security by Nicaragua. Libyan hitmen were wandering the streets of Washington to assassinate our leader – hispanic narco-terrorists. One thing after another was conjured up to keep the population in a state of constant fear, while they carried out their major terrorist wars.

Remember, the same people declared a war on terror in 1981 that was going to be the centrepiece of US foreign policy focused primarily on central America, and they carried out a war on terror in central America where they ended up with substantial responsibility for killing about 200,000 people, leaving four countries devastated. Since 1990, when the US took them over again, they've declined still further into deep poverty. Now they're doing the same thing for the same purposes. They are carrying out domestic programmes to which the population is strongly opposed because they're being harmed by them.

But the international adventurism, the conjuring up of enemies, that are about to destroy us, that's second nature, very familiar. They didn't invent it, others have done the same thing. Others have done it in history. But they became masters of this art and are now doing it again.

I don't want to suggest that they have no reasons for wanting to take over Iraq. Of course they do – long-standing reasons that everyone knows. Controlling Iraq will put the US in a very powerful position to extend its domination of the major energy resources of the world. That's not a small point.

But look at the specific timing. It's rather striking that the propaganda drumbeat began in September – what happened in September? Well, it's when the Congressional campaign began and it was certain that the Republicans were not going to win it by allowing social and economic issues to dominate. They would have been smashed. They had to do exactly what they did in the 1980s. Replace them by security issues and in the case of a threat to security people tend to rally around the President – a strong figure who'll protect us from horrible dangers.

The more likely direction this will take [after a war with Iraq] will be Iran, and possibly Syria. North Korea is a different case. What they are demonstrating to the world with great clarity is that if you want to deter US aggression you better have a credible deterrent. In the case of North Korea, massed artillery aimed at Seoul, and down the road, probably weapons of mass destruction [WMD], or else a credible threat of terror. There's nothing else that will deter them – they can't be deterred by conventional forces. That's a terrible lesson to teach, but it's exactly what's being taught.

For years, experts in the mainstream have been pointing out that the US is causing weapons proliferation by its adventures since others cannot protect themselves except by WMD or the threat of terror. Kenneth Waltz is one who recently pointed this out.[5] But years ago, even before the Bush administration, leading commentators like Samuel Huntington in *Foreign Affairs*, the main establishment journal, were pointing out that the United States is following a dangerous course.[6] He was talking about the Clinton administration but he pointed out that, for much of the world, the US is now regarded as a rogue state and the leading threat to their existence. In fact one of the striking things about the opposition to the war now, again unprecedented, is how broadly it extends across the political spectrum, so the two major foreign policy journals, *Foreign Affairs* and *Foreign Policy* have just in their recent issues run very critical articles by distinguished mainstream figures opposing the resort to war in this case.[7]

The American Academy of Arts and Sciences rarely takes a position on controversial current issues. [But, it] has just published a long monograph on this issue by its committee on international security giving as sympathetic as possible an account of the Bush administration position, then simply dismantling it, line by line, on very narrow grounds – much narrower than I would prefer – but nevertheless successfully.[8]

[There is] just a lot of fear and concern about this adventurism, what one analyst called "sillier armchair fantasies". My concern is more "What's it going to do to the people of Iraq?" and "What's it going to do to the region?" but these concerns are "What's it going to do to us?"

Matthew Tempest: Will the propaganda rebound if democracy is not established in Iraq after "liberation"?

Noam Chomsky: You're right to call it propaganda. If this is a war aim, why don't they say so? Why are they lying to the rest of the world? What is the point of having the UN inspectors? According to this propaganda, everything we are saying in public is pure farce. We don't care about the weapons of mass destruction, we don't care about disarmament. We have another goal in mind, which we're not telling you, and that is, all of a sudden, we're going to bring democracy by war. Well, if that's the goal, let's stop lying about it and put an end to the whole farce of inspections and everything else and just say now we're on a crusade to bring democracy to countries that are suffering under miserable leadership. Actually that is a traditional crusade, that's what lies behind the horrors of colonial wars and their modern equivalents, and we have a very long rich record to show just how that worked out. It's not something new in history.

In this particular case you can't predict what will happen once a war starts. In the worst case, it might be what the intelligence agencies and the aid agencies are predicting – namely an increase in terror as deterence or revenge. And for the people of Iraq, who are barely on the edge of survival, it could be the humanitarian catastrophe of which the aid agencies and the UN have been warning.

On the other hand, it's possible it could be what the hawks in Washington hope – a quick victory, no fighting to speak of, impose a new regime, give it a democratic façade, make sure the US has big military bases there, and effectively controls the oil.

The chances that they will allow anything approximating real democracy are pretty slight. There's major problems in the way of that – problems that motivated Bush No.1 to oppose the rebellions in 1991 that could have overthrown Saddam Hussein. After all, he could have been overthrown then if the US had not authorised Saddam to crush the rebellions.

One major problem is that roughly 60 per cent of the population is Shi'ite. If there's any form of democratic government, they're going to have a say, in fact a majority say, in what the government is. Well they are not pro-Iranian but the chances are that a Shi'ite majority would join the rest of the region in trying to improve relations with Iran and reduce the levels of tension generally in the region by re-integrating Iran within it. There have been moves in that direction among the Arab states and Shi'ite majority in Iraq is likely to do that. That's the last thing the US wants. Iran is its next target.

It doesn't want improved relations. Furthermore if the Shi'ite majority gets for the first time a real voice in the government, the Kurdish minority will want something similar. And they will want a realisation of their quite just demands for a degree of autonomy in the northern regions. Well Turkey is not going to tolerate that. Turkey already has thousands of troops in Northern Iraq basically to prevent any such development. If there's a move towards Kirkuk, which the [Kurds] regard as their capital city, aimed at really taking it over, Turkey will move to block it, the US will surely back them, just as the United States has strongly supported Turkey in its massive atrocities against the Kurds in the 1990s in the south-eastern regions. What you're going to be left with is, either a military dictatorship with some kind of democratic façade, like maybe a parliament that votes while the military runs it behind the scenes – it's not unfamiliar – or else putting power back into the hands of something like the Sunni minority which has been running it in the past.

Nobody can predict any of this. What happens when you start a war is unknown. The CIA can't predict it, Rumsfeld can't predict it, nobody can. It could be anywhere over this range. That's why sane people refrain from the use of violence unless there are overwhelming reasons to undertake it – the dangers are simply far too great. However, it's striking that neither Bush nor Blair present anything like this as their war aim. Have they gone to the Security Council and said let's have a resolution for the use of force to bring democracy to Iraq? Of course not. Because they know they'd be laughed at.

Bush and his administration were telling the Security Council back in November very openly and directly that the UN will be "relevant" if it grants us the authority to do what we want. To use force when we want, and if the UN does not grant us that authority it will be irrelevant. It couldn't be clearer.

They said we already have the authority to do anything we want, you can come along and endorse that authorisation or else you're irrelevant. There could not have been a more clear and explicit way of informing the world that we don't care what you think, we'll do what we want. That's one of the primary reasons why US leaders' authority [is] collapsing in the World Economic Forum poll. Other countries will presumably go along with the US war – but out of fear.

NOTES

1. This interview has been corrected for grammar and sense by the editor and Noam Chomsky. The references to sources given below were added by the editor.
2. See "What the World Thinks in 2002 How Global Publics View: Their Lives, Their Countries, the World, America", The Pew Research Center, 4 December 2002, <http://people-press.org/reports/display.php3?ReportID=165>; Gallup International Iraq Poll 2003, <http://www.gallup-international. com/docs/GIA%20press%20release%20Iraq%20Survey%202003.pdf>.
3. "Declining Public Trust Foremost a Leadership Problem: World Economic Forum Survey Reveals Data Before Leaders Meet in Davos", 14 January 2003 – Geneva, Switzerland, <http://www.weforum.org/site/homepublic. nsf/Content/Declining+Public+Trust+Foremost+a+Leadership+Problem>.
4. Maureen Dowd, *New York Times*, 23 February 1991, cited in Noam Chomsky, *Year 501: The Conquest Continues*, London: Verso, 1993.
5. Kenneth Waltz, "The Continuity of International Politics", in Ken Booth and Tim Dunne (eds), *Worlds in Collision: Terror and the Future of Global Order*, Basingstoke: Palgrave Macmillan, 2002. See also Harry Kreisler, "Theory and International Politics: Conversation with Kenneth N. Waltz, Ford Professor Emeritus of Political Science", part of the "Conversations with History" series, Institute of International Studies, UC Berkeley, <http://globetrotter.berkeley.edu/people3/Waltz/waltz-con0.html>.
6. See Samuel P. Huntington, "The Lonely Superpower", *Foreign Affairs*, March/April 1999, vol. 78, n. 2, <http://www.foreignpolicy2000.org/ library/issuebriefs/readingnotes/fa_huntington.html>.
7. See: <http://www.foreignaffairs.org/2002/5.html>; <http://www.foreign affairs.org/2002/6.html>; <http://www.foreignaffairs.org/2003/1.html>.
8. "Official Projections Underestimate Cost of Iraq War, According to American Academy Report", American Academy of Arts and Sciences, Tuesday 03 December 2002, <http://www.amacad.org/publications/ monographs/Iraq_Press.pdf>.

Notes on Contributors

Alistair Alexander is a journalist writing on politics and technology. He was also a press officer for the Stop the War Coalition. Email: <ali@ali303.net>.

Steve Bell's cartoon strip If... has appeared in the *Guardian* since 1981. A compilation of 20 years of his work, *Bell's Eye*, is published by Methuen (2000). Other recent books include *Chairman Blair's Little Red Book* (2001), *Unstoppable If...* (2001) and *Unspeakable If...* (2003), all published by Methuen.

Faisal Bodi is a senior editor at Aljazeera.net and a columnist for the *Guardian* specialising in Muslim affairs.

Rod Brookes is Lecturer in Media and Cultural Studies at Cardiff University. He is the author of *Representing Sport* (Arnold, 2002), and has also published a number of articles on the media and health scares and the media and national identity.

Steve Caplin is a graphic artist specialising in satirical photomontage illustrations for national newspapers. He is the author of three books on digital artwork.

Noam Chomsky, long-time political activist, writer and professor of linguistics at Massachusetts Institute of Technology, is author of numerous books and articles on US foreign policy, international affairs and human rights. Among the most recent books are *Pirates and Emperors: International Terrorism in the Real World*, revised edition (2002); *Manufacturing Consent: The Political Economy of the Mass Media*, revised edition (with Edward S. Herman) (2002); *9–11* (2001); *Rogue States: The Rule of Force in World Affairs* (2000); *The New Military Humanism: Lessons from Kosovo* (1999); *Profit Over People: Neoliberalism and Global Order* (1999).

David Cromwell is co-editor of *Media Lens* and a researcher at Southampton Oceanography Centre. He is the author of *Private Planet* (Jon Carpenter, 2001). He can be contacted at: <editor@medialens.org>. Sign up for free Media Alerts at <http://www.medialens.org>.

David Crouch is NUJ FoC at EMAP Greater London House and a member of the Socialist Workers Party. Visit the MWAW website at <http://www.mwaw.org>, or email <editormwaw@yahoo.com>.

Mark Curtis is author of *Web of Deceit: Britain's Real Role in the World* (Vintage, 2003). He is a former Research Fellow at the Royal Institute of International Affairs and the author of several books on British foreign policy. His website is <http://www.markcurtis.info>.

Stephen Dorril has been researching and writing on the activities of the security and intelligence services since 1983. Founder-editor of the widely respected journal *Lobster*, he is the author of *Smear!: Wilson and the Secret State* (with Robin Ramsay, Fourth Estate, 1991), *MI6: 50 Years of Special Operations* (Fourth Estate, 2000). He currently lectures at the University of Huddersfield.

David Edwards is co-editor of *Media Lens*. He can be contacted at <editor@medialens.org>. Sign up for free Media Alerts at: <http://www.medialens.org>.

Robert Fisk is Middle East Correspondent for the *Independent* newspaper.

Des Freedman is a lecturer in Media and Communications in the Department of Media and Communications, Goldsmiths College, University of London. He is the co-editor of *War and the Media: Reporting Conflict 24/7* (Sage, 2003) and the author of *The Television Policies of the Labour Party* (Frank Cass, 2003).

Maureen Gilmour is a teacher and works as a researcher at the Glasgow University Media Group.

Tim Gopsill is the editor of the National Union of Journalists magazine *Journalist* and joint Chair of the Campaign for Press and Broadcasting Freedom.

Edward Herman is at the Wharton School, University of Pennsylvania. Among his books are *Beyond Hypocrisy: Decoding the News in an Age of Propaganda* (1992); *The Myth of the Liberal Media: An Edward Herman Reader* (1999); *Manufacturing Consent: The Political Economy of the Mass Media* (with Noam Chomsky, revised edition 2002).

Patricia Holland's book *Picturing Childhood: The Myth of the Child in Popular Imagery* will be published by I.B. Tauris in early 2004.

Dr Abdul Hadi Jiad is a broadcaster and analyst of Middle East Affairs who has worked as war correspondent, producer, presenter and acting editor, for Reuters, the BBC and dozens of Arab and English papers and authored two books. The BBC's senior management summarily dismissed him shortly before the war against, and the occupation of his country of origin, Iraq, without warning, investigation or the right to appeal.

Douglas Kellner teaches at UCLA. His books include, *Television and the Crisis of Democracy* (1990); *The Persian Gulf TV War* (1992); *Grand Theft 2000* (2001) *Media Spectacle* (2003); and *From 9/11 to Terror War: Dangers of the Bush Legacy* (2003).

Phillip Knightley is the author of *The First Casualty* (Andre Deutsch, revised edition 2003), a history of war correspondents and propaganda from the Crimea to Iraq.

Justin Lewis is Professor of Communication at Cardiff University. He has written several books about media, culture and society. Among his recent books is *Constructing Public Opinion: How Elites Do What They Like and Why We Seem to Go Along With It* (Columbia University Press, 2001).

Tim Llewellyn was BBC Middle East Correspondent in the 1970s, 1980s and 1990s and is now a freelance writer and broadcaster on the region.

David Miller is a member of the Stirling Media Research Institute. His books include *Don't Mention the War: Northern Ireland, Propaganda and the Media* (Pluto, 1994); *War and Words: The Northern Ireland Media Reader* (co-editor, Beyond the Pale, 1996); *Rethinking Northern Ireland* (editor, Longman, 1998); *Market Killing: What the Free Market Does and What Social Scientists Can Do About It* (co-author, Longman, 2001); *Open Scotland? Journalists, Lobbyists and Spin Doctors* (co-author, Polygon, 2001). He is currently writing a book on global public relations and corporate power (with Will Dinan).

Laura Miller is the associate editor of the Center for Media & Democracy's *PR Watch*, where she writes on war propaganda and corporate public relations. She also has considerable experience in radio journalism, reporting and producing news for community and pirate radio stations worldwide. Laura's interest in independent media extends to video production. She is the executive producer of a new documentary on the selling of the Iraq war.

Julian Petley is Professor of Film and Television Studies in the Department of Performing Arts at Brunel University, and joint Chair of the Campaign for Press and Broadcasting Freedom. His most recent book is *A Young Citizen's Guide to the Media in Politics* (Hodder Wayland, 2002) and he is currently writing a study of media censorship in Britain since 1979, which will be published by Routledge.

Greg Philo is Research Director of the Glasgow University Media Group. His next book is *Bad News from Israel* (Pluto, 2004).

John Pilger is one of the world's most renowned investigative journalists and documentary film-makers. His books include *Heroes, Distant Voices, Hidden Agendas* and *The New Rulers of the World.*

Polyp has been drawing provocative political cartoons for *New Internationalist* magazine for ten years, as well as contributing to other radical publications. His book, *Big Bad World: Cartoon Molotovs in the Face of Corporate Rule* gathers together 150 of his best images.

Sheldon Rampton is editor of *PR Watch*. He is co-author of *Toxic Sludge Is Good For You: Lies, Damn Lies and the Public Relations Industry* (1995); *Mad Cow U.S.A.: Could the Nightmare Happen Here?* (1997); *Trust Us, We're Experts: How Industry Manipulates Science and Gambles With Your Future* (2001) and *Weapons of Mass Deception: The Uses of Propaganda in Bush's War on Iraq* (2003).

Yvonne Ridley is a senior editor at Aljazeera.net and author of *In The Hands of the Taliban* (2001). Her next book is *Ticket to Paradise* (Dandelion Books, 2003). She is also an active peace campaigner and has addressed lectures and rallies throughout the UK, North America, Canada, Europe, Australia and the Middle East.

Andy Rowell is a freelance writer and investigative journalist with over a dozen years' experience on environmental, food, health and globalisation issues. He is the author of *Green Backlash: Global Subversion of the Environment Movement* (Routledge, 1996) and *Don't Worry It is Safe to Eat: The True Story of GM Food, BSE and Foot and Mouth* (Earthscan, 2003). His articles have been published internationally; a selection of which can be seen at <http://www.andyrowell.com>.

Dr Nancy Snow is Assistant Professor of Communications at California State University, Fullerton and Adjunct Professor in the Annenberg School for Communication, University of Southern California. She is the author of *Propaganda, Inc.: Selling America's*

Culture to the World and *Information War: American Propaganda, Free Speech and Opinion Control Since 9/11* (both Seven Stories Press, New York). She is co-editor of *War, Media and Propaganda: A Global Perspective* (forthcoming, 2004) and is currently writing a book about media ownership and media activism in the age of terror and war.

Norman Solomon, a syndicated columnist on media and politics, is co-author of *Target Iraq: What the News Media Didn't Tell You* (Context Books, 2003). He is executive director of the Washington and San Francisco based Institute for Public Accuracy: <http:// www.accuracy.org>.

John Stauber is an investigative writer, public speaker and democracy activist. He founded the Center for Media & Democracy in 1993. He edits and writes for the Center's quarterly newsmagazine, *PR Watch*, and is co-author of four books, *Toxic Sludge Is Good For You: Lies, Damn Lies and the Public Relations Industry* (1995); *Mad Cow U.S.A.: Could the Nightmare Happen Here?* (1997); *Trust Us, We're Experts: How Industry Manipulates Science and Gambles With Your Future* (2001); and *Weapons of Mass Deception: The Uses of Propaganda in Bush's War on Iraq* (2003) <http://www.prwatch.org>.

Mark Steel is a broadcaster and columnist for the *Independent*. His latest book, *Vive la Revolution*, is published by Scribner.

Mark Thomas is the mouthy bloke who is often seen running at chief executives on the telly and is occasionally quite funny. He is also founder and director of the Ilisu Dam campaign and is currently campaigning to stop government support for the Baku–Ceyhan pipeline. Mark was in the Socialist League in the 1980s for a year, before being expelled for the theft of money from paper sales.

Granville Williams edits *Free Press*, journal of the UK-based media pressure group, the Campaign for Press and Broadcasting Freedom, and is the author of numerous reports on media ownership in the UK and Europe. He teaches Journalism and Media Policy at the University of Huddersfield.

Index